THE BARBER OF NATCHEZ

WILLIAM JOHNSON
(Reproduced from a daguerreotype by the Maurice Sackett Studio of New Orleans and identified by members of the family as William Johnson. Used here through the courtesy of Mrs. Mabel Johnston Carr, owner of the original and granddaughter of William Johnson.)

The

BARBER OF NATCHEZ

Wherein a Slave is Freed and Rises to a Very High Standing; Wherein the Former Slave Writes a Two-Thousand-Page Journal about His Town and Himself; Wherein the Free Negro Diarist Is Appraised in Terms of His Friends, His Code, and His Community's Reaction to His Wanton Murder

By

EDWIN ADAMS DAVIS
and
WILLIAM RANSOM HOGAN

LOUISIANA STATE UNIVERSITY PRESS
Baton Rouge

This edition of *The Barber of Natchez* is dedicated to the memory of William Ransom "Bill" Hogan (November 23, 1908–September 26, 1971)–who strongly believed that a man was a man, whatever his religion, his economic station, or his color.

Mr. Davis' research for this volume was partially conducted under grants from the University Council on Research, Louisiana State University; Mr. Hogan's research was partially conducted under grants from the American Philosophical Society and the Graduate School of Tulane University. These grants are acknowledged with gratitude.

Published by Louisiana State University Press
Copyright © 1954, 1973 by Louisiana State University Press
All rights reserved
Manufactured in the United States of America

ISBN-10: 0-8071-0212-1
ISBN-13: 978-0-8071-0212-1
Library of Congress Catalog Card Number 54-10885

The paper in this book meets the guidelines for permanence and durability of the Committee on Production Guidelines for Book Longevity of the Council on Library Resources. ∞

Preface

THE 1938 DISCOVERY by the undersigned of the 2,000-page personal and business diary of ex-slave William Johnson of Natchez, Mississippi, was an event of historical significance. Adding to the importance of this discovery was the fact that the attic of the three-story brick home which Johnson had built less than a block from the Adams County courthouse in 1840–1841 also housed many other significant papers: a nearly 1,400-item collection of legal and financial documents; personal and business letters; family papers of various types; sixty volumes of account books; bound and unbound issues of rare antebellum newspapers, two of which were not listed elsewhere; and over four hundred pieces of nineteenth-century sheet music—the whole collection spanning the period 1793–1937.

The publication of Johnson's monumental diary in 1951—the one hundredth anniversary of his death—secured for the Natchez barber and businessman a high place in the ranks of America's chroniclers.* Allan Nevins thought Johnson "one of the most . . . interesting of American diarists"; E. Merton Coulter called his diary "a human interest story unique in the annals of free Negroes." John Hope Franklin concluded his *American Historical Review* critique: "The history of Natchez and of the South has been considerably illuminated by this significant volume." Bell I. Wiley noted that "there is nothing like it in American historical literature"; and

---

*William Ransom Hogan and Edwin Adams Davis (eds.), *William Johnson's Natchez: The Ante-Bellum Diary of a Free Negro* (Baton Rouge: Louisiana State University Press, 1951). A two-volume, facsimile reprint edition of the diary was published in the Kennikat Press Series in Negro Culture and History in 1968.

Manly Wade Wellman, writing in the Raleigh *News and Observer*, called Johnson the "Dark-skinned Pepys" of the Old South. Hodding Carter concluded that "it is no over-statement to say that this is the most unusual record ever kept in the United States."

The publication of *The Barber of Natchez* in 1954 added to Johnson's reputation. Elsie M. Lewis wrote in Lincoln University's *Midwest Journal* that "again the editors of that remarkable document [Johnson's diary] have made a significant contribution." Dawson Phelps wrote in the *Alabama Review* that the authors "have endowed William Johnson . . . with a vivid personality" and "have recreated as background a remarkably accurate description of Natchez in which Johnson lived and worked," and then commented, significantly: "Free from the taint of either the nostalgic or the propagandist, it provides a commentary on the question as to whether the Negro can be assimilated into American society."

It must be remembered that both Johnson's diary and this biography were published before the *Brown* v. *Board of Education of Topeka* Supreme Court decision in 1954. With the gathering momentum of emphasis upon Negro history and biography since that time, it is strange that the Natchez diarist should have been overlooked by so many editors, authors, and historians. It is hoped that this edition of William Johnson's biography, together with the publication of this writer's sketch of Johnson in the forthcoming *Dictionary of American Negro Biography*, will aid in acquainting all Americans with one of the most unusual and most interesting men in American history.

EDWIN ADAMS DAVIS

Louisiana State University
21 February 1973

"*A few years ago we were ignorant slaves with nothing. Not even the rags on our backs were our own. Today we are educated citizens owning thousands of homes and farms and businesses. Our sons are officers and soldiers in the Army. We have thousands of doctors, lawyers, teachers, nurses and other professional people. Our workers have been accepted in the unions and work side by side with other Americans. The progress of the American Negro in so short a time is unmatched in recorded history. But I don't think we could have made these rapid gains if our fathers had not tried so hard to make friends with the whites, or if the whites had not appreciated their efforts to become good citizens.*"

(Statement by Dr. James Dickey, named the most outstanding citizen of 1953 by Taylor, Texas, and General Practitioner of the Year for 1953 by the Lone Star Medical Association. George Sessions Perry, "A Negro Doctor Wins Over a Southern Town," *Saturday Evening Post*, October 24, 1953, p. 80.)

"*The time has come to realize that the interracial drama acted out on the American continent has not only created a new black man, it has created a new white man, too. . . . One of the things that distinguishes Americans from other people is that no other people has ever been so deeply involved in the lives of black men, and vice versa. This fact faced, with all its implications, it can be seen that the history of the American Negro problem is not merely shameful, it is also something of an achievement. For even when the worst has been said, it must also be added that the perpetual challenge posed by this problem was always, somehow, perpetually met. It is precisely this black-white experience which may prove of indispensable value to us in the world we face today. This world is white no longer, and it will never be white again.*"

(James Baldwin, "Stranger in the Village," *Harper's Magazine*, October, 1953, p. 48.)

Table of Contents

PART I: THE MAN 1
1. William Johnson of Old Natchez 3
2. Slave Boy to Business Success 14
3. Barbershop Proprietor and Businessman 30
4. Farmer 44
5. Johnson's Apprentices and Slaves 54
6. Sportsman 69
7. The Family Hearthside 78
8. Community Position 91

PART II: A FREE NEGRO'S DIARY OF A TOWN 105
9. Chronicle of Everyday Natchez 107
10. Barbershop Gossip 118
11. Politics and Politicians 129
12. The Tranquil Streets 142
13. Pistols, Fists, and Bowie Knives 156
14. Fires, Fire Fighters—and a Tornado 168
15. Plasters, Pills, and Purgatives 178
16. Thespians and Clowns 188
17. Sports of the Turf 202
18. Aristocrats and Lesser Men 214

PART III: THE DIARIST APPRAISED 225
19. White Associates and One Great Friend 227
20. Colored Friends and Associates 241
21. Pride and Compassion 252
22. The Last Days—and Afterward 262

Part I

The Man

Wherein a Slave is Freed and Rises to Very High Standing

CHAPTER ONE

William Johnson of Old Natchez

WILLIAM JOHNSON of Natchez died a little over a century ago at the age of forty-two. While he was an exceptional citizen of the Old South, few Americans had heard of him until his diary was published in 1951. The book reviews insisting that he had written one of America's most unusual chronicles would have pleased and surprised him, for he certainly never expected posthumous recognition of the product of his pen. He simply would have remarked, "Well, after all, is a hundred years too long to wait?" and then would have set out to find his cronies, John Jacquemine and Robert McCary, in order to entice them into a short fishing or hunting trip.

He was not a professional writer, and the only things he published during his lifetime were a legal announcement or two and a series of newspaper advertisements describing one of his escaped slaves and offering a reward for his return. His personal and financial papers and records, together with his manuscript diary and a huge group of family dossiers, memoranda, archives, and trivia, were well guarded by the family and lay undisturbed and gathering dust in the attic of his home until the late 1930's. Nevertheless, the Natchez press eulogized him, both at the time of his sudden death, and during the ensuing two years when the man who had been speedily indicted for his murder was being cleared or placed beyond the law by each of three separate courts.

Johnson was a self-confident man, but he realized his

limitations and it is extremely doubtful that he ever thought of himself as a possible subject of historical investigation. Moreover, he did not write his diary with the idea of enlightening posterity about himself or his times. Had he envisioned his future status as an American diarist he would have given more time and thought to the style of the entries. With his respect for the value of the written record, he probably would have indited reminiscences of the little-known period of his childhood and youth; he would have left more than brief account books as a record of his young manhood; and he would have written specifically and at length about the most shadowy figure with whom he was associated, his father. He provided none of these, but his lack of self-consciousness, on the other hand, enabled him to think and write freely and occasionally with abandon.

His diary,[1] a significant document in Southern historiography, reveals important phases of general ante-bellum Southern life and free Negro–white relations. It also pictures the economic and social position of one individual, as well as his daily activities, his attitudes toward the slavery regime, and his thoughts and opinions on local, state, and even national and international affairs. The modern author Hodding Carter concludes that "it is no over-statement to say that this is the most unusual personal record ever kept in the United States."

Johnson never explained why he kept a diary during the years from 1835 to 1851, but certain aspects of his personal situation and character suggest a tentative answer. A precise knowledge of the dates and details of money transactions was a necessity if he was to expect prompt payments made in good will by individuals with whom he

---

[1] William Ransom Hogan and Edwin Adams Davis (eds.), *William Johnson's Natchez; The Ante-Bellum Diary of a Free Negro,* in *Source Studies in Southern History,* No. 1 (Baton Rouge, 1951).

had constant business dealings. Hence he used his diary, in part, as a means of keeping certain business records, some of which were later transferred in more formal fashion to his account books. This practice naturally led him to record information and conversations about contemplated purchases of farm land and town property and to note prices and sales of diverse sorts.

Perhaps an even more compelling stimulus to keep a journal arose from his almost isolated position at the top of his class. Unable to unbosom himself completely to anyone except one or two intimates, he used his diary as an outlet for the secret expression of the suppressed moods, feelings, and thoughts that most men would not have found necessary to stifle in public.

The daily continuation of a diary in nineteenth-century America was often regarded as a badge of distinction as well as an accompaniment of gentility. The numerous diarists ranged from the literary men of New England to the planters of the South and the host of political and military apologists of the Civil War generation. But among the Southern planters the composing of daily records of their actions, observations, or ideas was a more than common practice. Why they kept such records frequently was not clear even to them, nor has it been adequately explained by later scholars; but it is possible that there was a remnant of the spirit of *noblesse oblige* in diary-keeping and that a portion of Johnson's motivation stemmed from the same source.

Whatever the reasons, Johnson's broad range of interest in his home environment was equaled by none of the nineteenth-century diarists. His overwhelming curiosity was at least faintly reminiscent of Pepys and Boswell; he would have understood, and perhaps shared, Boswell's feeling that the making of a record was "the most meaningful portion of life itself." He knew Natchez, the surrounding country, and its citizens as few others did. The total effect of his diary is to evoke a substantial shadow of the flesh-and-blood life of one distinct area of the antebellum South. There are accounts of Presidential campaigns and small-town gossip, of duels and less dignified brawls, of the social affairs of prominent aristocrats, of disturbing evidences of thoughtlessness and cruelty, and of heartening proofs of fundamental decency. There are reports, too, of the race track and the tavern—and a few of the stories the Natchez wives weren't told.

An air of artlessness pervades Johnson's diary entries, which were written to no purpose except to record the day's happenings, to serve as a reminder of certain facts, to converse in private with himself, or to give expression to an inner compulsion that had been born of the society and time in which he lived.

The diarist was a conservative. He believed in those things which were conventional and traditional, and he was never conspicuous in any of his actions. Unlike some of his fellow citizens, he never marched in political torchlight parades giving vent to loud shouts and making wild gesticulations. He accepted slavery as he accepted everything else in the life around him. He was no intellectual, and it is equally obvious that he was no philosopher.

In short, accepting the view that in general American minds are remarkably uniform, Johnson fitted well into the pattern of his times. In his diary he rarely looked for a bloody fingerprint and, although he relished living and most activities connected with a well-rounded life, it was the workaday world of Natchez that attracted him. Nine tenths of the items that went into his diary, the things that absorbed his daily energy and gave his own life its meaning, are chiefly important or interesting today because they show that Johnson's daily life and habits were analogous with those of the ordinary Natchez citizen.

Was Johnson an accurate observer? His sources of information were ordinarily accurate, insofar as they went. He had the characteristics of a good witness—intelligence, the power of observation, and an insatiable curiosity. His mild prejudices were self-evident, his skepticism often led to a corroboration of facts, and his occasional flashes of temper were usually acknowledged. He attached the label "sly talk" to gossip. He frequently identified news as relayed from newspapers. And though his position on the social scale obviously barred him from taking direct part in many social events, he was a fairly detached observer in a surprising number of situations from which he would be barred today.

Johnson had few enemies during his lifetime, and these few were not of his own making. One of the remarkable features of his diary is the absence of vulgar or profane remarks about persons, yet he confided statements and opinions to it which he could not voice in public. His life was straightforward, boldly open. He walked a wide road where all could see him. His deeds were constructive, never destructive. He would have agreed that the man who acted properly need never fear the hereafter. His America has been called a kaleidoscope of creeds, but he never defamed any of them; his America had opprobrious epithets for many other nationalities, but Johnson used few of them.

Business success was his lifelong goal, for he accepted the view that the possession of wealth was the surest guarantee of recognition. He was ambitious to carve a distinctive position for himself and his family in the Natchez world, but when the hurdles were found to be insurmountable, his attentions were diverted in later years from the urban community on the bluff to his land, home life, and few close friends.

He could and frequently did refuse money for the sake

of moral satisfaction or emotional pleasure. He did not have what Francis Parkman once called the "national disease," for he was not "lean, starveling, nervous, restless, dyspeptic, hypochrondriac." He gained daily in worldly goods; his contemporaries correctly judged that he was prosperous. Yet he had the ability and the quality of mind to be comfortable, to take his ease when the day's work was done, or to avoid a day's labor if the mood struck him.

Johnson's life was never methodical beyond the requirements of rigorous necessity; complete regularity did not fit in with his scheme of things. He never formed the habit of most diarists, for example, of jotting down his thoughts or descriptions or impressions as soon as possible. Some of his entries were penned immediately after the day's events; some were written late at night after the household had quieted down; one entry was made during early morning hours while he sat at the bedside of a sick son; other entries awaited the moment when the diarist could register a week's happenings at a single sitting; and one series of recordings were not made until the events were a month old. It was the same with his life. There was complete order if order was necessary, as in matters of business; otherwise the problems of living more or less took care of themselves.

Johnson began his business career as the proprietor of a small barbershop in Port Gibson, Mississippi, but within a couple of years he moved to Natchez, where he spent the rest of his life. Here he acquired another and larger barbershop, followed within a few years by two additional barbershops and substantial holdings in city rental property, and during the 1840's large acreages of farm and timber land just south of Natchez. For the last several years of his life he operated this landed estate, the labor being done by his slaves and a few hired white men.

But his chief interest, in addition to his barbershops, was "buisness," as he usually spelled it—the buying and selling at a profit of anything that was marketable. By the end of his life he was a moderately well-to-do citizen whom the Natchez community respected for his fair dealings and canny business judgment.

Who was this William Johnson, this man whose penned chronicle made him, according to historian Allan Nevins, "one of the most remarkable and interesting of American diarists"? Who was this man whose death was lamented by Natchez townsmen, whose funeral was attended by many of the "most respected citizens," whose position was recalled with pride by the press which termed him an "esteemed Citizen" and an "excellent and most inoffensive man" and held up his life as "one well worthy of imitation by all of his class"?

William Johnson was a free Negro, a free Negro living in the heart of the ante-bellum South.

William Johnson's Natchez has generally been misinterpreted or distorted in literary and quasi-historical writings. Some of their errors have been accidental, some deliberate. In them the area has long been identified with the familiar literary stereotype of the ante-bellum South—large holdings in land and slaves, colonnaded mansions, imported furniture, and the rest of the plantation legend, all fused into a picture of an opulent, leisurely, and cultured way of life. Most of the "planters" had "princely incomes," lived a life almost "feudal in its careless magnificence." Natchez "had realized the southerner's dream of Utopia. It was the classic age of America and Natchez was the Temple of Victory on the Acropolis."

Conversely, the Natchez-under-the-Hill river front

has been depicted as the wildest hell-hole of the pre-Civil War Mississippi River, and even of the entire South. It was a "stale sordid sodden place" of "whores, boatmen, gamblers, bruisers," of "barrooms and gambling hells" and "brothels," heavy with the "reek" of "mud and garbage" and heavy, too, "with the more impalpable smell of sweaty lusts and savage passions."

Below the crest of "the Bluff" overlooking the Mississippi were bawdy glories of vice, "squalor on the steaming mud flats"; but after one climbed the hill and faced the town, there were "the tranquil streets—the elegance of the wind-swept heights."

These two interpretations of Natchez life have provided the patterned descriptive phraseology and basic elements of many an intriguing story or chapter. And the effect of this standard and conventional version has been to build the impression of a town with "a split personality."

The chief defects of this type of generalized analysis in black and white are that, like many good stories, it lacks the pedestrian virtues of accuracy and completeness. The truth is that the two extremes of the Natchez past were not in full glory at the same time. By the mid-1830's the reputation of Natchez-under-the-Hill was beginning to be replaced partially by one emphasizing its busy commercial water front, where river steamboats docked daily, where European goods were received directly from ocean-going vessels that had been towed up the Mississippi, and where cotton was often prepared for direct shipment to Liverpool or other English ports. The day of the stoical gambler and hell-raising flatboatman had by no means passed during the early years of Johnson's career, but it had undoubtedly begun to wane.

The life of the upper town had many other facets apart from the comfortable and luxuriant living of the upper middle class and aristocrats. Even patricians or would-be patricians occasionally participated in the frequent street fights or public house brawls that gave the "tranquil streets" a definite frontier flavor. And not all the houses of prostitution were below the Bluff.

An unmistakably cosmopolitan tone was also added by the town's Spanish and English background and by the presence of substantial groups of foreign-born Irish, German, Italian, English, French, and Spanish residents. The records of the census of 1850, for example, reveal that well over one fourth of the more than 4,600 citizens of the town proper had been born in foreign countries, that nearly 800 were "Yankee" in origin, that more than 200 were free Negroes, and that about one third were slaves.

Social and economic groups so overlapped in the entire Natchez region as to challenge glib analysis. While the plantation system probably reached "its zenith in Mississippi, and perhaps in the entire South," in the Natchez area during the 1850's, the wealthy planter represented only a small minority of the total population, and his plantation certainly cannot be accepted as typical of the Southern planter group. The plantation legend had at least a partial foundation in fact, however, for the Natchez area produced several millionaires during the ante-bellum years, and there were other families who almost achieved this goal.

In Natchez and Adams County the houses of the numerous small farmers, tradesmen, and businessmen were much less pretentious than those of the large businessmen and planters, and their lots and lands often intermingled. The economic interests of professional men, bankers, shipowners, commission merchants, and large plantation owners were inextricably bound together, often in the person of a single individual or family. Some of this top-layer group of the 1850's were men who had pushed and shoved their way up by law or medical practice, advantageous marriages, or ambitious expansion and speculation in land-holdings and slaves, just as some small planters had risen from the status of small farmers, overseers, and even squatters. Natchez and Adams County society was by no means static or immobile; it was alive and active.

We met William Johnson as the result of a series of accidents. But it must be admitted that for some years we had searched for historical traces of a man of his racial, economic, and social status—a literate free Negro, who lived during the ante-bellum regime and kept a record of contemporary activities as well as some of his own opinions and beliefs. It was at least unpredictable that his diary and other records were preserved by his family for nearly a century against the possible ravages of time, weather, fire, insects, rats, and the rainy-day-attic activities of children. It was also accidental that his son and grandson, together with their wives, had such a strong sense of family pride that they guarded the scores of leather-bound tomes and smaller manuscript volumes, as well as the trunk filled with loose letters, receipts, and other business records. The last accident occurred in 1938 when three persons were brought together—the quiet and gentle widow of Johnson's grandson, the local historian of the Natchez area, and a university archivist.

After the Johnson family papers were acquired by Louisiana State University, we set to work to discover everything possible about the life of the man and the community in which he lived. The research trail led to archival, manuscript, and library collections in Natchez, Woodville, Jackson, and other Mississippi towns, to New

Orleans, Washington, and New York. Our work continued over a thirteen-year period, a large portion of which was devoted to editing Johnson's sixteen-year diary, and culminated in the diary's publication in 1951.

During these years we became intimately acquainted with William Johnson. We discovered that, within the full possibilities of his color and station, he was a good citizen. We learned that he gained the confidence and respect of both the white and colored population of the entire Natchez area. We sat at his family hearthside. We became familiar with his moods, his thinking, and his opinions. We grew to respect him, as did his Natchez contemporaries, and to realize that he would have been an asset to any Southern community at any given period, and that the South today would be economically and spiritually stronger if there were more William Johnsons.

We also became acquainted with Johnson's white and colored neighbors. We came to know the Minors, the Surgets, the Marshalls, the Bingamans, and other noted families of the City of the Bluffs and the surrounding countryside. We met free and slave Negroes and a host of ordinary white citizens.

As we saw him in motion, as occasionally we were able to look through his eyes at the community in which he lived, as we came to understand him and his chosen pattern of life, we began to suspect that, although he was a distinct personality, he may have been representative of others at the top of his class in the ante-bellum South. This class, like the members of the poor and middle-class white groups, left few records. But William Johnson, the free Negro barber-businessman, did leave records, and through these and subsidiary sources, the man and his socio-economic position are revealed.

CHAPTER TWO

Slave Boy to Business Success

THE rise of William Johnson from slave boy in 1820 to successful young businessman in 1835 might have been patterned upon the plot of one of Horatio Alger's novels. That it occurred during the hurrying, materialistic 1830's, when "getting ahead" epitomized the American spirit, was not so unusual; but that it was achieved by a free Negro in a deep-South town in the midst of the slavery regime marked him as an energetic and intelligent young man, who took advantage of every opportunity for economic advancement.

The story of Johnson's life prior to the acquisition of his Natchez barbershop and the beginning of his systematic financial record-keeping in 1830 must be largely pieced together from a variety of legal records. And the same is true of the pre-1830 career of his Negro mother and the entire life of his white father. The opportunities for humanizing touches are few, because extensive personal papers do not exist, and the local or state government clerk was not interested in personalities but rather in the brief recording of facts. After 1830, however, the young Negro's records begin to bring his daily life and habits into focus.

But—let the records tell their story.

The series of events that was to liberate slave boy William began when he was five years of age. In early February, 1814, a certain white man, William Johnson of Adams County, Mississippi, crossed the Mississippi River from Natchez to Vidalia, parish seat of Concordia Parish, Louisiana, and conferred with the parish judge. There he made formal declaration that he intended to emancipate his slave Amy and that during the past four years she had led an honest life, "without having committed any robbing or without having been guilty of any other criminal misdemeanor." Amy was the mother of the future diarist. The next day the sheriff of the parish posted an official public notice, in both French and English according to Louisiana custom, which stated that William Johnson had filed his intention to emancipate his female slave Amy and that any person who might have legal opposition should voice it at the office of the parish court within forty days.

Six weeks later, no legal protest having been made, William Johnson had the instrument of emancipation executed according to the laws of Louisiana. He acknowledged that "for divers good causes"—and also in consideration of five dollars—that he had "released from Slavery, liberated, manumitted and set free my Negro woman Amy being the age of thirty years and able to work and gain a Sufficient Livilihood and maintenance." He bound himself to support the former slave should she ever be in want owing to sickness, insanity, or old age.

Four years later, in 1818, an authorized agent of William Johnson carried Amy's daughter, "a mulatto girl named Delia aged about thirteen years," to Philadelphia. With the written authority of the child's owner, the agent arranged for her liberation in Pennsylvania and brought her back to her mother in Natchez.

On January 21, 1820, the white William Johnson addressed an eloquent petition to the Mississippi General

Assembly (then in session at Natchez) asking that body to free Amy's son, William. He stated that because of her good conduct and fidelity, Amy had been freed according to the laws of Louisiana, but that he had been prevented from manumitting her son because of "his minority, and consequent incapacity to execute a Bond." He further certified that he was a resident of Mississippi and had no debts that would render the act of emancipation unjust. Emancipating the slave boy would constitute "that disposition of his property most agreeable to his feelings & consonant to humanity," he claimed, and would give "that Liberty to a human being which all are entitled to as a Birthright, & extend the hand of humanity to a rational Creature, on whom unfortunately Complexion Custom & even Law in This Land of freedom, has conspired to rivet the fetters of Slavery."

The following day an Adams County member of the assembly's lower house presented the petition. It was referred to a special committee, which reported a bill providing for William's emancipation. After being amended by both houses, the bill was passed February 10 and approved the same day by Governor George Poindexter.

Thus the mulatto slave boy became the free William Johnson, taking his former master's surname as his own, as was the custom. After reaching maturity he ordinarily used the signature "William Johnson," though on several occasions he inserted "T." as a middle initial. His marriage license was issued to "William T. Johnson," but he signed it "William Johnson"; and he once wrote "William Tiler Johnson" on a page of meaningless scribblings.

Who was this white William Johnson who had arranged for the emancipation of "the mulatto boy named William," of his mother, and of his sister in three different states within six years? The few records concerning him do not shed even oblique light on his personality, real character, and unadvertised activities. Singularly enough, the imprint that he made upon the public archives of Adams County, and even on the federal census records, was less distinct than that of any of the three slaves to whom he gave freedom. Even the heart-moving petition he addressed to the state legislature in behalf of his slave William might well have been written by an attorney employed for that purpose.

State and federal census reports reveal that he was not named as the head of a family in 1816, 1818, or 1820, although he was listed as a "white poll" in the tax rolls of the same period. The tax rolls also show that his taxable slave holdings rose from none in 1818 to eight in 1823.

Between 1820 and 1825 this William Johnson was engaged in more than a dozen civil suits, either as defendant or plaintiff. The majority of these suits were actions for the collection of promissory notes which ranged from $90 to $522, and the extant records indicate that Johnson was often the defendant and that many of the judgments were against him.

Diarist William Johnson did not definitely identify his father or furnish sufficient facts, either in his diary or in his extensive financial records, to identify him. There are references in both diary and cashbooks to a "Capt." or "Cap" Johnson. He once noted in a financial record: "To Cap Johnson for a watch $70.00." Was this Johnson the father? One day in 1836 he recorded in his diary: "Old Dad and his wife went Down to Woodville Left Big Waller, Little Clabourne, Jeorgan to mind the House. Wm wrides out there and comes home very soon—Some what hurt at the sight of things." Was it possible that "Old Dad" referred to his father? Other scattered references are equally obscure.

The only specific reference the Negro diarist made to his father was a brief notation in his cashbook in February,

1831: "To a Debt of Fathers $7.00." While this does not reveal the identity of the father, it may indicate something of the character of the son.

Following her emancipation, Amy, the illiterate former slave of this shadowy William Johnson, had established her household in Natchez. Under the name Amy Johnson she was listed as the head of a free Negro family in the censuses of 1816, 1818, and 1820. In 1819, according to the license record filed in the Adams County chancery clerk's office, she received a license "to retail in Natchez," and it is probable that she kept a small store or was a peddler. She acquired several slaves, and by 1838 the tax rolls listed her slave property as three women and two children, valued at $1,650.

Between 1816 and 1822 her name appeared in several court suits. In 1820 she was successfully sued for non-payment of a debt of $10.77½. Two years later she sued Arthur Mitchum for assault. Mitchum was a barber who had a shop opposite Winn's Hotel, where he advertised soaps, clean napkins, and double-toothbrushes.

Counsel for Amy charged that in May, 1819, the barber had spit in her face, had "greatly squeezed" and pulled her nose, had pulled out large quantities of her hair, had hit her with a brickbat and pounded her whole body with his fists, and had torn and caused $50 worth of damage to her "gown dress Petticoats shift and bonnett." As a result, counsel averred, she had been unable to work for some time, and he therefore asked that she be awarded damages in the amount of $500; but the court awarded her a judgment of only $27.50 and costs.

The record in this case does not show what Amy Johnson was doing or saying while her altercation with the barber was in progress, but in view of her children's later testimony as to her quarrelsome disposition, it is highly probable that Mitchum did not emerge from the fight without knowledge of what she thought about his character and antecedents or without injury to his clothing.

In the meantime Amy Johnson was doing a sound job of rearing her two children. In 1820 her fifteen-year-old daughter, Adelia, married a twenty-year-old Philadelphia-born free Negro barbershop proprietor named James Miller, who was a man of high moral character. In the same year Amy's eleven-year-old son, William, was freed by the state legislature and shortly thereafter was initiated into the barber business in the shop of his brother-in-law.

During the early 1820's young William Johnson learned the art of shaving and haircutting. The leading barbershops in the principal cities of the lower Mississippi Valley were operated by free Negroes, and during the decade James Miller became the most widely patronized barber in Natchez. The apprentice system of learning the barber trade was in vogue and young relatives often went through the process.

By 1827 James Miller had become a well-established and highly respected Natchez businessman. In that year forty-four prominent men of the community—including Dr. Ayres P. Merrill, Dr. Stephen Duncan, Alvarez Fisk, James Wilkins, Lemuel Gustine, and members of the city council—petitioned the state legislature to remove all his civil disabilities as a free man of color, except those which excluded him from voting and from jury and militia duty. The petition stated that Miller had lived in Natchez for nine years and had acquired property by honest industry, and that he "affords & has invariably afforded a good example to his brethren & that his conduct & demeanor are highly praiseworthy." While the legislature failed to take the requested action, it did strengthen his already strong free Negro position by passing an act permitting him to remain in Mississippi, "any law to the contrary notwithstanding."

James Miller not only taught young William Johnson the barber trade but also took the place of a father in teaching him the ethical principles which became a lasting part of his character. It was James Miller, too, who initiated him into the ways of the upper-class free Negro orbit of his existence, and who indicated many of the vaguely marked boundaries of his economic and social status in relation to the white Natchez community.

At the age of nineteen, William Johnson embarked upon his first independent venture as a businessman when he acquired a barbershop in 1828 at Port Gibson, Mississippi, a town about fifty miles north of Natchez. He operated this shop nearly two years. In 1830 he summarized his Port Gibson business career: "The amount taken in During my Stay in Port Gibson which was twenty two months was one thousand and ninety four Dollars and fifty cents, This was by Hair Cutting and Shaving alone."

But the young barber hoped eventually to establish himself in Natchez. He enlisted the services of his friends in looking for business opportunities. On March 6, 1829, Washington Sterns wrote him: "Old Jim wrote to you the other Day did he not what does he say about Letting you have the shop now." But the deal did not go through; young Johnson waited a year and a half before the opportunity came.

During the late 1820's Miller began to contemplate a move to New Orleans, though his economic position was as strong as that of any free Negro in Mississippi. Not only had a law been passed for his special benefit, but he had a thriving business in Natchez, owned four slaves, and had nearly $4,000 loaned at interest. Nevertheless on October

14, 1830, Miller sold the unexpired portion of the lease on his Main Street barbershop "and other adjoining Houses" and the furniture therein to William Johnson, his twenty-one-year-old brother-in-law, for $300, and moved to New Orleans.

Young William Johnson had at last established himself as a free Negro businessman in Natchez. His first purchases for his new shop were a dozen razors, a razor strop, and two bottles of bear's oil to be used as a pomade for men's hair.

The first five years of his Natchez career were years of intense activity. The young barber-businessman worked hard, but he expended just as much energy on recreation. He minded his own business. He paid his bills. In 1832 the Adams County Court and Police Board licensed him to remain in the state, for he had "Satisfied the Court of his good Character."

Johnson's Main Street business was originally located in an old brick building which he rented. By the fall of 1833 he had accumulated sufficient capital to purchase the building property, a lot partly occupied today by the United States post office. He made a down payment of nearly half the purchase price of $2,750 and gave a note for the remainder. Less than two years later, he retired the note.

During his first year in Natchez the young barber's total expenses, including rent and wages paid, were approximately $1,350. The second year they amounted to more than $1,500 and increased the third year to over $1,600. While the record of his income during this period is not complete, it is sufficiently detailed to indicate that it must have been at least $2,500 annually. By 1834 the Adams County tax assessor's roll listed him as owning one lot worth $2,700 and three slaves.

As the volume of Johnson's business increased, he

added improvements to his shop. He paid $26 for painting a sign. He periodically had the floor repaired and the walls repapered or whitewashed. And from time to time he bought new furniture and pictures to enliven the interior. In 1834 he expanded his business to include a bathhouse, which was erected at a cost of $170. This was equipped with four tubs and a device for dispensing the water, which was hauled to the establishment in barrels.

Johnson's charges were reasonable, even for that period. A shave cost a cash customer twelve and a half cents, while a haircut cost twice as much. The standard rate for shaving by the month was $1.50. The price of a hot or cold bath in 1834 was fifty cents, but in March the next year he raised the charge for a hot bath to seventy-five cents. While most of his customers paid cash, a large number secured credit and though most of them paid their accounts promptly, others let as much as two years elapse before settling their bills. But practically all eventually paid.

The young barber-businessman—never one to neglect any possible method of making an honest dollar—augmented his income with numerous business side lines. He lent small sums of money for short periods; he cannily bought and profitably sold numerous types of goods; in 1830–31 he conducted a toyshop in one of his vacant rooms; and he used two of his slaves to haul coal, sand, and street-watering barrels with horse-drawn carts. For a brief period he operated a drayage concern in partnership with one Henry Melin. He also speculated in farm land and began to acquire a small but steady income from city real estate rentals.

During these early years Johnson recorded even the most minute of his daily personal expenditures, occasionally entering them in two or even three different account books. These financial records reveal much concerning his personal habits and standard of living.

In 1831 he recorded purchases of barrels of flour for seventy-five cents each, and beef and steaks at twelve and a half cents, though on one occasion the steaks cost only six and one-fourth cents. Other "market" items included bread, milk, sugar, eggs, corn meal, lard, and similar staples. He drank beer and frequently bought whisky and occasionally other stimulants—cider, ale, gin, brandy, Madeira, and champagne. During the summer he drank a soda water almost daily.

His clothing outlay unquestionably made him a well-dressed young man. On February 26, 1831, he purchased a frock coat for $20, a vest and pair of pants for $10, and a pair of shoes for $1.50. The following day he paid $30 for a suit of clothes and later purchased another for $24. Subsequent clothing items included a pair of "satinet pants," six "Cambrick Hankerchefs," a white hat, and a pair of "Seal Skin Boots." He consistently noted the expense of mending and "scouring" his clothing.

There were numerous miscellaneous items among his purchases. He paid $1.50 for a violin and even recorded six and a quarter cents for a "Fiddle string." He acquired thirteen pictures, all of which may have been hung in his shop. He bought a sofa, a second violin, a "finger ring," and "a stamp of my name" for which he paid $1.00, and he expended $12 for the repair of his gold watch.

During these early years young Johnson was a gambler —with small change or part of his spare cash—and remained so the rest of his life. He regularly gambled small amounts at roulette and faro and in lottery ticket purchases. He bought numerous packs of cards and always had dominoes and checkers available for small-stake games. He backed his skill at shooting with bets, and carefully noted his losses in his accounts: "Lost shooting at the mark .62½." On one occasion he lost twenty-five cents in a fence-jumping contest. He was an admirer of horses and owned several by the mid-1830's; and he lost wagers ranging from twelve and a half cents to $14 at racing meets—beginning a twenty-year period of singularly bad luck in picking winners.

The theater was one of his favorite diversions until 1836. During February and March, 1831, he attended the theater on at least nine occasions, usually with a female companion (at fifty cents per admission), and several times he had "Coffee at Theatre." But he did not neglect the circus, as evidenced by one laconic account entry: "Dec. 18, 1831—Elephant Show .12½."

Johnson's various travels from 1830 to 1835 are shown by his expenditure records to have been chiefly pleasure jaunts; after his marriage in 1835 they were usually limited to business or family visits to Vicksburg or New Orleans. During the two years he lived at Port Gibson, he made numerous trips to Natchez to visit his family and friends and to court several girls with whom he was acquainted. In 1831 he spent a month in New Orleans. The following year he tarried in St. Francisville, Louisiana, for several days in company with a young woman in whom he was interested. In 1833 he spent between two and three months traveling in the East, visiting Philadelphia and New York. And during the entire period he was making infrequent trips to New Orleans to visit his sister, Adelia Miller, and her husband.

The 1831 visit to New Orleans was his most lengthy stay in that city. He recorded in his cashbook that he paid $10 for his steamboat passage and made numerous purchases of clothing, soda water, lottery tickets, and fruit. On July 19 he hired two carriages for $12 and drove "the Ladys" out to Lake Pontchartrain, where he paid $3.00

for dinner and also purchased whisky and two watermelons. On July 23 he played billiards. The next day he hired a gig, played billiards, purchased liquor, soda water, and oranges, and paid a "bathing" fee. Two days later he again played billiards, hired a carriage, and noted an expenditure of $3.00 for dinner at "the Lake." Once he varied his usual routine of expenditures by the purchase of a French-and-English spelling book. On August 5 he noted that $1.25 had been used for the purchase of a lady's handkerchief. Six days after this he crossed the Mississippi with "the Ladys," presented them with a $9.50 music box, played billiards, and purchased both whisky and wine.

On August 13 he took passage on a steamboat back to Natchez. He recorded that he had been away "during the whole of this month" and that his trip had cost him exactly $135.87½. But he did not begrudge the expenditure; he had thoroughly enjoyed his vacation in the "Paris of the Western World," "the great theatre of fun, frolic, flash, and fashion," as a reporter of the *American Turf Register* later described New Orleans.

The account entries for Johnson's Eastern trip are meager, but they offer at least a skeleton of his itinerary. He apparently traveled from New Orleans by river boat and overland stage and noted that the cost was $18—a sum considerably less than Gulf-Atlantic passage. On August 1, 1833, he noted, "I was in Philadelphia." Two weeks later he paid $63.65 for "perfumery" for his barbershop. He wrote that transportation from New York to Philadelphia had cost him $1.50, and that he had spent $1.50 for sundries in Walnut Street.

In early September he engaged passage to New Orleans on the ship *Archer* for $45, but departure time was still two weeks off; during that period he boarded with a Mrs. Becket, made a trip to New Castle, and bought a $30 violin. He later paid $8.00 for his passage from New

Orleans to Natchez. William Johnson had visited the East; the travel bug never bit him again.

During these years young Johnson was courting several girls. While identification is limited to only a few of the young women in whom he was interested, there is no doubt that several of them received gifts from him. A "Miss Catharine" received a pair of gloves; "Miss Mary Gatewood" was given a lady's handkerchief; "a present to Miss Amer Silk Dress" cost him $4.37½.

Johnson probably met Mary Gatewood, a free woman of color, in New Orleans in 1830 or early in 1831. For almost a year they corresponded regularly, and during one extended period she wrote at the rate of two letters a week. He saw her frequently during his 1831 visit to the Crescent City. The $9.50 music box, which he bought when he crossed the river with "the Ladys," probably was given to her. During the month's sojourn it is obvious that they grew fond of each other.

Then, in July, 1832, he received a letter from her, posted at St. Francisville, Louisiana. This river port was only sixty miles south of Natchez, and within two weeks the young squire had hired a horse, left his barbershop in charge of a friend, free Negro Robert McCary, and ridden the winding roads past Woodville to the Louisiana town.

For several days Johnson and Mary Gatewood renewed their romance. The young man noted in his accounts that he bought considerable quantities of beer at "Madam Scotts," probably a colored inn or tavern, gave a generous tip to the Madam for her "attention to us," and the day before his departure for home gave Mary $100 in "U. S. paper." His records fail to state what prompted him to give her such a large sum, but upon his return to Natchez he wrote in his ledger: "Francisville Francisville Good Good."

For at least six months after Johnson's return the

couple wrote frequently to each other, but not a single letter from "Miss Gatewood" remains in the Johnson Collection today, and there are no copies of his letters to her.

The woman Johnson was to marry was a resident of Natchez. Ann Battles was the daughter of Harriet Battles, an illiterate free woman of color who was a friend of Johnson's sister, Adelia Miller, and her husband. The first mention of Ann in Johnson's papers occurs in a letter which his friend Washington Sterns wrote to him in Port Gibson in March, 1829. It revealed that a mutual friend had wished him "great success" with Ann Battles. Apparently there was already some romantic interest between the twenty-year-old barber and the fourteen-year-old former slave girl.

Ann's mother had been the slave of Gabriel Tichenor. In 1822 Tichenor, who now claimed to be a citizen of Concordia Parish, Louisiana, filed notice with the parish judge that he intended to free his mulatto slave Harriet Battles, aged about thirty, whose conduct had been praiseworthy, and her seven-year-old daughter, Ann. Under Louisiana law only the mother could be freed, and this was accomplished when the manumission papers were filed and recorded in December. Nearly two years later the action was recorded in Adams County, Mississippi, and certified by the county clerk.

But Harriet's daughter was still a slave. Hence in April, 1826, Tichenor—who now claimed Natchez as his correct residence—appointed a Cincinnati attorney to emancipate Harriet Battles again and to free her daughter. On May 16 Harriet and Ann Battles, "both lately of ·Natchez in the State of Mississippi, but now of & at Cincinnati in the State of Ohio . . . in consideration of the faithful services of the sd mulatress and for other good considerations," were freed. Six days later the mayor of

Cincinnati added his official signature to the document.

That the mulatto mother and her daughter remained in the good graces of their former owner was evidenced by the fact that in August, 1829, Gabriel Tichenor and his wife deeded to Harriet Battles, for a consideration of $2.00, a Natchez lot across the street from Travellers Hall, one of the town's hotels. Her public conduct thereafter was exemplary. In 1832 the Adams County Court and Police Board licensed to remain in the state, "Harriet Battles a free mulatto woman about thirty five years old five feet six inches high having satisfied the court of her good character and honest deportment."

Shortly after his return to Natchez in 1830, young Johnson began to squire Ann Battles to public amusements. They became regular theater attendants and on occasion were accompanied by her mother. Soon Johnson began recording amounts paid for small gifts for the young woman. He bought her an orange, he furnished her guitar with new strings, he entered twenty-five cents for "Mending Miss Anns Breast pin," and he presented her with "three songs in Music." Though her name appeared with considerable frequency in his cashbook, he dated other girls, still much the young-man-about-town.

In 1832 Ann's mother began to do Johnson's laundry. Afterward he occasionally noted small payments to her for mending or small postal charges.

Finally, on March 24, 1835, Johnson noted in his cashbook: "To Bon [a Natchez tailor] for my wedding Coat $48.87½." On April 20 he secured an Adams County marriage license, and the next day he and Ann were married. No entry was made in his cashbook thereafter until May 11.

Twenty-year-old Ann Battles had ensnared the most eligible bachelor in her class in Natchez. Her husband was the hard-working, hard-playing, twenty-six-year-old owner of the town's most popular barbershop, building property worth at least $2,700, and several slaves. He was a man who was respected by the community for his integrity and good deportment.

Moreover, like many small men—his height was slightly less than Ann's five feet, seven inches, and his weight usually 135 to 140 pounds—he was meticulous in his dress. He carried an expensive watch, wore rings, paid a boy fifty cents to blacken his shoes for a month. He owned a well-equipped saddle horse, several musical instruments, some books, and he subscribed to magazines and newspapers.

Concerning William Johnson's other qualifications, Ann Battles was presently to be informed. Their sixteen-year union was to be blessed (in the thought and phrase of the times) with ten children, the last of whom arrived a month before the father's death in 1851.

Chapter Three

Barbershop Proprietor and Businessman

BARBERSHOPS, taverns, and coffeehouses in ante-bellum Natchez served as commercial meeting centers and informal men's clubs where business and social contacts of many kinds were made. In these places business deals were initiated, political opinions aired, and bets laid on impending horse races—all in an idiom invariably masculine and occasionally rough and profane. Even the odors of tavern bars and barbershops had common elements, but there was one marked difference. Both were redolent with the smells of the unwashed male and his whisky and tobacco, but in the barbershop these virile scents were partially counteracted by the fragrant tangs of lavender-water, rose-water, and other "perfumery."

As the town's leading business house of its type, the Johnson Barbershop was for forty years one of the vital institutions through which ebbed much of the everyday life of Natchez. One of its advantages was its location. When the young proprietor purchased his Main Street business property in 1833, he was either lucky or keenly perceptive in diagnosing trends for the immediate future in the development of the business center of town. Within three years, two of his immediate neighbors had erected new three-story brick buildings, and at the end of the decade additional business expansion in the immediate vicinity of the barbershop had made it a choice property.

By 1840 the young free Negro found himself surrounded by practically all of the town's important commercial and governmental structures. The courthouse was a square away. The three principal hotels—including the three-story, 120-room City Hotel, which was rebuilt in 1837—were within a block and a half; two banks, including one organized in 1839, were immediately across the street, and the remaining two were on the same street, in adjacent blocks. Two important firms also established themselves opposite the barbershop—Patterson & Wiswall's merchandising emporium in 1835, and the commission firm of McAlister & Watson in 1840. The pedestrian who strolled eastward past the shops came in the next square to the warehouse and exhibit rooms of the leading auctioneer, Jacob Soria, then to the store of John R. Stockman, and finally to the counting rooms and warehouses of a notable commission firm, Stanton, Buckner and Company. Intermixed with these and other Main Street stores were several dozen smaller establishments —fruit stands, bootmakers, tailors, auctioneers, drugstores, bookstores, billiard halls, and barrooms.

Meanwhile the young free Negro had seen the wisdom of keeping pace with his neighbors in improving the appearance of Main Street. His old brick building was neither sound nor sightly nor appropriate for a man who aspired to solidify his economic position and to be well thought of by his mercantile neighbors. Accordingly, in 1838 he contracted for the erection of a handsome new three-story building at a cost of nearly $3,400. Customarily a keeper of careful itemizations of expenditures and income, in this case he outdid himself by entering some of the construction records in three different account books as well as in his diary. He examined each brick and timber that went into the structure, unobtrusively watched every move made by the skilled workmen, all of whom were white men, and frequently talked with their bosses in amicable but firm tones.

The bricklayers were paid periodically, but in February, 1839, the principal contractor, George Weldon, agreed to take a note for the final thousand dollars, payable without interest within a year. A note outstanding against him always worried the barber, and it was typical of his business methods that he paid Weldon in full within six months. On July 11, 1839, he entered the payment in an account book, and recorded in his diary:

"To Day it was that I took up my note that Mr George Weldon held—I owed Him a Ballance of Eight Hundred Dollars which I took up in this way—I Gave him a Note on the Rail Road Banking Company for three hundred and sixty four Dollars, which he took, and I Gave him a note on Messrs Wood [and] Metcalfe for Three Hundred and nineteen Dollars, which he took—I then Gave Him in Cash One Hundred and seventeen Dollars which makes the Eight Hundred Dollars which He held against me, as a Ballance on One thousand Dollars that He had my Note for." Following the entry, which incidentally illustrates how promissory notes often were virtual substitutes for money, he pridefully signed his name.

By this time Johnson had found a tenant willing to pay $1,000 annual rent for a part of his new building—a section he referred to as his "Fancy Store on Main Street," and in another part he had refitted his own place of business. Eventually his shop contained six chairs manned by the proprietor and other free Negroes and a slave or two, two washstands, a coatrack and a hatrack, a table and a desk, and two sofas, while the walls were ornamented by four mirrors and more than thirty framed pictures, including several horse-racing scenes.

This barbershop, by far the largest in town, dominated

the trade. The opposition consisted largely of a small shop run by a free Negro friend, Robert McCary, and others opened by a half dozen or more transient French, Spanish, and "Dutch" barbers. Johnson watched them jealously but needlessly, for McCary was the only one who remained in Natchez more than a few months, and his two-chair establishment was in a location on the edge of the business district.

Competition was kept at a minimum not by cutthroat tactics but by the application of business principles that a later century would accept as most effective. The barber's success formula was simple: politeness, even beyond a customer-is-always-right attitude; reasonably satisfied employees, even though a few were slaves; cleanliness, as evidenced by a tidy and attractive shop, separate "shaving boxes" for rent to regular customers, and the linen coats of the barbers; and service, often exceeding minimum expectations of new customers.

The clientele generally had a choice of a variety of "perfumery," fancy soaps, and hair oils. These included lavender-water, rose-water, "lemon scent," cologne, rose soap, several types of "essences," "Cosmetique" perfumery and pomades, "Creme de Perse," bay rum, oil of orange, and Macassar oil. The less fastidious always found "rectified bear's oil" at hand for application to their hair.

The barber's emphasis on "perfumery" and sanitation made his shop a place of refuge from the collective stink of the numberless putrefactions that often pervaded the business district. The failure of nineteenth-century city governments to provide adequate garbage disposal and street-cleaning frequently left noisome stenches in the central areas of towns, and Natchez was no exception. Odors from the romantic magnolia and honeysuckle and night-blooming jasmine were overpowered by smells emanating from outdoor privies, from deceased and decaying horses, cows, hogs, cats, dogs, and rats, from decomposing offal and overripe eggs. Natchezans, like other American town-dwellers, were partially resigned to this huge symphonic fragrance along their main business streets, but William Johnson's generation was at least becoming aware of the luxury and possible healthfulness of the personal bath.

When, in 1834, the barber opened his public bathhouse as an adjunct to his principal business, he was both unconsciously reverting to a tradition of his trade and participating in a mid-nineteenth-century controversy concerning bathing. During the Middle Ages numerous European public baths had been supervised by a remarkable combination, the barber-surgeon. In the seventeenth and eighteenth centuries, however, much of the European and American world had experienced a stunting of the desire for cleanliness "and, in the broader sense, for regeneration" of the body through bathing. This attitude, which in part had sprung from a tendency to equate bathing with nudity and hence with sin, had been responsible for neglect of bodily care probably "without parallel in any other highly civilized period." But the decades when William Johnson operated his barbershop and bathhouse witnessed the beginnings of a struggle by health-minded reformers to introduce widespread bathing into the United States—by hydropathy (cold-water curative treatments), by steam baths at home, or in communal establishments, tubs, or showers.

Johnson was moved by no high-minded reform motives in opening his bathhouse. He merely knew that such establishments were being increasingly patronized in other urban centers, and he was enterprising enough to build one, largely as a money-making, summertime luxury service. Since most Americans of his generation were usually dirty, he probably would have been personally responsible for making local males more attractive if he could have induced all razor or scissors customers to take baths. But public patronage of the bathhouse did not remotely rival that of the barbershop except in a single inflation year when everyone was flush with spare cash.

Total bathhouse receipts for his most profitable year —which ended just before the monetary crisis of 1837— were almost $500. Thereafter the venture was much less profitable, although very infrequently a single day saw as many as twenty customers enjoying bathing and scouring themselves with flesh brushes and "fancy soap."

If the bathhouse was no great money-maker, it did bring its proprietor much good will from his clientele. American household plumbing was still in a primitive, non–mass production stage, and a few well-to-do men were the only persons in Natchez who owned bathing apparatuses, designed to be operated by servants. The barber's bathhouse account book therefore records the names of a number of prominent citizens who had sought occasional relief from the heat and dust of the unpaved streets. Bathers whose names were unknown to the proprietor were entered in the book under such whimsical, fabricated appellations as "Mr. Negro Trader," "Mr. Thermometer," "Mr. Sick Man," "Col. Troublesome," "Little Low Man," "Mr. Red Face," "Mr. Long Nose," "Mr. Frock Coat," "Mr. Silver Smith," "Mr. Italian Singer," and "Mr. from Texas." In 1840, Johnson noted in his diary the unusual circumstance that "the French Lady" took a bath.

As a further convenience to his customers and as a profitable slash at competitors, Johnson also opened two small one-man barbershops in addition to his principal establishment. One of these—located in the Tremont House, a small hotel just around the corner from his Main Street shop—was in operation from early 1840 through 1843. A Natchez-under-the-Hill business was begun in 1838 and continued in different locations there until 1851.

Both shops were rented by Johnson and were operated by free Negro employees or by two slaves, who bore the names Charles and Jim.

In Johnson's Main Street shop, customers could get their personal razors set or sharpened at the proprietor's honing table. They could also purchase Magnum Bonum razors, shaving brushes, and "metallic shaving boxes," as well as toothbrushes, cigars, and suspenders. And a plasterer could buy surplus hair at $1.50 per bushel.

Moreover, the shop always opened early and closed late. Sunday morning found the proprietor and at least one of his barbers on duty behind the chairs, and sometimes work went on as usual even on Christmas Day.

Johnson also performed special tonsorial services. Infrequently he shaved both male and female heads, measured them and installed wigs thereon, and sold hair powder to the wig wearers. He often rode horseback to nearby plantation homes to cut children's hair, and in 1841 he was paid $1.00 for curling the hair of a young lady. Late in 1836 he charged former Governor George Poindexter $6.00 for twelve shaves in his room "at the tavern." He collected $1.00 for shaving a sick man, even during a yellow-fever epidemic, and $5.00 for shaving a corpse.

This last operation also demanded tact and patience in collecting his bill. In 1845 Charles G. Dahlgren, a merchant-banker who was later to become a Confederate general, paid Johnson $5.00 for having shaved the corpse of his wife's first husband in 1838. The barber charged nothing for having assisted in making a plaster of Paris cast of the face of the corpse.

The Negro occasionally cemented a friendship with some prominent person by permitting one of his barbers to accompany the friend on a trip. The barber equipment needed by one of Johnson's slave barbers, who was to serve the speaker of the House of Representatives as valet-barber at a session of the state legislature, was recorded in a diary entry:

"I Bought the following Articles and put the[m] up for John to take up to Jackson

Eight Razors	$5.37½	2 Shaving Brushes	.50
One Razor Strap	.75	1 Metalic Shaving	
2 pair of sissors	1.50	Box & soap	1.00
1 Box Powder &		1 Flesh Brush	1.25
Puff	1.25	1 Comb	12½
2 Bottles Lavender		3 Cakes of fine	
water	.50	Soap	1.25
1 Razor Hone		1 Flesh Brush	
Loaned	00	Large	.75"

The barber also went out of his way to build up good will by other methods. Two excerpts from his diary in 1837 illustrate his willingness to assist white friends in a time of distress:

"Mr Sweney was to night a hunting for some one to write for him and I told him that Mr Abona was doing nothing and would Like such a situation and I sent for him up to the Jefferson Hotell—When he Came I introduce[d] him to Mr Sweney and he then told him that he herd that he was out of Business and Mr S. gave him Something to do."

"Last night about ½ after 11 Oclock Mr. Gellett Came and awoke me to get the Loan of my bath tubb for his Brother who was very ill with a Cramp in his Stumache. I got up and assisted him in taking it up to his house Neither of us had a hat on at the time."

In this year, the barbershop operator desperately needed not only good will but customers with cash, for the Panic of 1837 had crippled his business. Entries in his diary reveal that the Natchez male regarded barber services as an extravagance to be sharply curtailed in this time of financial stress.

This was all the more galling because the barber's income had mounted to its highest point in the two previous years. In 1835 and 1836, the beginning years of the diary, Johnson's daily receipts frequently totaled $15 to $20 in cash, and occasionally between $20 and $30. At the end of the second week of February, 1836, he recorded that his gross income for the week was $117.87½ and that his expenses were $50.94—both figures being not far from his average for this period.

Johnson's barber business was exceedingly poor for several months following the Natchez bank crisis of May, 1837. By mid-July diary entries typically reported "Buisness as usual very dull." In the first week in August he wrote to his sister: "Buisness is so dull that tis hardly worth Keeping shop open for what one can make, if I had Rent to pay it would Burst me wide open. 6 shops on the hill and two or three under the hill." On September 25 he wrote again: "There is nothing doing here now—1.50 is a big days work here now—I never herd of such times in my Life—I don't actually make my Expenses now—and have not for the last 12 days in my shop—tis the Case with all us in the trade." On October 12 he recorded that the past month had been the "dullest time for Buisness" he had seen in his seven years in business in Natchez, and four days later he took in only thirty-seven and a half cents—"the dullest of all days that I Ever saw in Natchez . . . Now dont that beat Nature."

Such was the impact of the money crisis of 1837 on the barbershop business in Natchez. But if that business was a reasonable criterion, the town experienced temporary recovery late in 1837 (after the fall yellow-fever epidemic had run its course). Johnson's business continued "good" throughout most of 1838 and 1839, but became very "dull" early in 1840 and continued so until the end of 1843. At one point in 1842 income from his barbershop was so low that he considered changing his means of livelihood. Recovery began early in 1844, and the barbershop proprietor thereafter was better satisfied with his daily returns, which, however, never approached the boom days of 1835 and 1836. After early 1844 he considered $5.00 to $10.00 a "tolerable fair" day's cash business for his principal shop, and $12.00 or $13.00 exceptional.

A number of Johnson's barbershop customers borrowed money from him as his moneylending and brokerage sideline expanded. It reached its period of maximum operation during the flush times of the middle 1830's. An analysis of his loans for the twelve months ending March 30, 1837, shows that in that year he lent nearly $4,700 and that on February 16, 1837, at least $2,100 was still outstanding. By September 12, 1839, the amount of his loaned money outstanding had been reduced to about $925. In the following year his lending activities dwindled even more; in 1844 the total of his loans was about $580; and in the late 1840's his lending consisted of only a few small loans each year.

The operation of a lending business, even on a modest scale, made it necessary that the barber keep well informed concerning the confusing variety of money then in circulation. Early in 1840 he noted that "To Day Silver, Silver, Silver is Deman[d]ed by Our Profession or two for One in paper." He used his knowledge of the money market to make small profits in changing one type of money into another. A diary entry late in 1836 read: "To day I made 1 dollar by changing two Hundred Dollars Bankable money, ½ per cent." Such brokerage fees supplemented the profit which he made from interest on loans. His interest rates varied from 5 per cent per month to

6 per cent per year. But it is doubtful that his profit from both sources exceeded $300 in any one year.

Johnson's largest single loan was $1,000 to the firm of Gemmell & Taylor. He also made others ranging in size from $660 down to $100 to such firms and business and professional men as Elijah Bell (a hotel proprietor), McAlister & Watson, Barlow & Taylor (a mercantile firm), A. Spielman (proprietor of a saddlery), John B. Nevitt (a plantation owner), Dr. John M. Hubbard, a Dr. Benbrook, Dr. Reed Potts, and former Governor George Poindexter. But most of his loans were smaller than $100 and very frequently for short periods. The prevailing money tightness was reflected in a number of loans for periods of one to fourteen days and the borrowing of small amounts by individuals supposedly well-to-do or rich.

Johnson rarely failed to collect money that was due him—partly because he was careful to make most of his loans to responsible individuals, partly because he was capable of being extremely persistent in his collections, even to the point of going to court in rare instances. In difficult cases he transferred notes to white men who could bring stronger pressure to bear on the signers of the notes or paid a man named F. Taylor to collect on a commission basis.

One semiliterate man once wrote a detailed explanation of the circumstances which had prevented him from paying a debt due the barber. But he promised to pay very shortly, and added, "Nead Sesity Drive a Man to Doe Sometimes to Doe things that he Does not wish to Doe and So it was the Case with me and I hope you will not think hard of me for so doing. . . . But I shal Be up soon and it will Be all Right with you."

William Johnson, successful as a barbershop proprietor and moneylender, also made money as a landlord. In 1836–38 he erected two new buildings and thereby increased his income from rentals. The first, constructed under contract by Thomas Rose in the latter part of 1836 and the first half of 1837, was built on a lot on the south side of State Street (a half block from the courthouse). This property was owned by Johnson's mother-in-law, but managed by him. The two-story, five-room frame building cost Johnson $2,952; and it brought in more than $1,500 in rent payments before it burned in late September, 1839. However, the structure was covered by insurance to the extent of two thirds of its value. The chief tenants prior to the devastation of the first structure by fire had been P. McGetterick, who operated therein "a coffee house" called "The Southern Exchange," and a business firm called Green & Blake.

From the rent of what Johnson called his "Fancy Store on Main Street," which was located in the same brick building as his barbershop, he received at least $2,500 in the two and a half years following its completion in 1839. But an analysis of his rents for the years 1844 and 1845 indicates that his two buildings on Main Street, one brick and one frame, brought him no more than $600 per year (above maintenance costs), and his income from this source continued at about this figure until his death in 1851. His Main Street tenants in the 1840's included Colonel D. F. Waymouth, a storekeeper; J. N. Staples, another storekeeper; Dr. A. A. Jones, who operated a "botanic" drugstore; Jones's successor, Dr. J. R. Applewhite; Arthur Kenney, a "boot maker"; "Mr. Bunting," who operated a tenpin alley; and several fruit-store proprietors, including Antonio Lynch and Joseph Meshio.

With such a multiphase struggle for economic position, the free Negro's daily journal naturally reflected his activities as interlaced with daily occurrences on Main Street. The observant and curious Johnson turned a quizzical eye on those among his tenants who were obscure immigrant tradesmen, but, with the exception of a Greek friend, he was less amused by the remainder of the quarter of the town's population that had been born abroad. In 1842, in the midst of a devastating depression that had ruined many of his best customers, he wrote: "Business dull. . . . [these] times are very different from what they were 6 or seven years ago—The City is full of French and Duch Jews—trading mostly in Dry Goods."

In 1835 and 1836—"6 or seven years ago"—Natchez had been furiously participating in a countrywide orgy of get-rich-quick speculation that inevitably preceded a major depression. Land, slaves, and business houses were sold at puffed-up prices that represented unreal values, only to be resold at a profit. This tempting boom market led the barber to speculate, too, but he managed to achieve escape without alarming loss in the debacle that soon followed. His initial profits came from purchases and re-sales of a 162-acre tract of land, a city lot, and stock in a new bank. "The Bank Stock of The Commercial Bank," he wrote, in 1836, "was Drawn for to Day—There was the Greatest Rush made for it by the people that was Ever Known in this place before   A very Grate many Persons did not get any shairs."

Then came the Panic of 1837. When the Natchez banks unexpectedly stopped specie payment in May, Johnson wrote that the "times are Gloomy and sad to day Money is no money . . . I know not what will become of us. . . . terrible times."

The impact of the depression that followed can be incisively traced in the barber's day-by-day recordings of the gradual though irregular transition from bustling fortune-making to successive money crises, public meetings to discuss currency fluctuations, street auctions to dispose of the household goods and merchandise of debtors, sheriffs' sales, and bankruptcies. The barber himself sustained a loss from an investment of $2,000 in a railroad company that built 25 miles of a planned 125 miles before it went into bankruptcy. In 1840, a year in which a tornado and the partial failure of the cotton crop compounded the current economic misery, he noted:

"There has been the Largest Crowd at the Auction of the Marshall and the Sheriff at the Court House that I have Ever Seen—the Property of Mr Brown, of Mr Barlow, of J Smith the Carpenter, of Perkins, of Lenears, of McMurtry and of others. There was no real good sales made—oh my Country, my Country, what are you Coming to."

Many businesses, including Johnson's barbershops, suffered severely during the money crises of 1837, but late in that year experienced an illusory recovery that lasted—at least in men's minds—until late 1839 or early 1840, when the depression hit with full force and "the land-bubble burst." This reflected the curious reluctance of the lower Mississippi Valley and Texas to abandon the fever of speculation that marked the late 1830's, even in the face of admitted and widespread monetary tightness. The total sales of merchandise in Adams County, as reported on the tax rolls, show what happened to Natchez merchants in this period: 1830—$823,000; 1835—$1,655,-000; 1839—$695,000; 1849—$1,183,000.

These figures show a drop in trade in 1839 that had a disquieting effect on Johnson's business in the following years, for prosperous merchants were necessary for a thriving barber trade. Yet he not only managed to remain solvent in the years of widespread insolvency, but rode out the baleful effects of the depression and left a considerable estate to his family when he died in 1851. Energy, patience, shrewdness, and occasionally opportunism had combined in a notable example of free Negro enterprise.

Chapter Four

Farmer

On October 12, 1835, twenty-six-year-old William Johnson opened his sixteen-volume diary with the notation, "Bought at Auction 162 acres of Land at $4.12½ per acre Belonging to the Estate of Mr Lewis." It was his first investment in rural property.

Like most Southerners of the ante-bellum period, Johnson developed early in life an interest in land. The ownership of a farm or plantation was one of the keys to social position and to success. Its possession was calculated to raise the economic and civil status of the barber in the Natchez community—a status already enhanced by his ownership of city property.

But the pride of rural property-holding did not deter the young businessman from his quest for quick profits. The next month he offered the 162-acre tract for sale at $8.00 per acre to Adolph Flecheux, "Engraver, Copperplate printer, and Jeweller," and promptly closed the deal. For the next ten years, though he consistently watched land prices in the hope of another good investment or speculative venture, he acquired no rural real estate.

During this period Johnson had become interested, through his hunting and fishing excursions, in the countryside six to eight miles southwest of Natchez, lying west of Ellis Cliffs and north of Hutchins Landing. Between the cliffs and the river was an extensive area then known as "the Swamp," consisting of swamp, timberland, several small lakes, and some cleared fields. Land here was cheap, and Johnson came to the conclusion that money could be made from its development.

The land fever hit Johnson during the early 1840's. He became interested in the Collier Place, but finally decided that the soil was poor and the farm too swampy. For a time several tracts were worthy of temporary enthusiastic attention. Then he changed his mind about the Collier Place and tried without success to purchase it. He tried to buy Natchez Island, but he and the owner's agent could not reach an agreement. On one occasion he wrote that he had "been in a terrible way" about the swamplands he had been wanting to buy.

Early in the 1840's Johnson had loaned $100 to William Mosbey, one of the farmers of the Swamp area, and during the years that followed Mosbey became further financially distressed and borrowed additional sums. Johnson's friends urged him to foreclose on his mortgages, but he refused and confided to his diary: "Poor Fellow I am sorry for him."

During the late summer of 1845, Johnson purchased from Winslow Winn for $600 a tract of 120 acres, called "Hard Scrabble," lying immediately south of Mosbey's property and thirteen months later bought out the unfortunate farmer, paying him $3,000 for 242 acres (a very fair price) and $100 "for his Corn & stock of Hogs & Cattle, farming utensils and Everything that He had about the Primises." Two months after this purchase he noted his third land acquisition: "I was at auction to day, the School Land Sales, and I bot 403.10 Hundredths acres of Land at 1.25 per acre." He had bought a ninety-nine-year lease on the school land for $500. This tract was less valuable than the others for it lay a section away from the river, and it was very swampy and split by a long, shallow lake.

Thus, at an expenditure of some $4,000, Johnson had

acquired nearly 750 acres of farm and timber land. From this time until his death, four and a half years later, he devoted much of his time and energy to the attempt to make his venture pay and to protect his timber rights against illegal encroachments by two of his neighbors. Shortly before his death in 1851 he added to his holdings again, although during the intervening years he had on several occasions bid unsuccessfully on tracts in the vicinity, and once on a 1,400-acre tract in Arkansas. In the spring of that year he acquired 2,400 acres of swampland near his farm, though after his death the title to two thirds of the acreage proved to be defective.

Since the barber could not devote all his time to farming, his first problem was to secure adequate supervision of his labor force. To this end he usually contrived to have on his place a white man who was expected to act as a combination tenant, overseer, and chief laborer. Early in 1847 he made an agreement with W. H. Stump, who had been living on a nearby farm, to manage Hard Scrabble: "Stump Commencd this morning to work and our bargain is that he is to have one third of what is made on the ground and one third of the Proffit that may arise from wood that may be Cut by Billy, Phill and Peggy [three of Johnson's slaves] and he to find his own Family and I to find my force." The next year Johnson paid Stump $15 per month to manage both his tracts and furnished housing and food for him and his wife.

By midsummer of 1847, however, Johnson's diary began to reveal a measure of dissatisfaction with Stump: "Stump on the Gallery as usual and the hands at work Cutting wood." In early January, 1849, his patience was beginning to wear thin. "I find there is Scarcly anything down thare done when I am not thare," he complained. "I found Mr Stump and Little Winn going down the Road when I Came down this mor[n]ing." Shortly after this Johnson had an end-of-the-year settlement with Stump, and they did not renew their agreement.

In the summer of 1849 H. Burke agreed to act as overseer for a stipend of $15 per month, in addition to food and housing. Burke proved no more satisfactory than his predecessor. By early February of the following year Johnson had written in his diary: "Burke is, I think, begining to Drink a Little too much for my Interest, It wont do at all, no Sir." On March 6 he wrote: "I found Burke up at the Point Fishing, him and Little Winn, and when he Saw me he started down from the Point and went to the house and Got the hoe and went to work on the Levy before the Door Oh what Rascally Conduct for a man that pretends to do Buisness." During Burke's sixteen months of overseeing, he did much fishing, hunting, and drinking, but the free Negro acknowledged that the overseer was able to do a fairly good day's work while partially drunk. Finally Burke and Johnson severed business relations. "Thus we are square to this date, and I Expect to Keep So," he recorded, and the same day he hired B. Wolcott to oversee.

From 1849 onward, Johnson hired a succession of white men to work on his farm. Beginning in March, Samuel Clark was employed to perform "Farming work of all Kinds" at $12 per month, but apparently he spent most of the next three months cutting cordwood and their relationship was terminated when he presented a bill for the wood-cutting which Johnson considered exorbitant. The same spring a "Mr. Strong" also assisted in farm work. In August Johnson hired William Langford "on Conditions, that is, he is to take no more Sprees." Langford was usually drunk or sick, however, and in October Johnson went down to talk to him: "we had but a very few words before I told him that I had no farther use for Him and that I wanted to Settle with Him, which I did." Still later

Gardner Lindar agreed to "do anything in The Shape of work" for $5.00 a month. For a period in early 1851 a "Mr. Coburn" was employed to dig drainage ditches.

The labor force usually included the chief white tenant or overseer, occasional white or free Negro laborers, and five or six slaves—most of them Johnson's. In addition, he temporarily augmented this force by hiring extra slaves from neighboring planters, agreeing "to find them there Clothing & Medical Bill for the year," and occasionally during planting and harvesting periods secured the help of his sons, one or two of his barbers, relatives from New Orleans, and free Negro friends. When Johnson remained overnight at the farm he often arose before daybreak and paced his hands in two or three hours labor before breakfast. Thus the farmer was usually able to throw a miscellaneous labor force of between seven and twelve hands into the fields.

Occasionally during slack seasons, Johnson reversed the procedure and hired a portion of his slaves to other planters. For three months during the winter of 1847–48, Peggy was hired to Mr. Ford, and during January and February, 1850, worked for Mr. Pearce. In late October, 1850, Phil, Sylvia, Anderson, and Mary were hired to Mr. Gregory to pull corn at the rate of $2.00 per day and their keep.

The yearly routine of Johnson's farm naturally evolved from its products—corn, vegetables, fruit, cordwood and timber, wool, and cattle. The late weeks of the old year and the first weeks of the new were generally devoted to enlarging the planting acreage by clearing. Potatoes, corn, and onions were planted during late February and March and the cornfields plowed. There the labor force planted peas, potatoes, pumpkins, watermelons, and cabbages. Additional ditching had to be accomplished, and some of the corn had to be replanted if the stand was poor.

June found the hands digging early potatoes and cultivating corn; in July and August, roasting ears were gathered and corn fodder stripped. In late August and September, turnips were planted, grass was cut, and corn shocked or pulled. In October and November, corn was shelled and sacked, potatoes were dug, and pumpkins hauled to town. Then the late corn was pulled, and the stalk fodder was cut. November and December witnessed the repair of buildings and fences, the cutting of wood, the digging of drainage ditches, and the other miscellaneous off-season tasks that attend farming.

Other products enabled the owner and his overseer to keep the farm hands busy at slack times. Some fifty to one hundred sheep had to be brought up occasionally, for they usually grazed "in the woods," as Johnson wrote, and in May or early June they were sheared. Hog pens had to be constructed and the pigs penned and marked, because they practically ran wild in the Swamp and some of the neighbors or his own overseers were not overly scrupulous in determining original ownership before they killed or placed evidence of ownership on unmarked pigs. In late March, 1851, Johnson wrote of one such incident: "Wm Wolcott [a neighbor] Marked them all   I mean all 6 of the Pigs that was Caught from my Sow, I find that is the reason that I have always been so unlucky in the raising of my hogs, I never Marked them in time." Johnson gave considerable attention to his cattle, and descriptions of many of them found their way into his diary: "Bob-tail old Cow, Redish Color, Branded E A," "Ball face old red Cow, very old, Same Brand," "A white Cow with Flesh Colord, Blue Spots, Branded as above." Many of them bore such names as Mary, Patuna, Adeline, Ellen, Jenny,

Ruffin, Pretz, Savanah, and Francis. Johnson had his own cattle mark, which was "a cross and under bit in the right Ear and a cross and Slit in the Left ear." Some time also had to be spent in the care of three or four mules, several oxen, and from twenty to thirty horses and colts.

Although numbers of rails and logs were needed for fencing and for the construction of cabins, barns, and sheds, the chief subsidiary product was cordwood. Some of the cordwood was cut by Johnson's labor force, but most of it was obtained under contract (usually at from 55 cents to $1.00 per cord) with white wood choppers or the owner of a small gang of slave wood choppers, or by the hire of white men by the month. Johnson's force transported it to the river bank, where it was sold to passing steamboats. The usual price was between $2.00 and $2.50 per cord, and the ordinary sale was between 10 and 40 cords. By 1850 this business reached such proportions that Johnson's overseer sold about 450 cords.

Johnson's expenses in running his farm were continuous and sometimes ran to sizable sums. He was called upon to furnish implements, tools, and other equipment—plows, harness, chains, sweeps, harrows, axes, and hoes—and they had to be replaced or repaired from time to time. Salt must be provided for the animals. Lumber was needed for buildings and tar to seal the roofs. One March day he sent down three pounds of buckshot, presumably for use against predatory animals and birds. The outlay for rations for the labor force was considerable, as several of the larger shipments by skiff from Natchez to the farm during the late summer of 1850 illustrated. On July 15, the skiff carried seven hog heads, seventy-seven pounds of side meat, one-half gallon of vinegar, one gallon of molasses, five barrels of corn, and one and a half bushels of meal. A week later it brought four barrels of corn, one and a half bushels of meal, seventy-six pounds of bacon, and thirty pounds of flour. On September 1 thirty pounds of flour, seventy-nine pounds of bacon, three bushels of corn meal, and sugar arrived. Meanwhile nearly every day saw the dispatch of smaller shipments. Not infrequently Johnson was led to make such remarks as "Now we will See how they will Last," or, "The Last Call I hope They will make this year."

While the vexations of planting were normally numerous, Johnson apparently had more than his share of troubles. The hands did not work well unless under competent supervision, and his overseers were frequently inattentive or not on the job at all. He often noted that very little work was being done, and after one such entry remarked, "Well I have my own trouble, That I do." Another time he was even more annoyed: "They are Pulling Corn or pretending to do so—has been at it all week—Oh what a time my Country." And his entries regarding sickness were numerous; either his land near the Swamp was unhealthful, or his slaves were a singularly sickly group.

His farm land and the vicinity of his house, quarters, and outbuildings also were subject to floods and even high water. On one occasion he had to use a skiff to cross from the house to the slave cabins.

A variety of additional vexations also plagued him. Oxen and cattle were lost, stray or wild dogs killed the sheep, and one May day in 1847 he reported that some of his hogs seemed "to be dying from Poison of Some Kind—tis very Strange indeed." The skiffs which he used for the transportation of goods or personnel between Natchez and the farm sometimes sank, and though no lives were ever endangered, the loss of supplies was both inconvenient and expensive. One of the farm ponds did not hold water very well. Thieves broke into his corn house. Neighbors appropriated his horses to ride to town. And raccoons had uncommonly good appetites for sprouting corn. Slaves were careless; buggy shafts were broken, tools were misplaced or lost, and once a slave lost control of a team, and the wagon crashed down a hillside. In June, 1848, Ellen "got the Ends of two of Her Fingers Ground off in the Corn Mill . . . I Cut the End of One of them off with my Knife." Later Fanny (a cow) ran off, and that night the Negro farmer wrote that "this has been a Day of Some vexations to me. I Flogged Sarah, Dicy and the Little mule all to day."

From the beginning of his farming operations, Johnson was confronted with these problems and headaches of planting and sometimes seriously thought of reducing his farming acreage. Pessimism often began to replace his earlier optimism concerning rural life. In 1847 he rented the improved portion of his northern, or Mosbey, tract for $100, and a house on the place for $50. In mid-September, 1848, he went down to Hard Scrabble and "Took a Look at things in General." What he saw did not please him; the potato patch was covered with grass, the pumpkin vines were bearing poorly, the sheep were lean. The next year he rented Hard Scrabble for $50, which was, however, a good return on his initial investment there. In late 1849 he was led to remark: "Oh I have had bad Luck this year in the way of Croping, very indeed."

Early in 1850 he contemplated renting Hard Scrabble to Gregory, one of his neighbors, but the deal never materialized. Late the same year he wrote: "Things Looks bad and I have a Strong Notion not to Cultivate the place the Coming year." Yet even with this dark outlook, Johnson continued farming operations on the Mosbey tract in 1851, after having rented Hard Scrabble for the sum of $35, and in the spring he purchased several scattered tracts of swampland.

Was Johnson's farming a profitable enterprise? An exact cost-and-profit answer is impossible, but it is certain that the expenses of feeding the considerable number of persons in his town household were substantially reduced by the use of produce raised on the farm. Vegetables, corn, eggs, and butter were often delivered to his town kitchen. His sheep brought a small annual profit and his cordwood business from $50 to $750 a year. In his six years of farming he probably made $700 above costs in sales of cattle and horses. In 1848 and 1849 he received not more than $250 annually from sales of corn and potatoes, a goodly portion of which was shipped by steamboat to New Orleans and sold by his brother-in-law, James Miller.

Regardless of whether Johnson's farming and timber operations had been reasonably profitable, his land investments brought a substantial return to his widow. On July 1, 1853, she sold the lands and lease to prominent planter James Surget for slightly less than $8,000.

CHAPTER FIVE

Johnson's Apprentices and Slaves

THE Natchez barber-farmer's restless economic enterprise and growing family responsibilities eventually led him in his last years to become the master of about two dozen Negroes and the employer of a few whites. Like any other man with expanding business affairs, a three-story residence, two aged mothers-in-law in his family group, and a new baby arriving every eighteen months, he needed labor assistance in quantity.

But even an affluent free Negro could not hire just anyone who wanted a job. In securing servants for his home and manpower for his shops and farm, he was restricted to three types of persons: other free Negroes, for skilled employment; slaves, largely for household and unskilled jobs; and an occasional illiterate white man who was not unwilling to take pay for half working, half malingering, on a colored man's farm. Of necessity, therefore, William Johnson chiefly used slaves and free Negro apprentices and journeymen.

His diary not only delineated his attitudes toward these assistants but, even more unusual in a Southern personal journal, also humanized several of the free Negroes and slaves by endowing them with distinctive and strikingly varied personalities. It further divulged his methods of operating the apprentice system, the only educational institution then available for many free Negro and poor white children.

The apprentice system furnished a convenient, if not

APPRENTICES AND SLAVES   55

invariably humane, solution to a problem for white men who had a paternal or court-designated interest in free Negro youngsters and for courts which had the responsibility of disposing of indigent orphans. In theory both black and white apprentices were to be taught a skilled trade and otherwise instructed and cared for. In practice whether they were maltreated and meanly exploited, or fostered and fairly treated, depended largely upon the nature and whims of the master to whom they were bound or upon the interest and community position of their original protectors.

Johnson and some other masters frequently allowed a would-be apprentice to work for a trial period before an indenture was signed. In one instance related by the barber, an influential white planter who was the legal protector of two slave girls—the planter's brother had ordered their freedom in his will, and they were then being tried out as prospective seamstress apprentices—allowed them to leave the service of a Miss Dowell, the only woman then advertising as the operator of a Natchez shop. They reported that they had departed because "the old Lady was too Foul mouthed Intirely. It would not do—" Court records show in other cases that free Negroes were apprenticed as "mechanics," hostlers, and bricklayers to white masters and as barbers to Johnson and possibly one other Negro shop proprietor, while white children were bound out to learn "the art, trade, and mystery" (in the language of the legal documents) of printing, the seamstress trade, bricklaying, and merchandising.

Most of Johnson's barbers were free Negro apprentices or journeymen. His younger barbers were selected from a number of applicants, and on more than one occasion the shop master refused to take prospective apprentices. The free boys he agreed to train were placed in the shop by their parents or white protectors when they were between ten and fifteen years of age. Until they were eighteen or twenty-one they served as apprentices or would-be apprentices, subject to the barbershop owner's discipline and control. In return for their labor services, he taught them the barber trade, gave them a rudimentary education, fed them, and in some instances clothed them. At the age of eighteen the apprentices were usually released to make their own wage agreements with him or some other proprietor. In the 1840's Johnson habitually paid $100-plus-shoes to $150 per year to his former apprentices who had graduated into the journeyman class and had elected to remain in his shop.

Johnson carried out his part of the apprenticeship agreements in good conscience. He disciplined his boys when he thought they needed it: he did not hesitate to flog them for being impudent, for "being so careless and passionate, whilst shaving," for smoking his cigars, or for taking absence without leave. He also regretted it when he caught two of them fondling a black slave wench. "Oh what Puppys," he wrote in his diary. "Fondling—beneath a Levell, Low Minded Creatures. I look on them as Soft."

On the other hand, he paid them small amounts regularly, made special awards for good work, and allowed them to attend "darkey parties," theatrical and circus performances, races, and church meetings. He was pleased when they did well in their studies; while he confessed to a "failing" to "Keep them at it" regularly, he probably fulfilled the educational clause in his apprentice contracts more faithfully than the ordinary master. And when they finally had become journeymen and departed to set up their own shops in a neighboring town or on a steamboat, he was apparently sincere in his hopes that the young men he had trained would "do well."

From the shop master's viewpoint, one of the most

disappointing proclivities of his apprentices and journeymen was manifested in their willingness to associate with slaves at "darkey parties." Selected free Negroes and slaves were invited to these entertainments, which were occasionally given in the Natchez vicinity by benevolent slaveowners to reward their slave cooks and personal servants for praiseworthy service. They were usually held in white residences, but at least one "Darkey Ball" was staged in 1839 in the ballroom of the Mississippi Hotel, then one of the state's two finest hostelries. Johnson would have been insulted at a suggestion that he attend; he wanted his charges to maintain a similar aloofness from associating with slaves on a social level.

If they insisted, he permitted them to attend. But not without scornful comment in his diary: "Bill [Nix] and Charles and Wellington all goes out to a Party Given by a servant of the Missis Evans out at there Residence—Butter, Butter will run in suitable wether"; "Antony Goes to Darkey Party to night, Birds of a Feather"; "I find that Antony & Jeff was at a Darkey Ball. Ferdinand Burns was thare   H Lee was thare too. It was Some where up at Sam Cottons, Oh what a Set."

Could some of this disdain have stemmed from unadmitted frustration that he could attend neither white nor black balls, from the loneliness of his abnormal position which left him suspended between two races, too proud to mingle with the servile but barred from participation in most social activities of the master group?

Only one of his free barbers followed his advice to remain away from "darkey parties." This sole exception was William Winston. This boy, whom he called "Bill Winston" or "Winston" in his diary (to distinguish between him and other "Bills") came closer to maintaining what Johnson considered correct attitudes and deportment than any of his employees, and eventually the two were firmly attached to each other by ties of affection, mutual interests, and long business association.

When Bill Winston came to work for Johnson in 1836 "to Lern the Barbers trade," he was about twelve years of age and still a slave. But his master, former Lieutenant Governor Fountain Winston, had made provision in his will for the freeing of Bill's mother, Rachel, and had added several provisions in behalf of the boy: "Believing Bill or William the son of Rachel too white to be continued in Slavery," he had directed that he remain with his mother until he was old enough to be bound as an apprentice to "some reputable mechanic." When he was twenty-one, he was to be freed. Fountain Winston further directed that his furniture should go to Rachel; $500 should be set aside to support Rachel and Bill (during the latter's minority); and the residue of his property (amounting to $3,000 plus land in Tennessee), except his library, should be held in trust for the boy—provided only that his habits should be good.

Soon after Bill's arrival at the Johnson establishment, he displayed a willingness to stand up for what he conceived to be his rights—a quality that his master admired. "To day Bill Wilson & Bill Winston has a fight in the Back Room. Winston has the Best of the fight tho," the barber related. "I Parted them Both and made a greate Deal of fun of Winston. Second Fight took place in the Back of the Yard and Bill Winston whiped him Fairly and he hollowed to have Bill Winston taken off of him."

Thereafter the relationship between master and apprentice grew steadily closer. The boy had to be chastised infrequently, but he was allowed to accompany the barber on horseback rides into the countryside, fishing and hunting outings, and jaunts to the race track. Johnson found him an excellent companion—lighthearted and quick-witted, but also steady and moral in his habits.

In 1842 Johnson had a conversation with the executor of the Fountain Winston estate about Bill Winston's future: "I Saw Mr W Burns this Evening and had a Long talk with him about Winston. He wanted to Know how he was ageting along &c and I told him that He was doing very well tho I was not at this time Learning him much in the way of his Book. He wanted me to do so and he thought that Winston was now about Eighteen years old and that he wanted to have him Learn to Read and write, so that he might be able to Keep his Books or accts when he became older Enough to do Buisness for Himself He thought that wages was and Injury to a Boy, that it would give them Bad Habits, and that he did not want him to have any but to work along as Long as he was satisfied. We Could agree I thanked him. He Said that he thought that there would be something Left out of the Estate and that if he conducted himself well that he would give him a start some day—I told him that Winston was a very smart Boy and that I Liked him very much indeed."

By this time Johnson considered Winston his most reliable barber and occasionally left him in complete charge of the shop. When he was twenty-one, Johnson agreed to pay his top journeyman wages, $150 per year, to Burns for the Negro's services. But the white man allowed his charge to keep the wages, even though he was still a slave, and during the succeeding year sent him to Cincinnati to be emancipated. He returned to Natchez and continued to work in the Johnson Barbershop long after the diarist was killed in 1851. Ohio freedom papers were by this time open to serious legal question in Mississippi, however, and in 1854 the Mississippi legislature passed a special law authorizing William Winston, free man of color, to remain in the state—a most unusual concession to a free Negro in the 1850's.

Some of the free mulatto apprentices, such as two Hoggatt boys and various members of the Burns family, were too young for close association with Johnson, but their work was carried on in an atmosphere of mutual respect. Two older free Negro journeymen, Wellington West and Washington Sterns, were also employed for brief periods. West, who also worked for Johnson's brother-in-law in New Orleans, was a satisfactory employee, but it was not altogether safe to allow Sterns access to the shop till and he drank too much to suit the shop proprietor. After Johnson fired Sterns, with whom he had grown up in Natchez, he wrote that he had "told him that I could not aford to Keep him any Longer and that his maner of doing buisness would never do. To be Drunk ½ of his time would never Suit me nor my Customers."

Concerning William Nix, another longtime apprentice and journeyman, Johnson wrote in 1839 that he is "up to this Day a pure pure Negro at Heart and in action, &c." The barber considered this a damning indictment —wasn't it obvious that ambitious free mulattoes ought to emulate the more exemplary individuals among the whites?—but Bill continued to disappoint his mentor. During his apprenticeship he was flogged more than once for stealing, his mother being "greatly Hurt" on one occasion "at the Conduct of Her Degraded Son." When Bill, who was of "light complexion," was a little older, he disgusted Johnson by yielding to the charms of "Black women" slaves. When he finally married, Johnson was not surprised to hear that his wife had previously been "made use of" by a white man.

Still Johnson continued to look for improvement. He recorded any inspiring suggestion of more creditable aspiration on the part of the younger Negro: Bill Nix had joined the Methodist church; he had gone to the Catholic church to learn to sing; he had been taking French lessons —although his English spelling and reading were admittedly poor. Moreover, he had unquestionably learned the mechanics of his trade. The barber's notations, made on successive days in 1844, about the termination of his business relationship with the apprentice had a note of restrained hope:

"Nothing new, more than that the Barber at Rodney is dead and the citizens wants another to Come up there, William Nicks is in a greate way to go up and take the Shop—I hope he may . . ."

"Nothing new. Buisness has been Tolerable fair to day. William Nix Left here this morning on the Concordia To open a Shop a[t] Rodney—in place of the Dead man, I hope he may do well, I Know he can if He will Only try, for there is money to made up thare and I Know it, We have not had a regular Settlement for thirty three months He has had in that time Cash to the Ammount Five Hundred and ninety three [dollars and] 82 cts and it was understood by us Some Eighteen months ago that he was very willing to work for the Same per month that Charles worked for."

William Johnson tried to teach the barber trade to several slaves, but was successful with only two, Charles and Jim.

The slave Charles was ten or eleven years of age when he was placed in the shop by his owner, Major S. Young. The original agreement concerning Charles contained provisions very similar to indentures governing free apprentices: The slave's clothing expenditures were to be at the Major's expense, while Johnson was "to Learn him the trade" and "to Learn him his Books &c &c Learn him to write also." Charles subsequently became an excellent barber by the time he was fifteen; he was also personable and well liked, and when he was critically sick with yellow fever in 1839, "Several Persons" volunteered to watch by his bedside.

In 1842, when Charles had passed his eighteenth birthday—the age when most free apprentices became independent journeymen, Johnson and Major Young had a conversation about the slave which incidentally illustrates how the barber conducted himself in a business deal: "I had a talk with Mag Young to day and He surprised me very much when he told me that the Boy's [Charles's] time has been out for some time &c. After Considerable talk He wanted me to say what His Services is worth and what they were worth for the Last year & I wanted him to do the same but he would not   So I told him that I would settle the Amount of a Debt that He told me that he was dunnd for up at Mr J B Nights Store—It was agreed on and He then wantd to Know how much I would give for Him for the next year. I told him that a good part of the time there was Little or nothing doing, 6 months of the year that was very Little to be done, so that I Did not in reality want Any One. Well, seys he, suppose we make and avarrage of what you think. Say about fifteen dollars, and we agreed on the Same." A few months later Johnson was paying Young $150 per year (less the medical expenses and the cost of clothing) for the slave's services, an arrangement that benefited both parties.

During most of the 1840's Johnson allowed Charles to run the one-man under-the-Hill barbershop with comparatively little supervision. The slave brought in his receipts every two weeks, and Johnson often gave him one tenth to one fifth of the proceeds. The barber came to think so highly of his work that he agreed to raise the annual payments to his owner from $150 to $200, a sum larger than the wages paid to the shop's free journeymen.

The slave was in fact as free in most respects as the journeymen, for he was not only almost his own boss in his shop, but he selected his own clothing and roamed about the town and made frequent visits to his Jefferson County "home."

The master barber nevertheless came to believe that Charles had a fatal weakness in a yearning for "darkey parties" and colored women beneath his "level." "Charles was over the River to day a fishing and came home Drunk," he wrote in 1843. "Wanted to marry an old Black mans Daughter and told the old man to Refer to Wheelock & Sayers, A. L. Wilson, or Erhart & Foster if he wanted to know about his character." Five years later his taste had not improved: "Charles disgraced Himself this Morning by Marrying Mrs Littles Servant Girl Mary Known to the City as being a Buster." After a few months elapsed Major Young was reported as "Down on Charles about Getting married against his Orders—He told me that Charles Should have to give up that wife or Remain a Slave all his Life."

If the major was a gentleman of unswerving convictions, Charles's "marriage" was annulled, for in 1851 Young arranged for him to be sent to a Northern state to be freed and to remain there. As an association of fifteen years thus came to an end, the barber-diarist noted the termination of Charles's employment with not the slightest expression of emotion except a halfhearted suspicion that the slave had lately "Humbuged" him by withholding some of his earnings.

The twenty-six-year-old slave Jim was installed in place of Charles in the shop "below." From the day in 1844 that Johnson had purchased Jim at a street auction, he was "very well pleased with him." As a laborer on Johnson's farm and later as a barber, this young man with a yellow complexion was invariably dependable in his work and strait-laced in his morals. Any attempted stigmatizing of all slaves as devoid of pride and discrimination in mating would be proved false by the evidence that Jim "seperated" from a slave wife when he became convinced that a former judge of Mississippi's highest court had taken "1st chances." Not once did he commit indiscretions that led him to feel the sting of the lash.

Each slave was more than a name at the top of a cost-and-return sheet in an account book. He was an individual with marked characteristics and his own prides and perplexities. Walker, a very black man who smiled broadly and usually became confused when addressed, disappeared and was never found. Had he been stolen or had he run off to Kentucky to rejoin his "wife" whom he had longed for? And old Middleton, the property of Johnson's sister who had moved to New Orleans, had been allowed to remain in Natchez on condition that periodically he would hand over a part of his earnings to Johnson for forwarding to the owner. But the slave became more of a problem than a source of income, as Johnson indicated in a letter to his sister:

"Dear me what must be done with old Middleton—he is now Lying—Sick way up town—and has been for God-Knows how Long—he has got a wife some where up town—and that is where he stays—I was up to see him about a week ago—and he pretended that he was unable to work or walk—So I left him he says that he wants you to take him for you to take care of him. the old Fellow has Killed himself—Drinking—he has not paid me a cent for I cant tell when. tho I will Look in his Book and Let you know—what must be done with him, he says he [can't] work nor walk."

But the diary notes regarding Steven are in another vein. Steven was an irrepressible fellow who caused Johnson more trouble than all his other slaves combined. He was a petty thief. He kept forbidden rendezvous with Negro girls. He ran off frequently. He shirked his tasks. Despite laws prescribing strict penalties for the sale or gift of intoxicants to slaves, he seemingly had little difficulty in securing liquor and he drank it to excess. Its consumption always caused him to perform some act which inevitably brought him a severe thrashing, a stay in the Natchez guardhouse, or confinement in handcuffs or chains.

Four entries in Johnson's diary in a single month in 1838 afford ample illustration of the derangement of the barber's affairs caused by the slave:

March 19: "Steven got drunk Last night and went of[f] and remained all night and was not Here this morning to go to Market. I sent Bill Nix to the Jail to see if He was there and He was not there. I then sent Him out to Dr Ogdons and in going there He found Him and brought Him Down and Left Him in the gate and he Jumped over the Fence and went threw in Judge Montgomerys yard. Bill He ran around the Corner and found him and brought Him in, I Kept him [in] the shop a Little while and then sent him to Help Mrs Lieper to move from the old House Down to the House belonging to Bill Hazard He ran off 4 times in about three hours and Bill Nix Caught Him Every time, so He Brought Him Home after a while and I went to the stable and gave him a pretty sefveere thrashing with the Cow hide—then he was perfectly Calm and Quite and could then do his work. Tis singular how much good it does some people to get whiped."

March 27: "Steven ran off Last night and God Only Knows where he has gone to, for I dont, tho if I should have the Good Luck to Get Him again I will be very apt to Hurt his Feelings—This is the second time he has ranaway in a week."

March 29: "To day I took one of the bigest Kind of a hunt for Steven But could not find the Rascal at all."

March 31: "I got on my Horse Early this morning and wrode Out to Washington in search of Steven but Could not find Him at all I also went Out again in the afternoon to Becon Landing but could not hear of Him. During the time that I was in sea[r]ch of him He sent me word that if I would Only Let him off without whiping him that he would never runaway again Durring His Life."

Steven was not unintelligent—he once cleared himself of a charge of stealing in a minute's testimony in his own behalf before a jury—and his master felt a secret sympathy for him. But his vice made his retention impossible, and the barber felt himself forced to make arrangements to sell him.

On December 30, 1843, Johnson wrote: "I Expect from what past between Mr Cannon and myself that he will take Steven On Monday if Nothing Happens—And what is the Cause of my parting with him, why it is nothing but Liquor, Liquor, His fondness for it. Nothing more, Poor Fellow. There are many worse fellows than poor Steven is, God Bless Him. Tis his Own fault."

The next day the sale was closed. "To day has been to me a very Sad Day; many tears was in my Eyes to day On acct. of my Selling poor Steven. I went under the hill this Evening to See him of[f] but the Boat did not Cross over again and Steven got drunk in a few minutes and I took him Home & made him Sleep in the garret and Kept him Safe."

On January 1, the diarist recorded: "I got up this morning Early and took Steven with me down to the Ferry Boat and gave him up to the Overseer of Young & Cannon. . . . I gave Steven a pair [of] Suspenders and a pr of Socks and 2 Cigars, Shook hands with him and see [him] go On Bourd for the Last time I felt hurt but Liquor is the Cause of his troubles; I would not have parted with Him if he had Only have Let Liquor alone but he Cannot do it I believe." Johnson had given a bill of sale and had received $600 for the slave who had been longest in his service—six hundred pieces of silver.

While William Johnson's Negro blood did not deter him from using severe measures in disciplining his slaves, neither was he among the masters who were despotically brutal. In this connection it should be noted not only that whipping slaves was generally thought to be indispensable for the maintenance of order, but also that flogging was a common mode of discipline of groups of whites, such as apprentices, criminals, schoolboys, and soldiers and sailors. In the case of William Johnson, he felt it necessary that reasonable labor returns should be secured from his slave investments, and his position as a prominent free Negro businessman made it imperative that his slaves behave themselves.

He therefore demanded seemly conduct, while at times he also manifested a paternalistic sympathy. In accordance with the policy followed by more enlightened masters, he never disrupted any of his slave families by the sale of one member; he fed his slaves well; and he allowed them to attend church meetings, "darkey parties," and circuses. The whippings he administered were always for misconduct or carelessness in the handling of property, but never for laziness. He punished Lucinda, for example, because she secured permission to attend church but instead "went off in some private Room, the Little Strumpet"; and several years later he again whipped her for hitting her "husband" in the street.

Thus William Johnson accepted and used the labor system as he found it. His slaveholding was not the "act of benevolence" which a highly respected modern historian concludes was often the case with free Negro slaveholders. No streak of self-condemning integrity obliged him to waver between the opposing forces in his heritage that might have contended for his soul. No queasy irresolution prevented him from wholehearted imitation of the more humane white slaveholders. When any of his slaves died, he did what was expected of any Christian slaveholder: he paid for a respectable funeral service and burial and prayed that the deceased would be "better off in another world." In slaveholding, as in all else, he tried to conduct himself as an honorable human being.

CHAPTER SIX

Sportsman

WILLIAM JOHNSON spent much of each day working at his trade or at one of his other business interests but found time also for hunting, fishing, and other forms of recreation. His statement that he was "always ready for Anything" was no exaggeration. He played shuffleboard and checkers, pitched quoits and dollars, played marbles and cards, shot at targets, raced toy boats, high jumped and broad jumped, took long or short walks about the town or the surrounding countryside, bought tickets in lotteries and raffles, and bet on horse races, elections, or any other event with a problematical outcome.

He relished competition and managed to bring it into every sport in which he engaged. If he hunted alone, he took as much pains in making accurate shots as if he were shooting a match against strong opposition. If he fished, either alone or with his sons or with friends, he tried to catch large numbers. If he practiced his marble-shooting, he tried to knock every little ball out of the circle. If he had no opposition he competed with himself.

Winning in any type of competition became a matter of pride, and he usually recorded whether he was winner or loser. If he lost, he admitted defeat; but his strong competitive spirit usually carried him to victory, and that night he wrote of the incident with gusto. In one of his diary entries he referred to himself as "the old Shark," and once, when reporting a hunt, wrote: "I always Beat the Crowd that I go with, and no mistake."

On the other hand, he was a highly social individual and sought companionship when tramping the woods and swamps in search of game or fowl or when casting his line for fish, and on most occasions managed to find a friend to accompany him. While he took pleasure in excelling in the activity, the companionship counted heavily. "When I got home," he wrote after one hunt with "Mr F. Thomas" and his close friend, McCary, "I found myself prety tight."

Hunting was his favorite outdoor sport, and the rolling, timbered Natchez countryside tempted hunters with deer, rabbits, wild hogs, alligators, ducks, snipe, quail, pigeons, raccoons, squirrels, turkeys, and other small game. Lying close to the river south of Natchez were swamps and lowlands not conducive to large-scale plantation operations; further eastward and southward were precipitous, forested hills, still a virgin pasture for wild and tame animals alike. And across the river, in Louisiana, were heavy stretches of timber and swamp that were unofficial game preserves.

The hunter owned a variety of shotguns, rifles, and pistols. Some of these weapons were named after their former owners, as was "the Meshio gun," and were sometimes traded for superior or imagined-to-be superior pieces. He was meticulous in the care of his firearms and loaned them infrequently, for experience had taught him that borrowers were careless of their well-polished surfaces and often returned them in bad condition. But he was too kindhearted a man to ignore appeals from white or colored friends. In 1840 he recorded that a group had returned from a "weeks Hunt on the other side of the River—They gave me a shoulder of a deer. Mr B[arland] Had my Rifle over with him."

Startling numbers of animals and birds were killed by Natchez sportsmen during this era. On one excursion in 1835 the diarist and his friends Barland and McCary killed "about thirty Aligaters" and numerous ducks. On a day in 1840 he noted that several hunting parties had been in the swamp, and added that "it will make 90 ducks that Came out of the Swamp in one day—the Greatest Quantity that Every I herd of Coming Out of the Lakes in one day before." Three years later he wrote that he "Killed to day Sixteen Squirrells" and some birds.

The variety was also amazing. In 1836 he recorded one bag: "Mc Killed 1 King Fisher, 1 Owl, 1 Little Swaller, and the Dogs caught a Rabit—I killed 1 Squerrel, 1 wood pecker, 1 wood Cock, 1 Little fat Bird." Three years later he noted: "Killed by Mr Whip, 1 Blue Indian hen, 1 white Crane, smaller One, 1 Frogg—Mr Ruffner, 1 Black Squirrel, 2 Large frogs, wounded, 1 Snake, caght 3 Aligators, Young Ones, with a Hook—I Killed 2 Squirrells, 1 white Crane, 4 or 5 young Aligators, 2 tolerable Large Snakes and 1 very Large one, water Mockersins, 1 frog."

Some of the hunts were notable in that the hunters carried veritable banquets with them. On one occasion, when Jacquemine and McCary accompanied him, he listed "Our Fare for the Day" as "Boil Bacon, Ham, Crackers—Beef stake, Buisket, Liquors, Whiskey and Brandy, good water, Segars, Venison Stake, Sauserage—aples—&c. Sweet milk."

While most of the hunting trips were free from accidents, there were times when bad luck dampened the enthusiasm of the hunters. In 1841 Johnson stated that he "wrode up on the old Quigless place, shot a Bird or two, then got as wet as water," while wearing his broadcloth satin vest. At other times accidentally discharged guns caused horses to jump and unseat their riders, and in 1839 Johnson wrote that he "went into the Swamp and took with me my three young Hounds and I started a Deer and in geting off my Horse I fell flat on my side and rolle[d] over on my Back." The rest of the hunt was uneventful and the results insignificant—four crows bagged and a new lake discovered.

Though Johnson seldom bragged about his marksmanship, he usually gave the bag of each hunter and let the numbers speak for themselves. Of one hunt, however, he noted: "I Killed one of the Largest Kind of an Aligator in the Aligator Lake. He was a Buster in any Country, I tell you." Though he rarely belittled the abilities of his companions, he once observed that "Brustee did not Kill a single thing, came back to town Just as he went and did not Kill a thing. I never saw Just such another Hunter as he is."

Judged from frequency of mention in his diary, Johnson's fishing excursions were considerably less numerous than his hunting trips. One reason may have been that few good fishing spots were to be found in the immediate vicinity of Natchez. St. Catherine's Creek was a comparatively small stream, the lakes south of town near the swamp were shallow and frequently dried up during hot summer months, and the Louisiana lakes across the river were not easily accessible. Some fishing, of course, was done in the Mississippi, but Johnson never recorded that he ever dropped his line in its waters.

The diarist infrequently mentioned the angling activities of his neighbors and friends, sometimes with a note of skepticism. When Izod, Woods, and Griffin reported that they caught thirty to forty fine fish, he wrote laconically: "I doubt it." Another day he said that "Sterns went across the river to Day to Fish and Came Home old Fashion."

Occasionally he took his apprentices or his sons out to St. Catherine's Creek for an afternoon of sport, but he seldom was able to report a large catch. In 1836, when a party of eight went out, he noted that "we only caught only 5 Fish in all—I caught 2, Mc 1, French 1, John 1."

In 1837 he recounted the story of a long-remembered fishing trip across the river. "I arose very Early in the morning and took Bill Nix and Bill Winston and mounted Our horses and crossed the River and went a Fishing in the Concordia and Cocodria Lake—Mc, J. Lacrose and G. Butler went along at the Same time and when we got Over to the Lake we found Messrs Levi Harrison, Pond, Rufner, Cambell, Stevenson, Noyes and Some Darkeys and after a short time young Bell and H Austin Came Down. Young Bell got Drunk and Lye down and went to sleep and Caught no fish of course tho all the persons that were over there caught a Greate many. My two and myself Caught 4 Doz and 4 fish Mc Caught as many or more prehaps than we three did—I Left Mc at the Lake a fishing We Reached town quite Early in the Evening and got home in time to have Our fish Dressed for Supper."

Three years later he again crossed the river to fish. He noted that the company included, "Mr McCary, Mr Lancaster, Mr Alderson, Mr Jno Jackomine, myself and Mr Noyes and two or three Small Boys" and reported that "we Caught a Greate many fish indeed Mc caught 66, Mr Alderson Caught 87, I caught 94, John 24."

After acquiring his farms south of Natchez he occasionally tried his luck in one of the shallow swamp lakes but reported little success and soon lost interest in the sport.

Johnson placed wagers on his prowess in many activities. He was an excellent rifle shot but was less skillful with a pistol. He once rode out to "Minor's Pasture," where he "Took Several Shots with a Pistol and then we Shot for Liquor and I made a tolerable Shot. I then Shot for Mr Thayer and Caused him to Loose the Liquor, it was so Dark that I Could not see to take good Sight."

But his winnings with the rifle more than offset his losses with the pistol. One of his favorite opponents in these shooting matches was John Jacquemine. In 1838 the diarist related that he "had a match with John the Greek to shoot 25 yards with a Riffle, 3 best in five for One Qrt. Box of Segars and I Lost the Cegars—I shot afterwards with him and Mc and beat them Both—they both shot with my Riffle." In 1842 he "went Out this Evening near Mrs Lintons and Shot a Mach With Mr Jaquimine, the 3 best in five, for One Barrell of Oysters—I won them with Ease." And on one occasion, he made this note regarding an unusual match: "Nothing new that I know of Except that I won 5 Cegars from Mc a shooting with a Blow-Gun this Evening."

Johnson found no pleasure in watching cockfights and made few entries concerning them. In 1837 he recorded that he went to the Natchez Landing and "Bot 1 Bale of Hay, 4 Sacks of Oats I also Bot a game Cock I payed five Dollars for him, thus it is ten Dollars for Provender & five for the chicken—I put him down in the yard and the Frizeling chicken whiped him So I find he is not much." Finally, in 1849, appeared a brief note: "I wrode out this Evening To the Tract to See a fight of Chickens and I saw 3 fights and Lost 2.50 and it is a Sport that is to me Disgusting in the Extream, I Shall not go to See any more I Promise." There is no record that he ever did, although by 1851 the Hutchens Livery Stable, only a few blocks from his shop, boasted a cockpit.

The diarist had little skill in pitching quoits and dollars. One day in September, 1841, he lost five fifteen-cent cigars to Joseph Meshio, who "Beat me Easy" in tossing quoits. A few days later he noted: "I was pitching Quoits a good part of to day with Jackomine, Meshio, Mr Rogers & Mr Antonia. I Came of[f] Even." Two weeks later, he "Pitched Quoits a part of the afternoon and Lost 75 cts worth of Cigars with Mr Jaqumine I then took him and we played against Mr Kenney and Meshio and they beat us Out of One Dozen Cigars." Another day he spent the greater part of the afternoon in pitching dollars "with John Jackomine and Mc and all Quit Even"; but Jacquemine usually "took" him, sometimes for as much as $5.00 per game.

Cards interested the free Negro, although he did not play as often as might have been expected. Some of his free Negro cronies were customary opponents, and he backed himself with his money as usual. There is insufficient evidence to venture an opinion as to his card-playing abilities.

Johnson was fond of horseback riding, and late afternoons frequently found him astride one of his horses on one of the country roads near Natchez. Although occasionally he rode alone, usually he had companions, one of his friends or one or more of his children; his wife "rode out" with him very infrequently. Sometimes he took a book along and dismounted to read under a tree for an hour. He picked berries along the roadside or in the fields, or simply "got Some magnolias and Came Home."

His rides were varied with short or long walks about the town or its environs. He walked to the old Spanish fort with McCary, went out to the edge of town where he and two of his sons "got Some grapes, Muskadines," or, at the day's end, strolled the few blocks to the Bluff where he watched the sun set to the westward over the Louisiana swamps and the river.

When he and his friend Bob McCary hiked together, their mischievous natures could get the better of them. "After 12 Oclock to day McCary and myself took a walk together and went Out by the Spanish Bayou, and there we found Some Boys playing Cards—We got Mooles to Load up his Gun and Hallow at them and Shoot at the Same time which he did and oh what runing you never Saw. They Left a Knife and 50 cts and there Cards, which

Jeff went down thare and got when they ran off." And on other occasions they took several of their children along. "I walked Out into Minors pasture this Evening with Mc and His two sons, William and Robert, and I had my Little William along also—We had Each of us a pupy to give them Exercise—The pup that I had Could Out run Mcs puppy very Easy indeed—We Eat Black Burries for a while then Came around by the Cricket ground and Came Home."

The diarist enjoyed playing with his children and boy apprentices. He hunted and fished with them and joined in their boyish sports. One day in 1843 he recorded: "I made a Jump or 2 with the Boys this Evening and beat Bill Nix about 6 inches in a ½ hamon Jump." He played marbles with them and with McCary, and McCary usually won. In 1839, he wrote that he and McCary had played sixteen games and that McCary had won ten out of the sixteen and "I have not been so tyred for some time As I am now from playing those Marbles." Three years later his game had not greatly improved for "Mc And myself played a good many Games of Marbles this Evening and He won a good many more Games than I did He Can beat me Easy." It was not an easy admission for the strongly competitive barber.

Early in 1847 the toy-boat-sailing craze reached Natchez. Small sailing boats, their white sails fluttering in the breeze, were to be seen on many of the Natchez ponds during late afternoons and on Sundays and holidays. The free Negro entered eagerly into the competition. On February 21 he noted: "We went Out to the Pond and there we past off and hour I Suppose in Sailing Little Boats accross the pond to amuse the Small Boys and ourselves too. My Boat out Sailed Mcs untill he found Out That I had a rudder on mine and then his Boat Out Saild mine being Larger than mine." And again on March 21: "I sailed Boats this Evening with Mc and the Boys and Mc[s] Boat Beat the old Shark at Last. It was a new One that he made."

Still another entry, made a month later, is revelatory of the diarist's character: "I Took my 3 Small Boats and went Out to the Pond of Mr John Johnson and Sailed my Boats alone to see which was the fastest, The Long Boat Rough & Ready beat the party Easy Enough. Good many Scotchmen was present, old Hardy, Hamilton Johnson and a good many others."

Johnson's competitive spirit was active, even when sailing miniature ships on a Natchez pond while he was alone on a warm spring afternoon.

CHAPTER SEVEN

The Family Hearthside

DURING the 1840's William Johnson's three-story brick home occupied a prominent location in a section of the town that bustled with social and business activity. Main Street was only a block northward and two blocks west was the river bluff and the old Spanish parade ground where Natchez folk walked on pleasant evenings.

The title to the lot, which dated back to Spanish days, had been acquired in 1829 by Harriet Battles, the mother of Johnson's wife. The barber built his first house, a frame building suitable for rental purposes, on the site during the latter part of 1836 and the first half of 1837. This structure burned in late September, 1839, during a period when a yellow-fever epidemic had forced the Johnson family to retire to the country. The fire gutted the entire block bounded by State, Canal, Washington and Wall streets.

A new house on this site was built under Johnson's immediate supervision between August, 1840, and November, 1841. His slaves performed most of the rough labor; the carpentry, bricklaying, and plastering were done by local white artisans; but William Johnson acted as his own chief contractor. Aside from a dancing master who occupied a room or two in the building for a few months in 1841 and 1842, Johnson's records do not indicate that any portions were used for rental purposes. It has been the family home for more than a century.

Some thirty feet behind the house was the servants'

two-story brick house in which one of the downstairs rooms was used for the family kitchen, as was the Southern custom at the time. A frame walkway connected the second stories of the two buildings and beneath it was a partially bricked patio. In the patio was the cistern, which was dug at a contract price of $125. On November 8, 1842, Johnson bought a "Cistern Bucket," had it fastened to the windlass and "Drew out a Buckett of the first water, and took a Drink of it, that Ever was Caught in the Cistern— It was pleasent and good." The backyard was filled and graded, and a hole for the new "back house" dug and the house built over it. Near the back of the lot was a stable and perhaps another small frame building or two, for Johnson kept horses and a few other animals. No new outbuildings were added until the spring of 1850, when Johnson built a small frame structure at a cost of slightly over $200.

Johnson furnished his home well and continually improved the quality of its appointments by purchase or trade. His accounts and diary entries indicate that he acquired pictures, sofas, mirrors, a secretary, bookcases, a pair of dining tables, chairs, and other items. Some of the furnishings were purchased at private or public sales at bargain prices, but occasionally he was deceived. "I find out to day that Mr Waller cheated me Sharply in Selling me the Sofa yesterday," he recorded in May, 1850. "It has but 3 Legs Very well, I must get Even with him if I Can." But he persisted in attending sales, and bought all manner of smaller items—glasses, a mattress, buckets, pots and pans, coffeepots, strainers, dish covers, flatirons, lamps, and tumblers.

His passion for bargain-hunting led him to purchase an amazing variety of goods for general family use. Among his acquisitions were a "dress patron of Calico, price $5.50," linen shirts, twenty yards of cotton, an ice cream freezer, eight small aprons, two table cloths, a keg of white lead, and a piece of "Maddrass Hank." At an auction at Mr. Dolbeare's he was the successful bidder for "16 forks and 22 Knives, 2 Dishes, with Covers, and a market Basket." A bargain was a bargain regardless of the immediateness of the need for the item.

According to a modern Johnson tradition, the barber saw to it that his family was provided with a superabundance of food. The records of the family marketing, which was mostly performed by the father, indicate that the food on the Johnson table was both plentiful and varied. In addition to general staples, from time to time the larder contained quantities of luxury items: eighteen bottles of lime juice, nine bottles of London mustard, a barrel of oysters, two bottles of lemon sirup, two boxes of tea, two gallons of peach brandy, "a very fine half Keg of Gocian Butter," and a "Barrell of Cranburys." Purchased food supplies were supplemented by the produce of a well-tended vegetable garden and by milch cows and a few hogs and poultry.

The barber recorded all manner of home-life trivia. There were references to a new riding horse or a new buggy secured for the family's use. In 1844 he bought a low-bodied, folding-topped barouche, which was the fashionable vehicle of the day. He noticed that martins had made their first appearance, or that Lake, a milch cow, had a new calf. A new "back house" led to the entry, "We had a hold Dug yesterday and we Bricked it up and to day we Built a House on it and finished it off in Stile." He swung a new gate and "made Some other Improovments." He put up a new fence, removed a few old bricks from the patio, planted a few "Cabage" seed, and had the boys whitewash a new shed which had been built on the back of the lot.

The Johnsons had within their own home cultural opportunities far greater than those enjoyed by most white or free Negro families of the ante-bellum period. Whether as a result of the father's desire to emulate the Natchez aristocrats or of his own inner yearnings, he unquestionably made a serious attempt to elevate himself and his family. His children were sent to private tutors and schools; they were encouraged to read from the dozens of volumes and the magazines and newspapers that lined the bookshelves; they were given music lessons; and at least one of them studied art. The family musical instruments included a piano, a music box, and violins. Occasionally the father, who was a modest performer on the violin, gave an impromptu recital.

Johnson's home life was quiet and happy, and although he mentioned his wife infrequently in his diary, there were evidences of strong bonds of affection between them. She evidently managed the household to his satisfaction and left him time to concentrate on his various business affairs. While it is difficult to determine the manner in which household expenses were handled, it appears that Johnson paid most of the bills. Several diary entries, however, indicate that Ann had or was given money of her own which was kept separate from the principal family operating fund. In July, 1836, for example, Johnson noted that he paid a gambling debt by borrowing $10 from his wife.

During the early years of their marriage the young couple shared many of their pleasures. They continued to attend the theater and other places of amusement and took walks and horseback rides together, but as their children arrived Ann gradually went out less and less with her husband. She probably had a small circle of women friends, for she frequently entertained. "Good many Ladies at our House Last Night," Johnson reported on one occasion, "old Mrs Brustee, old Miss F. and young Miss F., Mrs Amie & two daughters, Miss Henrietta, Some other Miss of Jerman Extraction, Mr. Brustee and all our own children They Kept up the sport until 11 Oclock." Ann and the children also made irregular trips to New Orleans to visit the Millers and were sometimes accompanied by her mother.

Only once did Johnson indicate that there was friction between himself and his wife, and on this occasion he cast himself in the role of aggrieved husband. "I had Last night and this morning together several Quarrels with my wife," he wrote. "She Commenced it of course I did not have a great deal to say—all amounts to nothing any how for I Cant say that I said anything to Her to Hurt her feelings that I believd myself whilst I was talking. I only did it in a Spirrit of Retalation—that [is] all so Help me." But he did not state the cause of the family quarrel.

The most galling irritant in the home life of this free man of color was the general conduct of his illiterate free mulatto mother, Amy Johnson. Johnson evinced devotion to her, but she seemed to possess few attributes that would move her son to compassion or love. She had keen business sense and constantly dealt in birds of various kinds, traded in a wide variety of small items, and bought and sold slaves and other property. Her son frequently lent her money and was quite willing to assume financial obligations for her. At times Johnson found it necessary to pay her bills in order that the family financial standing should not be impaired. In 1843, for example, a member of the firm of Patterson & Wiswall spoke to Johnson "to Know if they Could by any way Collect $40 that Mouthers owed them for goods." Two days later John G. Taylor inquired about collecting an account which dated back to 1836. Johnson either succeeded in getting his mother to pay the accounts or paid them himself.

But the son could not prevent his mother from gossiping maliciously or spreading false rumors concerning him and other members of the family. Neither could he restrain her from arguing with tradesmen or with neighbors, from causing family quarrels, or from brawling in the streets. Her conduct was most embarrassing during the summer of 1837. On the last morning in June, she "Commenced as usual to quarrell with Everything and Every body," and her son gave her a few flicks with a whip as "the quickest way to stop it." She thereupon advanced upon him and dared him to strike her, which, he said, he "would not do for anthing in the world." During the next six weeks Amy was often in a terrible temper, and until August 12 she and her son spoke not one word to each other. On the seventh of that month she climaxed the quarrel by throwing "Salt all on the floor at the door, Quarrells and makes all maner of fuss for nothing at all." Johnson made one of his mother's servants "scour it up," but he did not "Say a word to the Old Lady about it." That night she commenced a "Terrible Quarrelling" and abused her son for punishing one of the slaves for misconduct. Partial reconciliation was effected through the good offices of Johnson's brother-in-law, James Miller, who was visiting him at the time.

Her conduct improved during the last of August and the month of September, and on the twenty-fifth Johnson wrote his sister, Adelia Miller, to "tell Mr. Miller that Mother does a great deal Better than I expected she would—She has quit running out in the streets to complete her quarrels—now she does pretty well—about 3 quarrels or three fusses a week will satisfy her very well —and before he came up here she used to have the bigest Kind of a fuss Every morning." But her good behavior came abruptly to an end on November 23. "The old woman is on a regular spree for quarrelling to day all day," he noted. "Oh Lord, was any One on this Earth So perpetually tormented as I am." During the rest of the month she was a fairly peaceable person and on December 1 paid to her son, without argument, $25 on a loan.

Despite all their quarrels, when his mother died in 1849 Johnson arranged a burial befitting a parent of the town's leading free Negro citizen. He rented seven or eight "hacks" or carriages for the funeral procession, and her remains were interred in a plot purchased in the white section of the town's leading cemetery. "Today has been a [day] of Great trouble to me and all of my Family," he recorded of the day of her funeral. "The Remains of My Poor Mother was Burried, oh my God. My Loss is too Greate. Oh my Poor Belovd Mother is Losst to me forever in this world." Several days elapsed before the diarist regained his accustomed composure.

Johnson was fond of his ten children. He noted their births and many of their birthdays. He helped nurse them in sickness, allowed them small sums of weekly spending money, and was more than indulgent in clothing them. When "Little Richard by Accident pulled down the Large Picture of the Last Supper & the Glass was badly Broken," he was a forgiving father; but, while he was usually tolerant of their childish misdemeanors, he occasionally wielded the strong hand of discipline. He once gave "Little William a very seviere whiping . . . for his bad Conduct, Throwing Brick and so forth, and sent Him Down Home," but had to reassure himself later that his action was correct. He taught his sons to hunt, fish, and ride horses, instructed them in reading and writing prior to their attendance at school, and gave them their first lessons in the barber trade at an early age.

He carefully observed their scholastic achievements and once proudly recorded that "Richard and William wrote their first Letter to day that they Ever wrote." And like all parents, he was disappointed in their failures. "The Letter from N. Orleans to day states that my Little

Anna did not make her Speech at the Examinatun as was Expected She would, Thus I am Disappointed," he wrote regretfully. He accompanied them on walks about the town or rides in its vicinity, and picnics were not unusual. Of one such excursion in 1844 he wrote: "I worked untill 12 O'clock, then closed and after Dinner I took All the children that I could well get in my Carriage and Drove Out in to Col Bingamans Pasture On the Woodville Road, I thare cut 3 water Mellons . . . which was more than we could all Destroy."

Like most parents, his anger rose when his children were abused or got into difficulties. When a slave "Black Boy," who was the property of a white neighbor, slapped one of the barber's sons, the father "got near Enough to give him a very seviere Kick on his but." A few years later he wrote: "Nothing new of much Moment. More than I have been very Mad nearly all Day Tis about my Son William It appears that he went out to Drive a calf to the Commons and it farther appears that 2 of Dr Jones children Got in a fuss with Him and what Ever name they Called Him he returned it and it then is Said by a man who I would Hate [to] believe on his Oath, I mean a Certain Horse Drover, by the Name Foreman."

While generally blessed with exuberant good health, the Johnson family was not entirely exempt from periods of sickness when the diarist became the tender father and husband. Home remedies were the rule for minor ailments, but at the first sign of serious illness one of the family doctors was consulted. Ordinarily Johnson followed their advice and gave the medicine prescribed but on at least one occasion, after Dr. Hogg had ordered "Sperrits of nitre," he decided that the medicine was "too strong." Ann was rarely incapacitated for more than a few hours and apparently responded to bleeding and the popular "Cook's Pills" or other medicines. When his son

Richard lay gravely ill in 1841, Johnson remained at home to attend him and late one night penned a poignant diary entry: "Tis now at the time of my writing nearly 4 Oclock in the morning and I am now setting by the Bed Side of Richard who I thank God appears a Little Easy in his Sleep." The Johnsons lost only one of their children, Phillip, who died soon after birth in 1844. Except for an accident or two and a few attacks of temporary illness, one of which rendered him practically blind for a few hours, the diarist had little to say about his own health.

Aside from his contacts with his immediate family, Johnson's closest personal family relationship was with his sister, Adelia, and her husband, James Miller. The Millers had moved to New Orleans in 1830 and there accumulated an estate which thirty-five years later was appraised at more than $20,000. The Millers and the Johnsons frequently visited each other, usually with their children and a servant or two, and constantly corresponded. During the summer of 1842 Johnson's wife, with the youngest children, spent over two weeks visiting in New Orleans, and in August, Miller journeyed up-river to Natchez. He and Johnson spent the day of his arrival in eating, conversation, playing the violin, competing at shuffleboard, and riding. The following days they took a steamboat trip to Vicksburg and went hunting several times. Before Miller's departure, Johnson invited Robert McCary to dinner, and the three friends "Sat prety Late at the table Drinking wine &c," after which they saw Miller off on "Bourd of S. B. Maid of Arkensaw." When Mrs. Miller and her children arrived, the two families and a few friends usually had a party, and after the purchase of his farm in 1845, Johnson frequently arranged for carriages to take everyone to the country for an outing.

The families often exchanged gifts—four dozen peaches, two or three jars of preserves, two hundred oranges, three or four "pine aples," a barrel of potatoes, a barrel of corned beef, a holiday turkey, "One Dog puppy," or similar items. There was also an exchange of accommodations in business arrangements. Johnson furnished the Millers with garden and field produce from the Natchez area, and Miller in turn purchased barber supplies at advantageous prices for his Natchez brother-in-law and in the late 1840's handled the New Orleans sale of corn and potatoes from Johnson's farm.

The two men wrote intermittently and exchanged ideas on a wide variety of subjects. Miller was primarily a materialist and his views were often expressed with a wry twist. In 1848 he wrote to Johnson: "I Have no News of Enny a Count to send you tho we Have a town fool of Peaple they are such as has Come to Look for that Main thing Money so it does Not Make Money Circulate as they are All Looking for it." And after the brother-in-law's death, Miller wrote to his widow: "Mrs. Johnson there is some members in My family that Has very Little regard for my whelfair More than for what they Make of Me &c People that wait for ded Mens shose gose a Long time Barefooted some times you no."

Adelia's letters were generally concerned with complaints about the conduct of free Negro apprentices, requests that the Johnsons send various kinds of food supplies, news about her children, and ordinary gossip. Yet a tone indicating forcefulness of character runs through her letters, leaving an impression that is reinforced by a contemporary newspaper account of an examining trial in New Orleans in which she was accused of assaulting a Dutch dyer, with whom she previously had had a minor lawsuit. According to the account in the New Orleans *Delta,* which Johnson read in Natchez, the Dutchman had been informed that Mrs. Miller's slaves were beating his daughter. When he had rushed out of his dyehouse to save his child, he had been confronted by Adelia, who had told him, he testified, "dat he vos a shdinking Dutch devil, and knowed nothing about the matter." He had replied "dat she had petter as been to work in the field, dan insulting one of de American bobulation." The free woman of color had thereupon "committed an assault" by shaking her fist in the dyer's face. Despite the testimony of several character witnesses that she was orderly and respectable in every way, the judge required her to give bond for a later trial on the charge of having insulted a white person. The charge was subsequently dropped.

But Johnson's intimate relationship with his sister and her husband did not deter him from criticizing their children or becoming impatient with their actions. When the Millers' daughter Lavinia was being courted by William McCary, son of his closest friend, Johnson complained: "Tis now after ten Oclock and Them infernal fools are Seting in the Parlor—Oh What fools—for God Sake, I mean the Gum Sucker & Lavinia." After Miller gave his consent to the marriage Johnson commented: "I am affraid that both of the young Ones are Small Potatoes, I feel So. Cant help it."

Despite this feeling, when young McCary went down to New Orleans in early December to assist in preparations for the January wedding, Johnson loaned him $14, though he remarked at the time, "The Gum Sucker, went Down this Evening on The Natchez. Oh what a green Creature he must be." But Johnson need not have worried about young William McCary. In the 1870's he became sheriff of Adams County, and his record in that office was far better than that of most Reconstruction officeholders.

Johnson suffered all the irritants which plague a man in his daily life, and he sometimes gave vent to his feelings. He was bitten by a new horse he had purchased. His mares were pestered by one of John Jacquemine's horses.

"Some infernal Rascal tyed a tin spout to my Bay Horses tail, also a piece to my Grey Horse's tail—If only knew who it was I wont say here what I would do." The rats ate his "Trubiale or Mexican Bird." "The white Pig" turned "Over the Churn We Lost the Butter." Another minor disaster was reported when "The Billy Goat fell in Our Cistern yesterday Evening and was not found untill this morning, drowned of Course." Slave Jim was delegated to drain and clean the water reservoir.

Livestock frequently got out of their pens or pastures and wandered off, or were stolen. Two of his calves "fell in The Sewer." Sometimes the recovery of strayed animals led to suspicion on the part of the diarist, as when one of his cows wandered off, and "Mr Seltzar, the Butcher" offered to find her for $2.50, which he did within a few hours.

Occasionally, as with all men, an entire day went wrong, but Johnson usually refrained from comment. His entry for December 5, 1840, however, reveals how much he had been plagued. "A Day of Singular Coincidences The following Are a few of them. In the first place, my 2 Turkeys were Stollen & my 2 Cows were Left Out and Ranaway   I had 1 Calf to Die—Steven Ranaway—All of those I was pestered with   I intended to have gone a Hunting but for the fact of all those things Runing away &c I was prevented and all for the Better I hope   Yes, and I had my mare Kitty Fisher Badly Hurt by John in Looking for my Cows." But the day was not without its recompense, for he rented one of his houses for $1,000 a year.

There was little that was unusual about the home life of William Johnson, though he had more outlets and more interests than most of his free colored or white contemporaries. He gave his family all the advantages he could afford. He and Ann reared their children in an atmosphere of respectable morality, and none of them ever departed from its precepts. The family ties were close, and the group tightly welded together. When the barber died, the Natchez press had ample reasons for printing long notices praising the free Negro's character.

CHAPTER EIGHT

Community Position

ALTHOUGH William Johnson was a substantial figure in Natchez business, there was no role for him to play in many aspects of the town's life. He was a part of the community and yet not a part of it. He watered his own streets, joined the bucket brigades in helping put out fires, and made contributions to fund-raising drives. He had amicable relationships with his neighbors in their joint concern about such problems as cisterns, flues, paving, fencing, cow lots and cow sheds, wells, property lines, and retaining walls. Yet he did not vote and could not participate in civic meetings; he did not belong to a local militia company, nor did he ever hope to become a member of the board of selectmen.

Johnson's character and personality offer convincing proof that he tried to be a public-spirited member of the body politic and that he would have succeeded if his skin had been of the lighter shade. As he was a member of the free but disfranchised group, however, his daily activities were customarily concentrated on more personal matters; though he wrote about numerous matters affecting the welfare of the entire town, he was necessarily more directly interested in the well-being of himself, his family, and his friends and acquaintances.

Perhaps the most important battle of Johnson's life was his successful attempt to gain a position in the top rank of Natchez free Negroes. He had serious competition in this struggle, for others were equally ambitious, but by the late 1830's or early 1840's he was unquestionably the leader of the small, select group at the top of the town's colored citizenry.

Johnson not only conformed to the social pattern of this group but also helped set its high standards. He permitted members of his family to associate only with those who passed rigid inspection. He guarded his apprentices, watching their movements carefully and constantly. Nevertheless they misbehaved at times, and all of them, with the exception of Bill Winston, crossed him by attending what he termed "darkey parties." When other free persons of color did not behave discreetly, they also became subjects of his criticism.

While the white citizens of Natchez recognized that he was at the top of the free Negro ladder, that he was a businessman whose word could be depended upon, that he was community-minded, that he read considerably and was quite a literate fellow, there was a demarcation line that he could not cross in his relations with them, a dividing line that was sometimes tenuous and indistinct and was inclined to change location. Johnson himself made only indirect mention of this unwritten code that limited his range of action, and the white citizens of Natchez who left comprehensive personal records did not comment on the terms of their association with the free colored group or with William Johnson. They undoubtedly knew him, visited his barbershop either regularly or infrequently, perhaps had business dealings with him, but no single incident in this relationship prompted a personal notation.

His status in the Natchez world had a certain core of definiteness, however, even though it was bordered with intangibles. The location of the free colored strata in the social pyramid could be pointed out without much difficulty; and he was at the top of these strata. The lower free white strata were technically just above him. But the social dividing line between William Johnson and lower-class whites, or even with some of the higher elements of the white group, was never kept clear-cut and distinct. Analysis of his position can therefore be specific in some particulars but must be marked by an irritating and fuzzy tentativeness in others.

Johnson constantly tried to conduct himself according to the standards of a white gentleman. He walked and talked with proper demeanor and decorum, and even with dignity. He dressed expensively but with propriety. While he rarely made impulsive remarks when associating with white men, there were occasions when his tones were strong and his language pointed.

The social tradition of birth and wealth was an accepted part of his normal thinking, though he made few direct references to such matters in his diary. The nuances and patterns of his thinking usually were delicately revealed, but there were times when subtlety was deliberately abandoned. When writing of the marriage of a young lady who lived a few miles away at Washington, he noted that she was "a teacher of inteligence" while her new husband was "a wine merchant of this City—Enough Said." And occasionally he pointed out members of the respected, top-ranked class by name and rank.

Even more important than birth or station, the conduct of a person had to be continuously circumspect, in Johnson's view; and he must never advertently or inadvertently attract extraordinary attention. When people sitting in the balcony at the theater failed to conduct themselves with proper decorum, he wrote that he had made up his mind "not to go up there any more untill there was some Regulations made up stairs."

He considered personal bravery a highly desirable attribute. His remarks on this subject left no doubt as to his opinions. When one white man showed the white feather the diarist significantly concluded his account of the incident, "this he did from fear." Another individual took a beating and "Cryed Like a Child but would not fight." And once he saw "a Young man by the name of Horton Kick a Young man by the name of Brown On the Back Side and made him run out of the House and he did not resent it Oh that a man Can stand some things is most true."

Though Johnson set up these high standards for his own conduct and religiously followed them, the line of social demarcation was constantly present. Johnson almost never ate with white men except under certain rather well-defined conditions. He employed an overseer for his farm, and there were times when the white employee and the Negro employer ate at the same table. Upon occasion white men hunted in the area and on his land. Of one such hunt Johnson wrote: "Dr Broom & Mr Gay Came Down to day and was Hunting Game—They Both took dinner with me." But such an entry does not necessarily mean that Johnson ate with them, although under such conditions dining with them would have generally been approved. Black and white hunters could eat together in the field or whites might eat at the table of a colored man when in rural areas, but the Negro did not eat with them unless the friendship was a close one.

The color line prohibited the barber from riding in a public or private conveyance with white men and from sitting with them at public gatherings. When the Reverend John Newland Maffitt, a noted Methodist pulpit orator, came to Natchez the diarist recorded: "I went to the Methodist Church and Listened on the Out Side of it at Mr. Maffitt Preaching—He is a splendid speaker, The best I Ever herd in all my Life."

But there were situations in which the line of demarcation between Negroes and whites became almost invisible, occasions when William Johnson was treated by white men as an equal, or very nearly an equal. In his manifold business activities Johnson was generally dealt with by the whites as if he had been one of themselves, and as his reputation for honesty and integrity grew they came to respect him above many of their own color. His position was demonstrated by the trust that many individuals placed in him. In an age when a man's word was supposedly as good as his bond, Johnson fitted into the pattern, for many of his business agreements with white men were verbal and were faithfully carried out by both parties. Had Dun and Bradstreet been operating at that time they would have given Johnson an excellent credit rating, for he would have presented strong recommendations from those with whom he did business. Johnson unquestionably discussed his financial and business problems with white men and received friendly advice from them.

One tribute to his integrity was the confidence they had in him. He entered into business relations with numerous whites, and some of them kept no records of the transactions, preferring to accept the records and figures of the free Negro. In one instance Johnson recorded that he had had a settlement, the first in several years, with a prominent physician. Johnson prepared a statement which the doctor accepted, but two days later Johnson noted that he had made a mistake and told the medical man "of the mistake that I made the day before yesterday when we had a Settlement." The doctor approved the new set of figures and paid Johnson $342 to settle the account. Another entry in Johnson's diary speaks in the same tenor: "Maj Young was in Town To day and I paid him One Hundred Dollars for Charles wages   I wanted to Know of him how we stood and he Said that he had Kept no acct. whatever and I told him that I had the acct but had not Looked over my Books to See."

Whites trusted him to attend to items of business for them, and though these cases usually involved small amounts or were of slight consequence, at least once the matter was financially important. Early in 1850 Dr. Luke Pryor Blackburn became interested in acquiring a plantation. Believing that if he dealt directly with certain whites the asking price would be higher than if the prospective buyer was a colored man, he secured Johnson's assistance. Johnson recorded: "Dr Blackburn wants me to see what Mr Whitcom will take for the Gilbert Place." Two days later his entry ran: "Dr Blackburn & Dr Fox wrides down to the Waltern Plantation to Look at it, They Came back and Dr. B told me that he would give four Thousand Dollars for it, ie $2000 in Cash and the other in One and two years—I am agoing to make the offer for them for I should Like them to get it."

Johnson was the recipient of many tokens of esteem from white men, among them such prominent and respected individuals as Colonel William Robertson, Major Henry Chotard, Colonel Adam L. Bingaman, Dr. Stephen Duncan, and General John A. Quitman. None of these would have performed favors for the barber had they not respected the man and admitted a measure or more of personal regard for him. During a period when some of the free Negroes of Natchez were under pressure to furnish sureties for their good behavior, one young aristocrat visited the diarist and "said if I wanted any assistance or if he could do anything for me to Let him Know." Much correspondence was delivered to the barbershop proprietor, or to the individuals to whom he wrote, by white friends. In 1840 he wrote that "Gen Quitman handed me a Letter to day that was given Him at Jackson for me. He did me proud, He did me proud." Further, he exchanged gifts from time to time with certain members of the aristocracy, one of the most remarkable examples of his relationship with whites.

Routine business favors from white men were common. The incident of the lost note is a good illustration. In 1841 Johnson borrowed $220 from George Weldon, a white contractor, but when he paid the note it was found that Weldon had misplaced it. About three years later Weldon found the document among some papers. "He had Lost it and had Just found it and he brot it to me for which I thank him."

It was natural that there should be conversations, discussions, and arguments among the white customers at the barbershop awaiting their turn for haircut or shave. Johnson was permitted to participate in some of these discussions, for he was probably as well informed as the average tradesman or planter-farmer who patronized his place of business. There were times, moreover, when a single individual or several would remain after closing hours to discuss the topics of the day. Johnson made an entry concerning one such incident in 1842: "Mr T Rose Came in the shop to night and we began and ta[l]ked untill After ten Oclock—The Subjects, Banks & Banking—prospects of war—money Loaning—insolvent people. England and the English—Slavry—Texas & Mexico." The barber and his friend were covering a lot of territory.

Men occasionally proposed that he enter into combination bets with them, bets in which all the participants except one were white men of good standing in the community. One day "Mr S Woods called to See if I would not go in with Several of them in a $500 bet, ie for me to go in $100. I did not Consent Exactly but told him that I would Like to go in about $30. So we did not Say any more."

One of the most revealing entries in his diary was written on September 2, 1836, less than six years after he bought his shop in Natchez. Its first revelatory fact is that within six years from the time Johnson began business in Natchez he had gained the respect of at least a certain group of businessmen and tradesmen of the town. His entry read:

"At a Raffle this Evening at Rowlands Coffee House for a gold watch valued at $150.00 I won it by throwing 41. The number was 16, taken by L. S. M. Bon. Therefore it was to be divided between us—I had two other chances and I got Mr Pulling to throw for me and he threw Low numbers   I then threw for Mr Muchaster and threw 37. Mr Walker threw 40   After wining the watch I called for a Basket of Champane wine. The Company Drank Eight Bottles which amounted to $20. I made Bon pay the half of the Expences."

The next day he completed his explanation of the incident: "I settled with Mr Bon for his part of the watch that we won & I paid him in cash $35 and in horse hyre $20 which is up to the 30th of this month."

It is apparent that Johnson was the only colored man participating in the raffle, that he and a white man—the tailor Bon—jointly won a watch, that the two winners then treated the crowd, and that later Johnson bought the tailor's interest in the watch. The record did not disclose whether Johnson was actually one of "The Company" that "Drank Eight Bottles" of "Champane wine."

Johnson's home and lot on State Street was a single colored island in a white section of Natchez. Prominent businessmen Gabriel Tichenor and Peter M. Lapice, who also owned plantations, were immediate neighbors. Directly across the street was William Parker's well-known Mississippi Hotel. Around the corner to the left on Wall Street was the home of William Newton Mercer (a noted philanthropist, who later moved to New Orleans), a two-story Georgian house where Andrew Jackson, General Thomas Hinds, and other personages were entertained. Around the corner to the right on Wall Street was Lawyers' Row, where many of the Natchez legal fraternity had their offices. Near the end of that block was an old mansion built during Spanish days, and just across the street from it was the Conti House, where David Holmes, last territorial and first state governor of Mississippi, had lived. Within three blocks were the homes of banker W. A. Britton and Peter Little, one of Mississippi's pioneer lumbermen, as well as the Adams County courthouse, the Catholic parish house of San Salvador, and the Presbyterian church.

Johnson kept on good terms with his neighbors. At least once there was a difference of opinion over a boundary line, but the matter was settled without difficulty. The problem of a retaining wall at another time caused continued negotiations. In 1843 the diarist recorded that "Officer Samuels told me to night that Some of my neighbours Had Complained to him that a Stove pipe was Sticking through the Roof of my Kitchen [which was in a separate four-room, two-story building just back of his house] and that it was Dangerous as it stood &." The Negro hastily made the necessary repairs.

His neighbors, in true neighborly fashion, attended to his interests in his absence if things went wrong. In 1844, when a thief attempted to steal a white sow, Thomas Rose came to the rescue of Johnson's property. The would-be thief said that he had acquired the pig from Dr. Ayres P. Merrill, whereupon Rose hunted up the doctor, who said that he had "never Sold him any Such Hog and made [him] let her go."

When Thomas Henderson, acting for an estate which owned the large corner lot just west of Johnson's house, decided to sell, he gave the diarist first refusal of the property. "Mr Thom. Henderson Calld today to inform me that he had been offered Seven Hundred Dollars for the adjoining Lot to me and he promised me the refusal of it, I thanked him for it Kindly I must See to morrow what I Can [do] as towards making The Purchase of it." Johnson bought the lot.

Johnson's friends and neighbors treated him, where the institution of slavery or other free Negroes were concerned, in exactly the same manner as they did white owners. When French William, a free Negro apprentice, made a nuisance of himself by peeping through Thomas Evans' fence at one of his colored servants, Evans simply came into Johnson's shop and complained to him as he would have to a white master.

The diary entry concerning one of Johnson's horses, Paganini, is also illustrative: "To Day it was that I Found Old Pagg. in possession of a Black man belonging [to] Mr Barber. The Boys name was Patrick, I Brought him Out of his yard with the Saddle, Bridle, Martingale and all on the Horse. I got on him and rode home on him, After having showed the Horse to his master he promised me that he would pay any Damage that I seen proper to Charge him for the Horse."

One would have expected the incident to have ended here. But the next day Johnson recorded: "Mr Barber sells the Black man Patrick that stoled my Horse, he Sold him on that account alone." As far as the institution of slavery was concerned, William Johnson belonged to the slaveholding class.

Although the diarist customarily guarded his language so as not to give offense, there were occasions when he talked soberly but forcefully in conversations with whites. An incident in December, 1837, was an excellent case in point:

"To day Mr F. Taylor Told me that there was to be a tryal on Saturday next at The Court House and the Question was to be this—That himself and Dr Guinn and Mr. McAlister had signed a paper in behalf of Robert Smiths having a right to stay in Natchez and he said if the people of Natchez would not Let Smith stay here that he intended to prosecute the Ballance and that none should remain in the place—He also said that He believed Robt. Smith to be an Honest and as correct a Coloured Man as there was in Natchez."

Thus far the account might have been that of a white man of good standing in the community defending a deserving free person of color, and explaining his position to another man.

But Johnson continued his entry: "I then told him that I Knew R. Smith Better than he did and I knew that at this present time he was run off from New Orleans for Buying Goods from a Slave Negro and that when he came off he Left five hundred Dollars in Mr. Johnsons hands to pay his Bale for Johnson went his Bale—He confessed that he had herd some thing of it and I told him that he was wrong I thought in trying to make others suffer because he Could not gain his point."

At other times the Negro presented arguments, and perhaps offered bribes, to secure unusual free Negro privileges. When he or members of his family journeyed to New Orleans he ordinarily had little difficulty in securing good accommodations on river steamboats; on other trips, however, they were difficult and sometimes impossible to secure.

In 1842 the diarist recorded one incident involving his wife:

"I Spoke to A. L. Willson the other day to procure me a passage on the Steam Boat, Maid of Arkensaw, which he promised to do and to day when the Boat Came I went down to see about it and I saw him and He told me that he had spoke to the Capt. and that he had Refused to Let a State Room, But that my wife Could have the whole of the Ladies Cabbin to Herself but it was a Rule on his Boat not to Let any Col[ored] persons have State Rooms on Her—I askd him to go with me on Bourd—He went on Board and showd me the Capt. and I asked him if could not spare a State Room and he told me that He Could not spare one that it was against the Rules of His Boat and that he had said it once and that was Enough and that he was a man of his word and Spoke of Prejudice of the Southern people, it was damd Foolish &c, and that he was a doing a Buisness for other people and was Compelld to adopt those Rules—I did not prevail by no means—He then said that I Could Have a State Room on Conditions which I told him would answer."

Johnson's strategy, whatever it had been, had succeeded. His wife made the down-river trip to New Orleans in style to which most free Negroes were certainly not accustomed.

Some few whites claimed friendship for the Negro only when they were in need of financial assistance and had been deserted by white friends. When one young Natchez blade came to him for an endorsement of a $2,000 note to enable him to purchase a store, Johnson recorded that "I Could not Come it Sure." The young man had been in various kinds of trouble and was having difficulties with his family, and Johnson advised him to make apology. The following day Johnson had another "talk with Him and I find Him Still proud." On another occasion a man "sent for me to day to go On his bail and take him Out of Jail," but Johnson promptly informed him that he was not "in a situation to do anything in that way at present," that he was "under a Pledge to not go Security for any One at all for no shape nor maner." He did, however, take the time to secure a lawyer for him.

Perhaps the most ironical case illustrating this phase of Johnson's life occurred in September, 1837. By this time Johnson had acquired reputation for industry and good deportment, and it was well known that he had sufficient money to make loans. One day a white man sent word for Johnson to come and see him, saying that he was "unwell or he would come down."

As Johnson recorded the incident in his diary: "I promised him to come up . . . I Knocked at the door, it was opened by his Miss, She showed me in to his bed Room where he Lay asleep She Commencd Calling him by saying, Willy, Willy. He at Length awoke and she told him that a Gentleman had came to see him He saw me, shook hands together, he then got up, invited me to take a seate, I did so, wanted me to drink, I refused, We then talked about One thing or other In the mean time the Miss walked up Stairs He after awhile came to the Point —he wanted to Borrow a hundred and fifty Dollars from me, I told him that I had not the Surplus about me and that I could not."

William Johnson could never change the color of his skin. There were times during the early years of youthful ambition when he believed that if he maintained high standards of conduct, if he never slipped from the narrow path of rectitude, the day might eventually come when some of the white citizens of Natchez would, to some degree, accept him socially. That day never came.

As the years passed Johnson realized that he had failed in his quest for satisfactory social recognition. As he gradually exhausted the scraps of privilege that he could catch from the abundance of the planter aristocrats, now and then he may have become more than a trifle bitter. The Johnson of the early 1830's was hardly the sometimes complaining Johnson of the late 1840's. But even then he kept faith with himself and with the white code of ethics and morality which he had appropriated.

Ironically enough he had one moment of complete triumph over a member of the dominant race, but it was an empty victory that Johnson must have recognized for what it really was. When that moment came the Negro allied himself with his own people.

There was a lawyer in Natchez who had once been prominent in his profession. Evil days came upon him, and the Natchez Negro recorded that he "this day has Gotten two dimes from me and as good [as] beged me for them; he is nearly in rags and is gone from the paths that he Once mooved in   How the mighty has fallen, but a Short time ago and he was a sworn persecutor of the Poor Friendless Colord."

Part II

A Free Negro's Diary of a Town

Wherein the Former Slave Writes a Two-Thousand-Page Journal about His Town and Himself

CHAPTER NINE

Chronicle of Everyday Natchez

WILLIAM JOHNSON'S barbershop was a clearing house for Natchez news. Men awaiting their turn for haircut or shave talked about local politics—the election of a new constable, a justice of the peace, or a member of the board of selectmen; the price of cotton or slaves; problems of planting; horse racing and other sports; or important visitors in the city. They discussed all varieties of minor local occurrences in complete and serious fashion. Although the free Negro barber did not always participate in the arguments, he was an eager listener. He absorbed all that was said and at night conveyed many of his impressions to his diary.

He was fascinated by the entire range of Natchez life; his interests ran from murder and sober transactions to tomfoolery and social functions of all classes. Few happenings of local importance escaped him and his record: births, deaths, weddings, family quarrels; lodge functions; conventions; local political campaigns; departures of young men for Texas or California and of the well-to-do for resorts or for Europe; holiday celebrations; militia musters; parades; horse races; cockfights; theatrical and circus performances; concerts; balls; "darkey parties"; trials; jail breaks; the opening of a section of the new railroad; steamboat arrivals, departures, and explosions; the terror of the yellow fever epidemics of 1837 and 1839; the cholera epidemic of 1849; and the ravages of that "Demon of Destruction," fire.

In many of these events, as Johnson recorded them, the names of obscure foreign-born tradesmen, free Negroes, and ordinary folk commingled with better-known and noted names. A man might not be of sufficient local importance to gain a place in the pages of the *Free Trader* or the *Courier*, but he could find a place in the diary of William Johnson.

Weddings interested the recorder of Natchez events, but in most cases he gave few details: "Maj Shields gets married to night to Miss Surget"; "Mr Geo Mandeville was also Married to Miss Postlethwaite up At the Residence"; "Mr Thom Bradford Gets Married To Night To Miss Bisland"; "Mr Garnet Howell gets married very privately to Mrs Minor, the widow of Mr Steven Minor Deceased"; or "Miss Jane Rabee was married this Evening to Mr Poindexter and they Left this Evening in an hour after the marriage on the S. B. Natchez."

If a man married a lady who brought him a considerable dowry, or if he apparently married above his station, the diarist sometimes expressed an opinion. In 1840 the son of Colonel Adam L. Bingaman, one of the community's foremost citizens, married a lady from New York and brought her to Natchez. Johnson, a close friend of the colonel, reported: "Nothing new that I know of Except that Mr. Louis Bingaman is married to a Miss A Livingston of New York. The N P. [newspaper, or Natchez press] speaks of the wedding Dress Costing $2000 And of the marriage Contract or Settlement $100,000—Not bad to take." In another instance the diarist wrote more pointedly: "Mr Parson Boyd gets married to night to Miss Raily Tis a big Lick for him."

While the chronicler did not often indulge in humor, except in an artless or wry manner, one wedding called for an irrepressible remark: "Mr George Fox gets married to night To a Miss McAlister, They were married Out at

Mr Warrens. Both of there Heads are red and all the Little Foxes will be Red of Course."

As in his wedding notes, Johnson ordinarily gave few details about deaths and funerals of Natchez residents. Usually he simply noted the essential facts: "The corpse of Mary Mercer arrived in a Steam Boat, it came by Sea"; "Old Mrs Minor was Buried this Evening Out at her Home place"; or "Mr H L. Conner Died Last night at his residence." On occasion he gave the cause of death. When Chapman, "The Ranger," died he wrote that it was "Said to be the Effects of Disapation"; upon Colonel R. L. Throckmorton's death he noted simply, "apoplexy."

Though the diarist was well acquainted with only a few of the persons whose deaths he mentioned, he knew something about most of them. Some he respected, others he had little use for. But only in exceptional cases did he voice a personal opinion or make remarks other than those of sympathy. When he recorded the death of "Poor old Mr Bracket," a man who had drowned while on his return trip to Natchez from California, he closed the entry, "Poor old Gentleman." He used almost the same words when he wrote, "Poor A G. Carpenter Died at 3 Ocolck this morning." Though he did not expressly say so, he was voicing strong sympathy when he noted that "Mr H. Mandeville buried his Second child to day ie, the 2d one that he has Lost this week."

When fraternal or other organizations assisted in a funeral Johnson mentioned the fact: "Mr Benj. Walker was Buried this Evening . . . Odd Fellows, Masons & Temperance Cocietys turned Out." And if the procession was a large one that information found a place in his diary: "Greate many Persons thare at the Funeral," or "It was a very Large Funeral indeed   The Largest Ever Known in the place," when Mrs. Charlotte C. Bingaman was buried.

Routine accidents—some humorous, some commonplace, some fatal—were steadfastly noticed. In 1835 he wrote that "A Bear belonging [to] Mr Phiffs Killed a Little Yellow Child Down at Mr Parkers Hotel They had to shoot him Dead to Loose him." The next year he reported that "Young Mr Alfred and John T Gellespie got Drowned in Second Creek at Mr Calvin Smiths plantation—they were in a swiming with Mr John Rouths son." In 1845 he noted that "Capt Minor Cut the End off his finger with the nail, by striking his Hand VS the Lamp-Glass," and two years afterward wrote that "Amsted Carters Hack turned over this morning with his Family in it but none of them Got Hurt."

Johnson mentioned two serious falls suffered by prominent Natchez citizens. In 1847 Captain Barlow either "Jumped or fell from the uper Stairs parts of his House, and was very much Bruised." The accident proved a fatal one, for the captain died the same night. Eleven years before Johnson had recorded the amusing but serious accident which befell the noted Mississippi lawyer and politician, George Poindexter. On November 15, 1836, Johnson had written that "Gov. Poindexter Last night in going to his Bed Room, mistook his way and Fell out of the End of Mr West Tavern He fell about 14 feet and Broke his Leg and one thy and sprained his ancle."

Natchez was almost wholly dependent upon the Mississippi River for communication with the outside world. The diarist therefore took special notice of steamboat disasters, and his entries are sufficiently numerous to indicate that they occurred with some degree of frequency. His accounts did not always coincide with published versions, but in some cases they probably were more accurate even though they represented current town talk.

One night in early December, 1835, he recorded that the steamboat *Walk in the Water* had burned: "She took fire about 8 Oclock at night—The Charleston caught on fire also but they succeeded in puting Out the fire, The Cotten that was Burned on the Walk Amounted to 1200 Bales. The amount of boat and Cotten was Estimated a[t] one Hundred and ten thousand Dollars—There was a runaway Boy Burned up and a pet Bear, also Harden, the Bar Keeper, Capt Glover commanded the Boat." In after years he noted boiler explosions and the burning of the *Ben Sherrod,* the *Louisiana,* the *St. Louis,* the *Oregon,* the *Webster,* and numerous others, and reported disastrous wharf fires at New Orleans, St. Louis, and Natchez.

Natchez businessmen, politicians, and members of the community's aristocracy traveled frequently—to New Orleans, Vicksburg, Memphis, and other towns along the Mississippi; to the state capital and elsewhere in the interior; to various northern cities and resorts; and even to Great Britain and Europe. While some of these journeys were for business reasons, most of them were for pleasure.

Johnson usually reported the embarkation of a party of sportsmen for the New Orleans races or to other sporting meets: "To day Col Bingaman and a Large party of gentlemen Left this place for New Orleans to see the Races Mr Lee Claibourne takes down Antilope & two other nags." When "Mrs Linton, Daughter &c" departed for a Northern sojourn in the spring of 1842, the diarist made a brief entry concerning the event. When "Mr F Surget & Wife &c" and a "Good Many Persons" started for the North, and some of them for "Urope," in May, 1851, he reported their departure.

The diarist was just as faithful in reporting their return to the community, but most of the entries were routine in form: "Messrs Bush, Marshall & Dr Merrill returned Home from the North"; "Mrs Lintons Family & Dr Duncans & Maj. Chotards Families Came Home from the North"; "Several familys arrived yesterday from the north,

Mr Samuel Davis and Family and Several others that I dont Recollect at all—W A Britton and his Brother also Came"; or "Dr Mercer & Frank Surget got up from New Orleans Last night on there return from the North   Bill Nix and Peet Coleman were the Domestics &c."

Occasionally Johnson included a bit of personal news about the returning traveler. When Merrit Williams arrived from Kentucky, Johnson wrote that he looked well and had not been in Natchez for some eight or nine years. When George Stanwood returned to town, it was recorded that he had been in California for a "year or two." While personal comments were infrequent, Johnson did mention that, when Walter Guion returned after a lengthy absence, he had "mustoshes and whiskers on his face."

He picked up all sorts of local trivia. He heard that Henry Patterson had "petioned his pocket to Buy a Mocking Bird." On a day in early August, he reported that "I Know Several gents that put on there winter Cloths." On another August day he wrote that "Lynch, the City Guard, in talking and raving threw up his stick or the End of it and broke the Glass in a Large Frame and had, as I thought, no money to pay for it." Once he commented: "Our Editors are abuseing [each] other Daily as is usual with them, Natchez is not improving much Any One may See."

He reported a joke played upon himself, a French barber, and choleric Samuel T. McAlister, who owned a store just across the street: "To night Mr [Grabbo], I believe, took my pole and Carried it around to the Little Frenchmans & took his pole and put it up at Mr McAlisters door   He Came Out and threw it Down and cut it up—I herd him then saying to Mr Grabbo—I Don't thank any One, Sir for it, I dont thank you Sir for it nor no other man, to play such tricks—I never played such a trick with you nor any One Else and no One Shall play them with me,

Mr Grabbo Commenced Excuseing himself but in so Low a voice that I Could not hear him where I stood."

One day he had a conversation with a man who lived south of Natchez, "and he then set in to tell me what was his Suspitions." The man feared that one of his neighbors and "a Boy of his" were conspiring to take his life. He had found a freshly dug grave in his field and he supposed that it "was done to Bury him in." Johnson manifestly tried to dissuade the fellow from his fear of impending assassination, but he had little success, for the suspect was forced to give a peace bond in the amount of $500. Johnson closed his entry, "Tis bad tis Bad." The barber-diarist knew many of the intimate secrets of the Natchez inhabitants, for they frequently confided in him.

In addition to keeping a fairly complete record of the weather, Johnson wrote much about the physical aspect of the city. The condition of the streets gave opportunity for comment: "Streets very dusty"; or "Our Streets are very muddy." Lack of rainfall led to the report that the "Cisterns all over our City is Out or Nearly So." In August, 1841, he found "Buisness very dull and Snakes are very thick Even in Our Amediate Streets." Several years later he noted that "A Large Piece of the Bluff" had fallen on the road which led to Natchez-under-the-Hill and that it was believed that "Firing the Cannon for Gen Tailor was the cause."

One day in December of 1836, the diarist recorded that about forty feet of track of the new Natchez railroad had been laid and that a crowd of men had been on the Bluff running a car "Backwards and forwards." Three days later he and his friend McCary rode out in the afternoon to see the railroad's "Boiler or Ingine," which oxen had hauled up the Bluff from a ship; a "Greate many Persons were present." In 1837 the "City Hotell opened for the First Day. They Kept open House for Every Boddy to

Day." On a Christmas Day he observed that "The City is full of overseerers at present Looking out for new Homes." In 1844 he reported that "the Catholic Church was Struck and a very Large hole made in it Was Struck away near [the] top Knocking off Some of the Staging and doing Some Considerable Injury to the Base or portions of the Steple, Some portion of the thunder bolt poped Down on the tin guter on the South side of the House." When the "Lottery Came off for the Piano That Mr McMicheal put up at $500," he noted that E. K. Chaplain had won the prize. Few incidents in the city's existence escaped the observations of the alert chronicler.

In view of Johnson's success as a businessman, his interest in transfers of Natchez real estate is not surprising. In some instances, as in 1847 when a Mrs. Meeks bought the house and lot next to his State Street residence, he was probably concerned about the acquisition of a new neighbor, but in most cases his interest in exchanges of money or property arose from his belief that they served as a barometer of business conditions.

He noticed the sale of all forms of real estate. When the Parker tavern was sold to Mr. Gildart of Woodville, Johnson reported the selling price as $80,000. Mrs. Merrick's house on Main Street sold in 1835 for $5,080 and a year later Dr. Braselman sold his house for $8,000, with terms granted for six, twelve, and twenty-four months. The Elms, the residence of "Parson" Potts which was sold at auction and purchased by Colonel Sessions, brought $32,500.

Johnson manifested keen interest in private sales and auctions. In June, 1836, a tract of nearly 10,000 acres was sold under a deed of trust in order to pay a debt due one of the city's banks. In the fall of the same year "Old Gridley" sold his city property for a little over $10,000 in order to raise money. Two months later "Hendrickus" was forced to sell for he had been indicted for retailing liquor without a license. Occasional slave sales warranted interest. In 1849 he recorded one of the largest slave transactions in Adams County history: "A very Large [sale] took Place to day at the Court House It was the Slaves belonging to Alexander Dunbar, at the instance of Capt Frank Surget and they all Sold very high and was nearly all Bot by the Captain, Tis not more than a week ago that he Bot the Plantations of Jessy Guice, Thom Gilbert & Mrs Denny." The captain was in the process of creating one of Mississippi's huge estates.

Johnson had many attributes of the hero-worshiper, and like most ordinary folk he was always interested in the visits to the city of noted men of the day. When they paraded up Main Street he observed the procession carefully; if they stopped at one of the city's hotels he got a closer view; if they were connected in any way with politics and spoke on the courthouse lawn he was an attentive listener; when he shaved them or cut their hair he took advantage of the opportunity for closer scrutiny. The possibility of making their acquaintance was an advantage which he had over the other free Negroes of the city. But whether he met them or not, he was interested in their activities and sometimes made detailed entries in his diary concerning their visits.

He recorded the visits of the state's governors, though these entries were usually brief: "Gov. McNutt is in Natchez at Present. Came I presume to review the Malishe [Militia] Muster"; or "Nothing New more than Gov. Brown arrived this Evening in our City and there [was] Considerable Firing of Cannon &c." When President-elect Zachary Taylor journeyed to Washington for his inaugural, Johnson noted that "Gen. Tailor Past up To day. I was on Bourd but did [not] See him I saw His white Horse and took a hair from his tail."

When notables visited the town and were accorded "a Splendid reception," Johnson was as enthusiastic as the next citizen and usually wrote of the incident. On January 4, 1840, he wrote: "Gen Jackson is Expected Down in the morning But I dont believe that he will be here at all." He did not give the cause of his skepticism. The next day: "The Bluff is covered with persons waiting to see Gen Jackson." Then on the sixth he bragged that "I with the rest of the Good Citizens of this City had the pleasure of seeing Genr Jackson on His way to New Orleans, He having stoped at the Landing a short time." Nearly two weeks later, on January 14, he noted that the city was awaiting the visit of the general on his return voyage up the Mississippi and that the militia companies had "all turned Out this Evening to receive Genr. Jackson but he did not come up." The following night he wrote briefly of the general's visit: "Gen Andrew Jackson Came up Last night and this morning came up to the Town and in the fineest Kind of Stile—oh what a Splendid reception."

Three years later Colonel Richard M. Johnson of Kentucky visited Natchez. "Col R M Johnson Came Last night and this morning at 11 Oclock the Different Companies turned out and gave Him a Hearty welcome to our city—Col A L. Bingaman made him a beautiful Little address and afterwards the Old Col J. made an answer or speech of Considerable Length. The Company that turned Out was Large an[d] respectible   The Court House would not have held them all."

The same year he recorded the visit of the renowned Marshal Henri G. Bertrand, a visit which gave the diarist a degree of personal satisfaction: "Marshal Bertrand arrived in this City   Considerable respect was Shown him, fireing the Cannon a Greate number of times and all sorts of small guns was fired at the Same town [time], he Landing at the Quarrantine grown [ground] and came ashore. Wrode in the Carriage of Major Chotard, Drawnd by four hansome Horses—I met him and touchd my hat very gracefully and his Son nod[de]d and the old Gentleman touched his hat to me very respectfully and passed &c."

Johnson devoted considerable space to the visit of Henry Clay to Natchez in 1842. "To Day Our City was visited by the Hon. Henry Clay, he Came soon after breakfast, The reception was rarther Cold for a Community to have been so Long apprised to his near Approach to Our City, He was receivd by the Fencibles, this being the Only Company in town that turned Out, He was Escorted up in town by old Dr McCreary, Capt Minor & Mr S. Cotton, They all wrode up in the Same Carriage Drawn by 4 fine Horses. They Halted at the City Hotel. There Mr Lee Claibourne made or deliverd a Short but hansome Adress, after which Mr Clay arrose and made Answer to said adress and Spoke of [the] Citys Misfortune, meaning the tornado, and some other few remarks &c., then walked into the saloon of the Hotel and thence to the Drawing Room where he was visited by the Citizens Generally— After a Stay of an hour or so he was then taken Out in a Carriage drawn by a pr of fine Bay Horses to the Residence of Mr St John Elliotte where He Dined &c."

The next day the streets were "full of People and a greate many of them has came to town mearly to see the Hon. Henry Clay, He was in town again to day to receive visitors and a Greate many was in to see him, Just before dinner he [was] taken Out again to Mr St. J. Elliottes."

Henry Clay made two subsequent visits which were recorded by the diarist, but they warranted only brief accounts. Johnson had lost his early interest in politics and by the time of Clay's last visit had become absorbed in his farming venture.

Chapter Ten

Barbershop Gossip

ONE of William Johnson's striking traits was a deep and sustained interest in people—their activities, their triumphs, and especially their perplexities. He was sympathetically concerned about the welfare of almost everyone he knew. Free and slave Negroes, as well as certain white tradesmen and professional men, made him a confidant and often sought advice concerning difficult business, social, and even intimately personal problems. During times of stress some of the wealthy and aristocratic also confided in him.

Johnson knew many of the town's most closely guarded business secrets. His position as one of the leading ready-money loan negotiators in Natchez gave him unusual opportunities to hear harrowing hard-luck tales from would-be borrowers. But he was close-mouthed—a fact known and appreciated by his Natchez friends and business associates—even in the privacy of his own bedroom with his own diary, and he recorded few of their commercial secrets.

As the town's most popular barber, he had an opportunity enjoyed by few to hear current talk and gossip. And, though he constantly kept an ear to the ground for off-color news and sly rumors, he was certainly no scandal-monger. Further, he never made personal capital of information secured in confidence.

In general, while his diary does much in bringing to light the day-by-day, neighborly news of ante-bellum

Natchez, it is strange that Johnson did not emphasize the scandals that must have occurred in a town of that size during a sixteen-year period. Either the Natchez citizenry —for all their boisterous energy and drive, enthusiasm for living, and their own brand of American individualism —must have generally been a moral lot, or the Negro diarist must have deliberately neglected to record many accounts of their indiscretions.

A steady stream of news and local gossip passed through his shop, colored according to the personal inclinations and enthusiasms of the narrators. Johnson, stopping to strop a razor or to speak to an incoming customer, edited it according to his own knowledge and prejudice. After further acquisition of facts or hearsay and the lapse of several hours or even days, during which he might have pondered the incident and the various versions which had come to him, he set down the particulars.

At times he separated truth from falsehood and put the record straight. On other occasions he doubtless thought the incident of insufficient importance for recording. Or he simply wrote what he had heard.

Thus William Johnson, with his knowledge of the citizens of his community and with his own sharp perceptions and honesty, balanced and judged the gossipy tales and, if he found them interesting enough, reduced them to writing. But he often used such phrases as "I am told," "It was to day I herd," or "So says report current this morning." The diarist was making clear his position as a mere narrator of what had been told him or what he had overheard being related to someone else.

Much of this barbershop gossip was of the small-town-news variety, and so Johnson told it. "Old Mr Vanison I am told is Courting Mrs Purnell"; or "I herd Mr Prentice [Seargent S. Prentiss, Mississippi orator and politician] gets some glass in his throat by Biting a wine glass. He was then very ill." Occasionally he gave no clarifying explanations, noting simply, "Considerable Humbugery going on in town." Or a college boy's misfortune was set down: "Buck Woods Came from Colidge yesterday and was Dissmissed, Expelled."

On April 28, 1841, Johnson recorded: "Mr S S Prentess Gets Shaved twice To Day—Something Out. I think I Know." Here the diarist was indulging in a bit of personal gossip. Nearly a year later he observed that "Mr S S Prentess was married this morning to Miss Mary Jane Williams and has Left on the Sultana for New Orleans."

Weddings were regularly material for barbershop talk and the diarist occasionally gave bits of enlightening information: "Mr Bandurant was married this Evening To Miss Jones, who he has Long Courted," or "Young Mr. Howard West of Woodville and Miss Dunbar was married Last night It was a ru[n]-away match." Occasionally he got in a sly punch, as when he wrote of one marriage and reported that the young lady was only fourteen years of age. And, being the recordkeeper that he was, when he reported the birth of a "fine Daughter" to one young married woman, he added: "She got married 24th May 1849. Thus it is 9 months and 5 days."

There were times, then as now, when Natchez parents took preventive measures. Johnson noted without comment on one such occasion that "her Father came Down and put a stop to it."

But marriages sometimes had immediate and somewhat peculiar aftermaths. In 1842 one couple crossed the Mississippi River to Louisiana, secured their license, and were wed. But "they were not married but half hour before she had Left him and Came back to this side of the River again and the man has been in persuite of her all day—Every body Laughing at the trick he plaid on her or she on him, I dont Know which." Another Natchez couple were married early one morning, and the young groom "went up the River amediatly and Left his Lady for a few hours, Strange I think."

Another couple eloped but were caught near Rodney, and the citizens of the community came very near lynching the would-be bridegroom. Four days later there was still talk of a lynching party. Johnson's last entry concerning this case stated simply that the suitor gave the father of the young lady "the plain Talk about His Daughter &c." The diarist did not explain further. The Adams County marriage records do not show that the couple ever succeeded in marrying.

Charivaris (or shivarees, as they are still called in American rural communities) sometimes afforded Johnson a relaxing moment, but it is doubtful that he ever accompanied (even at a distance) the parties of young Natchez swains who sang and paraded for newly married couples. The diarist, however, heard the reports of such expeditions: "A party of Persons Shelverdereed Mr John Williamson Last night—They were Finally Stoped by the Shirriff and Police officers—They have never had a chance at him since He married before and this they Gave him because he had made use of some Language that some men did not Like when Mr Patterson was married—They were dressed in all maner of Shapes One was Dressed to Look in shape Like Mr Williamson with a Large Corporation and another was Dressed Like his wife [the bride] with a behind as Large as they Could well make it to Look The thing went of[f] well I am told."

During the years of the 1830's and 1840's Natchez was a drinking town. For evidence of the prevalence of the use of alcoholic beverages, one has only to examine the diaries and daybooks of the wealthy aristocrats and the charge accounts of the middle and lower economic groups at the town's general stores, which in those days sold everything from hair tonic and saddles to furniture and grocery staples. Men in every walk of life "took" a little wine, or intoxicants in some other form; and even the clergy were not outdone. But with the exception of a number of professional bottle grabbers and young-men-about-town, drinking was done with discretion at hotel bars or in the privacy of individual homes. Members of the Natchez aristocracy did not often make public spectacles of themselves.

Johnson's notations of drunkenness during the sixteen years of his diarykeeping were comparatively meager. But he seemed to pull no punches in recording this form of gossip. He recalled that "Dr Dally has been drunk for the Last two days and nights and is Drunk this Evening—Dr Lyle Took him home this Evening and put him to Bed," that four of the town's citizens "were all Drunk to night driving a team of oxen up the Main St.," or that "A pascel of young men [were] very drunk at Mr West tavern . . . They acted very much Like Fools." He reported that one of the town's second-flight citizens "is Drunk to night and is Cutting up all Kind of shines, hallowing and cursing at Dr Broom['s]. Oh it is ridiculous to hear him, Sure."

Long-winded accounts that Johnson heard at the barbershop led to equally detailed diary entries: "The white Haired young Fellow that Drives the Hack Drove up to Mr Parkers door to night and Mr Cary from Woodville was in it—He had Lost his hat and cap and he was chaseing the Hack Driver around the Hack to whip him—so the fellow to save himself from whiping he ran off and Left his Hack—His friend that works at Lankershires Came up and Cary cursed him and would not permit him [to] take the Hack away so the fellow ran off to get a pair of Pistols—He came back again and the man Cary Gave him a wonderfull kick—The fellow ran Back and drew his Pistol But the friends of the drunking man took him in the Tavern."

One day Johnson's friend, Robert McCary, told him a humorous story about Washington Sterns, one of their mutual free Negro friends. "Yesterday whilst we were a Fishing On the other side of the River Sterns got Drunk and went Out into the yard to Sleep and he fell off of the chair that he was setting On. Made water in his pantaloons." And the diarist chuckled to himself: "That I think is a Little a head of anything that I have herd of Lately."

But the free Negro did not laugh at tragedy. When a well-known citizen of the community died he wrote: "He Died Out at his Residence, where he has been Confined to his Room for Six weeks, Drinking Whiskey: tis said that it was Liquor that took him."

Human misery always attracted the kindhearted barber, and he reported a few incidents in some detail. During the late 1840's the daughter of one of his farm neighbors came to his house without shoes, having escaped from the irons her father "had chained her in to Keep her from Geting Married." The following day Johnson found out that she had left her father and had gone to live with a neighbor family, but the next day noted her marriage on the other side of the river in Louisiana.

One May day in 1839, Johnson heard a resident of Washington tell Colonel Adam L. Bingaman, one of the leading citizens of the Natchez community, about the "unmercifull treatment" of a little seven-year-old girl, who lived with a woman in Natchez. As Johnson related the story:

"The Child is about To be Taken away from Her now since she has treated it so badly Here is the Particulars as they were stated by Mr McFarren. It appeared that the Child had missed going to School One Day and that Mrs B. Told the School Mistress That She would Call and

Take Her Home in the afternoon and Take the Child Home and would Give Her the worst whipping that she Ever had in her Life that night and that in the morning she would whip her again and then send her back to School by a Black Girl and requested the School Mistress to whip her again. She did accordingly send the Child by the Girl and when she arrived at the School House, the School Mss [mistress] Examined the Little girl and Lo the Child was whiped and cut from her feet up to the pole of Her neck —observed that she Could not whip her any more for she was so badley abused—she sent of[f] Amediately for a Doctor and several other Gentlemen to Come and see the Child and when they Came they Had the Old Lady arested and the Result was that She had to give Bail for Her appearance in the Sum of One thousand Dollars."

The colonel was so impressed that he interested himself in the case, eventually securing possession of the child pending court action.

Occasionally a citizen would leave Natchez suddenly and without prior notice to his friends. In these instances Johnson simply recorded that he had "ranaway from this place," or had "Fled the City or Left it a few Days ago." If he left creditors or departed under some other financial cloud, Johnson would report that he "wran off Last night in Debt to a good many of citizens. They were in Search of him but Could not find him." Writing about a brother of one of the town's businessmen, he reported that the fellow had "Sloped off with the stakes of Several Gentlemen to the amount of ten or fifteen Hundred Dollars." But he qualified the accusation by adding, "so seys report." In another case he wrote that the rumor had reached him that one of the town's physicians had collected $350 for a man and "had not paid it over to him, and that the people was much hurt at the thought of such conduct for he Denied having collected the money."

The plight of a Mrs. Ganson aroused the sympathy of the barber: "He Sold Out his Liece [lease] & groceries the other day To Henderson the Carriage maker for $3500 He got the cash in hand for what He Sold & then Fled the City—Left his wife behind him in a particular situation."

But he was never sympathetic with a man who ran from a fight: "This morning Little Hastings was making some remarks in the presence of several gentlemen about Mrs Horn or the Miss Edmundsons and it hapened that Mr Horn was present and Hastings did not know him—he Just Caught Hastings by the nose and pulled his nose for him then Kicked his back sides—so says report current this morning—I am told too that the way he ran was the right way."

On November 3, 1836, an elaborate ball was given aboard the ship *Powhatan,* then tied up at the Natchez wharf. The Natchez *Free Trader* reported: "Among the crowd of gentlemen we discovered planters, merchants, mechanics, and politicians—Whigs and Democrats, all joining joyously in the general melee, as though pleasure was their only business. Nothing occurred to mar the festivity of the occasion."

But the worthy reporter deliberately omitted two incidents that did "mar the festivity of the occasion." At any rate William Johnson heard about them:

"There were to night on Bourd of the Ship Pohatan a Large Ball She was Lying up at or above the uper Oil Mill, The Party or Ball was given by Mr Lillar & the Captain, I am told they were at Least three or four hundred pursons, Mrs Dunbars Carriage turned over and it Broke her wrist and Bruised her head or face a Little, Mr Clays Carriage upset also but did not hurt any One Mr A. L. Gains and Mr Lawyer Baker had a quarrell. Dr Hog Said Something in behalf of Gains for which Mr Baker got offended and Drew his Dirk on the Dr   He was held by Some of the gentlemen or Else the old Dr and him would Have been to gether for the Dr told them not to hold him —to lett him go as he was not at all affraid of him."

Johnson became more moral during the later years of his life. As a young man-about-town in Natchez during the early 1830's he had occasionally noted in his cashbook small outlays for "sensuality" or "sensual pleasure," but he later wrote of such things in a general tone of disapproval.

He was in ill-humor when he wrote that one of his apprentices had "acknoledged that he did Stay with a Black woman by the name of Lucinda that Belonged to the Gemmell Estate." When the same apprentice became a journeyman barber and subsequently married, he wrote that he had heard that the young man's bride had once been "given" to one of the town's solid citizens in return for the promise of a house and lot, but that afterward "he would not give it." Johnson did not pass judgment nor did he even speak positively about the incident, but simply closed his entry, "So Seys report Current."

Considerable gossip about free Negroes living in the Natchez area circulated among Johnson's acquaintances in town, and the more interesting of the stories the diarist transferred to his notes. He made no effort to verify such items but usually entered them into his diary without comment. He did pass judgment upon a group of free Negroes living near Natchez when he wrote that one of their daughters was "Kept" by a man and that one of their number had informed him that he was going to pay "a Short and his Last visit to night" to the young woman. Johnson wrote: "God Knows how true. They are all a pack of Strump—What I thought they was."

Touches of humor enlivened some of these occurrences. When one colored girl unexpectedly delivered a baby boy her mother was properly shocked; she "Like to have Died" when she found that her daughter had "had a child instead of the Dropsey."

One of the amazing features of Johnson's diary is the paucity of gossip concerning scandals among the white population of the Natchez country. Such few morsels as found their way into the diary were written briefly and succinctly with no effort at elaboration and with no evident joy in the telling. None of them concerned the aristocracy, though occasionally a lawyer or doctor or tradesman became the subject of barbershop conversation.

Once he said that a free Negro woman told him that a white planter's widow was "in the Family way by her Overseer." The widow planned to go north "To have the Child I presume." The Negro gossiper reported that one of the widow's daughters told her mother that it looked bad because the overseer was a married man, but the mother replied that she did not care for he was "only married to a Negro."

Other spicy incidents were related briefly. One Natchez man and a married woman not his wife were "Caught" together; "Report Seys it was One of the plainest Cases in the world"; "Her husband gave her a wonderfull whiping." When a white citizen of the town was "caught in bed with Mr Parkers old Big Black woman Buster" and another man was "Caught in bed with old Lucy Brustie," he commented, "Hard times indeed, when Such things Ocur."

Thus the citizens of Natchez—lawyers, merchants, planters, and men of a dozen other vocations—all came into Johnson's barbershop on Main Street, spoke to their neighbors, lighted their cheroots and pulled deeply from the weed, and began to talk. They talked of crops, of the price of cotton or slaves, of general business conditions, of what President Van Buren was going to do about the banking situation or how various members of Congress were going to vote on the Mexican question, and invariably their conversation included items of gossip. The barbershop proprietor, hovering nearby with his razor and his comb and his hot towels, listened intently, and later transferred such portions as he thought of interest or worth to his diary.

It was everyday small-town talk—sometimes malicious, sometimes benign—but it was and is today an essential feature of American life.

CHAPTER ELEVEN

Politics and Politicians

DURING these robust ante-bellum years the Commonwealth of Mississippi lived in a continual political maelstrom. Therein revolved issues, planks, and political dogma and theory, continuously agitated by the machinations of energetic and sometimes ruthless practical politicians. The waters were strong, for they were compounded of national as well as state and local ingredients of widespread diversity.

The personal and party struggles over public improvements, state banking laws, repudiation of state bonds, organization of new counties, problems of county representation, and other local as well as national issues kept Adams County and Natchez in a state of recurrent excitement. Men argued, campaigned, made speeches, wrote articles for newspapers, lost their tempers, and fought quick, bloody fights. In few states of the union had personal and party politics reached such combative perfection as in Mississippi during the 1830's and 1840's.

The potent flavor of Mississippi politics, and particularly of what Johnson called "all the Pomp of Nonsense and Splendid Foolishness" of political rallies, parades, and speeches, was reflected in many of his diary entries. Beginning in 1836 he faithfully recorded presidential elections, as well as other political events on the national scene. By 1844, however, his personal concern about the outcome of Democrat-Whig strife had lessened, and subsequent campaigns lacked the intense drama and appeal of that of 1840, but political maneuverings and high-flown speeches still greatly interested him as one manifestation of the human comedy. After he acquired farm holdings during the late 1840's and became absorbed with agriculture, his political zeal cooled even more and the campaign of 1848 found him apathetic. But the vigorous debates and speeches over the state of the union in 1850 were sometimes reported in his diary. During the entire period his interest in county and local elections mounted or waned according to the intensity of individual campaigns or according to the degree of his acquaintanceship with some of the candidates.

If politically minded William Johnson had been white, he would have taken an active part in Democratic party politics. But he was forced to watch these activities from the side lines. Like the greater percentage of his free Negro brethren in the Northern states, he could hold taxable real and personal property; unlike them Johnson could and did own taxable slave property. Like them he could sue and be sued in the courts, and there is no evidence, either archival or personal, that he was ever discriminated against by a court because of his color. Like most of them he never served on a jury, trained with a militia company, or held even the lowest political office.

At various periods in a few of the Northern states, some free Negroes, always a very small percentage of the total colored population, were permitted the right of franchise. This was one of the few evidences of citizenship granted the Northern Negro during the ante-bellum period, and, as Thomas Low Nichols admitted, was "almost the only one of a popular recognition of their humanity." While William Johnson, free black Southerner, fared no better politically than the majority of Northern Negroes, he probably fared no worse.

By 1836 Johnson had established himself in Natchez,

was a well-settled married man, and had begun to keep his diary. He took some notice of the Presidential campaign of that year, though national issues did not much interest him. But Andrew Jackson was his political leader, and he mentally aligned himself with the Democrats and a surging democracy. From his aloof position he probably dreamed of a future when a free Negro who was literate and economically successful, who minded his own business and guarded his deportment, might aspire to a greater degree of political emancipation.

On November 7, 1836, he noted that "To Day is the First Day of the Election," and briefly described John A. Quitman's courthouse speech at "a meeting oposed to the Election of Martin Van Buren." Five days later he recorded that former Governor George Poindexter had heard that Franklin County had given a three-hundred-vote majority to Van Buren and had said that "if he was a going to Sellect One hundred Fools in the United States that he would make the draw for them on Franklin County." But thereafter he wrote little about the national election and only mentioned the state campaign in a note showing that he became overcautious in reconsidering his $20 bet against John A. Quitman and transferred his bet; soon afterward he reported a rumor that Quitman had been elected to Congress, but the official election results subsequently proved the rumor false.

The Presidential election campaign of 1840 was one of the most spirited in American history, and Johnson had more to say about it than any other. Several possible partial explanations present themselves: The current economic depression had forced undesired leisure time upon him; he had not yet become interested in farm lands, except as a possible quick-turnover investment; and his closest white friend, Colonel Adam L. Bingaman, was one of the important Whig leaders in Mississippi and president of the Tippecanoe Club of Adams County. Probably more than all else, Johnson was attracted by the lively drama of the campaign, by the attacks of the local Democrats upon "aristocratic county Adams and city Natchez," as the *Free Trader* described the Whigs, and on the national scene by the fight of "Old Tip," the "Log Cabin and Hard Cider Candidate," to defeat the "Red Fox of Kinderhook." He was amused by the Whig log cabins, each with its barrel of cider or keg of whisky and its live coon tied outside. And he probably hummed with the Whigs,

> What has caused this great commotion–motion–motion
> The country through?
> It is the ball a rolling on,
> For Tippecanoe and Tyler Too. . . .

as they pushed their giant ball through the Natchez streets as a means of arousing party fervor. "Tippecanoe and Tyler too" put on a good show.

The party of Harrison "out-hickoried" the party of the Hero of New Orleans. "Little Van" was a gentleman; he had never fought or killed an Indian; he had never lived in a log cabin; he had never shot a coon out of a tree with a rifle. He was much more likely to drink vintage wines or champagne than hard cider or whisky.

Vice-President Richard M. Johnson, who was running for re-election, made up for some of Van Buren's deficiencies; he had been a noted Indian fighter, and it was said that he had actually killed the noted warrior Tecumseh. But it was also rumored that he had lived with a mulatto as his mistress and had given her daughters an education usually reserved for ladies. With some voters the glory of having killed Tecumseh paled.

The Whigs began their campaign early in Mississippi. In early August, 1839, Johnson mentioned speeches by

Reuben Davis and Colonel Bingaman. But the campaign proceeded slowly and Johnson had little to say.

A year later, however, "A Log Cabin was Brought to town," followed by a small train of Whigs, including the doughty Colonel Bingaman. Two days later he wrote humorously: "Considerable Shines Cut in the way of Flags, Shines of Every Kind." In August he noted that "The Good Whig Citizens of this place is very active in Building a Log Cabbin on the Bluff this Evening, geting it ready for to morrow, for to morrow is the Grand Log Cabbin day. The town is all Excitement, oh what regoiceing."

One aspect of the campaign that disgusted the Natchez barber was the active participation of the ladies: "I am sory to see the Ladys Join in the Foolery." But other observers approved. Orator Seargent S. Prentiss likened the array of ladies on the Whig band wagon to the "rainbow of hope adorning the storm cloud of political strife," while the editor of the *Courier* wrote that "When the historian talks about the political conflicts of these times in after years, the brightest chapter of his book will be that which records the patriotism of our ladies."

As the campaign became more heated Johnson began to write critically, humorously, and sometimes cynically about the antics of the Whig politicians. Of one speech he wrote that "there was a Greate Burst of Eloquence in a particular point of view—Bull Rushes and Palmettoes of La [Louisiana] was very Sublime." In September he recorded that at one Whig meeting Colonel Woods had "in the Estimation of Every Body" made a "Diry [dry] Speech," that Mr. Mandeville's was "very abusive" and that Mr. Mathewson had told "a few stale Anecdotes," and that Mr. Hewit had made a speech "that had but Little or no bearing on the Leading Principles of Government." In late October he reported that the Whigs had "Droped the Log Cabin, they Say it is too Cold." The barber was getting in his licks with a vengeance.

At times Johnson was more objective and was willing to give some Whig speakers credit for effective and logical oratory. One August day, he listened to speeches made at an important Whig rally:

"To day I went Out to the woods of Mrs Bingaman where the Speeches was Delivered by Different Gentlemen. The First I Herd was by Mr McMurran, it was a chas[t]e and Gentlemany Speech, the Best that I have Ever Herd by a Wig. The Language was Beautifully and Every Charge he made was I thought well Explained—After walking about for some time I returned to the spot and found a Mr Gill Martin adressing—I herd Him through. His Language was of a very Elloquent Nature, pronouncitons good, His Denunciation strong and I thought him rarther an Irishman than otherwise from the accent. Quite a Flowery affair—We then had a National Song by Young Duffield, assisted by Holton and some other Genius—The Song was good Enough—The Next Called to the Chair was the Elder Duffield. He made quite a Lengthy Speech—Sir Giles over reach—Richard the third, King Leear and Several other Greate men of Ancient times was represented by Him in Part and Poor Van Buren was made Everything of: King, Lord, Master, Tyrant, Usurper, Rober, and Every thing that Could be Conceived or Imagined. I was much Disappointed in the man and I have very Little Doubt but what the argument made use [of] changed many to the opposite side."

So the campaign continued. Mr. Dobins called the President "George the Third" and said that if Van Buren was elected he was willing to shoulder his musket and wage war against him; and a few Whigs left the party and joined the Democrats, "Disgusted at the Log Cabbin Speeches."

The night before the election Johnson reported the mounting waves of excitement about "the Election that will Commence in the morning at 9 Oclock." He went "under the Hill" and found that "half of the Citizens from off the hill was down Electioneering in Every dirrection."

On election day business was bad, "oh remarkable Dull and there is such a Large Concourse of Persons in the City too—To day is one that I thought we would have a fine Days work but the Contrary is the fact and no mistake sure." At one time he saw more than one hundred and fifty persons enter the courthouse yard to vote and "all were at that time Followers of the Tumble Bug Ball, properly named I thing." The next day Johnson reported that "The Greate Hum Bug Ball was stollen Last night by Some One that has more sense than the man that made it, and Demolished the thing, an rolled it Down the Bluff."

On the morning of inauguration day, 1841, the diarist reported that the citizens of Natchez had assembled "to hear a Long Studied Speech from Young Mr Mathison of this place, a Laboured article. Great Effort Doubtless made to produce Effect—To Day Gen Henry Harrison is our President, Sure." The election of 1840 had passed into the realm of history.

Harrison lasted but a few weeks as President, and John Tyler, a hitherto little known Virginia Democrat, succeeded to the office, immediately becoming known in some quarters as "His Accidency." In 1844 the Whigs nominated Henry Clay and the Democrats James K. Polk of Tennessee, "Young Hickory" as some called him. This time popular democracy was on the side of the Democrats. Hickory poles were raised, banners displayed, and the faithful began a singing campaign:

> O! Poor Cooney Clay,
>   Alas! poor Cooney Clay,
>   He never can be President,
>   While Polk is in the way.

And they clamored for the annexation of Texas, the "reannexation" of Oregon, and, if necessary, war with Great Britain.

But William Johnson was apathetic. Early in the summer he listed the names of the candidates. In July he told of the Whig barbecue held on Pine Ridge, north of Natchez, where "The party was pleasent indeed very, no One Drunk." He attended a Democratic meeting, at which a Capt. Johnson spoke; "The two Basonets got offended at Some remarks that was made, and has Join the whig Partee. (Who cares)."

He made a small wager on the election with one of the Whigs. It was a safe bet, and Johnson did not lose.

He watched the Democrats parade and went to their barbecue, where everything "passed off in Beautifull Stile and so pleasent   Did not see a realy Drunkin man on the ground   Dempsey P. Jackson came near geting in a fight by offering to Bet rarther too Loud." On the fifth of September, the day of the big barbecue in "Capt Minors Pasture," Johnson was more interested in the fact that business was good than anything else, although he did record that between four and five thousand persons were on the ground and that in the afternoon he heard several speeches, including one by Seargent S. Prentiss. He noted later that there was "Considerable to do about the Ellections" and that "both parties are Scared, Greatly Scared." But he was no longer concerned. He did not even acknowledge the election returns.

The annexation of Texas and the Mexican War followed; in 1848 Henry Clay again lost the opportunity of the presidency, this time through the nomination of Zachary Taylor of Buena Vista fame. General Lewis Cass, the old War of 1812 fighter from Michigan, became the standard-bearer of the Democrats, but Taylor's more recent victories on the border and in northern Mexico and the defection of Van Buren cost him the election.

Johnson had little to say. He confirmed the nomination of Taylor and Fillmore and listed a few political meetings. On November 7 he noted simply that "this is Ellection day and a Good number of People were in town."

Johnson usually noticed political and military events which affected the national scene. He rarely omitted the local publication of a President's inaugural address or his messages to Congress, though on most occasions he offered no comment.

Like most Southerners, William Johnson was interested in Texas. Shortly after he began keeping his diary in the fall of 1835 he noted that a "Rail Road & Texas Meeting" had been held at the Adams County courthouse, and from that time Texas notes appeared at irregular intervals. He was much concerned about the outcome of the Texas Revolution. He noted in April, 1836, that "Gen Houston was surrounded by the Mexicans and was thought to bee in Greate Danger of being Cut to pieces by them, also that 15 hundred Indians had Joined the Mexicans." But in early May he wrote with enthusiasm: "Greate news from Texas, that they had captured St Anna and killed 500 of his men and had taken about six hundred of them as prisoners of war." And later he noted the passage of Santa Anna, the self-styled "Napoleon of the West," up the Mississippi on his way to Washington.

For some years afterward Johnson had little to write about the Republic of Texas, except that individuals from the Natchez district had emigrated there or that emigration parties had stopped in Natchez or some other river town: "a party of Texans or men from Tennessee Camped Out in a public Square in New Orleans—Could not get a House to Stay in. They were on there way to Texas."

But Texans lived in turbulence, and during the early 1840's the diarist wrote numerous entries about the frontier republic. He reported the failure and capture of the Santa Fe Expedition and the taking of San Antonio by the Mexicans: "news . . . seys that on 11th San Antonia was taken by the Mexicans—It Seys that Court was in session at the time that they were all taken." Later he noted that "Gen Santa Ana had made a propsition to Texas to acknowledge her Independence upon Certain Conditions." In 1844 he wrote that "There is a greate deell of talk at this time about Texas being anext to the United States," but gave as his own opinion, "I dont believe anything of the Kind for I dont want to see it myself."

His notes on the War with Mexico were usually limited to the departures of Natchezans for scenes of hostility, but he listed a few major victories and in early September, 1847, wrote that "Gen Scott has Surrounded the City of Mexico and Can March in if he thinks Proper."

In September, 1850, Johnson heard that Natchez had received word of the passage of "Several very Important Bills," as well as other news: "The Texas Boundry Bill, The California admited into the union, the fugitive slave Bill, and the Death of the King of France." Three months later he wrote that "Gen. Foote adressed the Citizens of this place to day Made a Long Speech and at Night made another adress To them, I have not seen a Larger meeting in the Court House for a Long time if Ever . . . Mr Hillier he made a very fine speech Was much applauded. Cesesion & the union was the Subject."

Johnson felt little concern about state elections. His notices were usually brief and to the point. Only occasionally, when he was a friend of a candidate or when one of the issues was of striking importance, did he write extensively. His remarks were actually mere notices: "The Election Came on for all The officers in the State & County"; or "The Dayly Paper anoncees the Result of the Election Col Bingaman & Mr McMurran, Representatives"; or, "News from Jackson that Mr Vannorman is Elected President of the Senate." So the entries ran.

Infrequently he gave details. When word came that Charles Lynch had been elected governor he reported that "Col Wilkins, Mr Vick, Poindexter & others has a wine Drinking at Bells." When the railroad charter bill was passed by the legislature, the city was "Lit up in the most splendid stile," and there was a "Big dinner at Mr Bells Tavern." That prominent orators could hold audience attention for several hours is suggested by his entry of October 21, 1843, when Prentiss spoke on repudiation: "Oh he was very Seviere indeed, He spoke from ½ past 7 untill ½ past 10 Oclock to a full House." When Robert J. Walker was elected senator in 1836, the barber reported that William Parker, a Natchez hotelkeeper, kept "open house for three Days." And after the election of 1843 he noted that he had won "two dimes" from one of his friends as well as "two Cows and Calfs, tho he objected to paying the Calves."

Except for the rule of personal interest in certain candidates, he was just as laconic about local campaigns, though he reported the election of mayors, justices of the peace, road inspectors, members of the board of police, judges, selectmen, constables, and other local officials. One group of local regulatory ordinances inspired this comment: "To day They passed Some of the meanest Kind of Laws Respecting grocers, fruit and so forth." When the *Free Trader* called a Whig editor and politician "a Dirty Fellow about town and Demi John on Legs," the diarist was amused, though when his friend Colonel Adam L. Bingaman was running a losing race for office, he wrote that "If he Could only Come it, I would be Glad, but alass he belongs to the wrong party to Come it."

The birthdays of living statesmen were sometimes celebrated in ante-bellum Natchez, a custom long lost in American life until it was revived during the 1930's. On March 15, 1845, Johnson wrote: "The Democracy of this City Celebrated this Day by the Firing of Cannon and One or two Public speeches this being the Birth Day of Gen. Andrew Jackson. He is now Seventy Eight years Old, There was a turn Out among the Boys and men too. Gen Quitman and Mr Vanhozen Spoke."

After the death of Zachary Taylor, funeral services were held throughout the nation, and Johnson briefly described the Natchez ceremony which was held in the courthouse yard: "The Mock funeral of Gen. Taylor Came of[f] to day and there were a greate many Persons in the City to day. Prayer by some one I know not, a Sermen by Parson Drake, Oration by Mr North, All past off very well indeed."

So William Johnson, free Negro citizen of Natchez in the Old South, recorded the political happenings of his day, reaching into national and state as well as local politics for his notes. Though he followed the results of state and national elections, he made no serious attempts at political analysis. He never explained why Natchez was a stronghold of Whiggism. He gave no explanation for the fate of the Whigs in Mississippi during the 1840's. He did not even give adequate explanation of his personal political views.

Johnson was a lifelong Democrat, though of course he never voted, made a political speech, or held an office. But politics and politicians interested him. He stood on the side lines of battle, and insofar as his own political beliefs would permit, hoped that the better man would win.

On June 30, 1837, he summed up his political creed. Neither the ideas nor the phraseology were his own. He did not claim them, but he stanchly believed in them:

"The Basis of Our Free Insti[tu]tion
No Privileged orders—Liberty of Speech—Freedom of the press—The rights of conscience—Strict Construction of the federal Constitution—Universal Sufferage—Responsibility to the people—No Imprisonment for debt —And a general Diffusion of Knoledge among all Classes of the People
       Richard M. Johnson
       By William T. Johnson"

CHAPTER TWELVE

The Tranquil Streets

WHEN Thomas Low Nichols wrote in his nineteenth-century reminiscences, *Forty Years of American Life,* that "crimes of violence are far less common in America than in England," he set forth a generalization that was unproved but possibly true. When, however, he left the impression that shootings except for formal duels were almost nonexistent in the United States, when he continued that "a blow is very rare, and a kick unheard of," that "there are traditions of rough and tumble fights . . . but the rule of American life is order and security," his observations were almost completely contradicted by the Natchez of the 1830's and 1840's.

William Johnson's diary furnished a very different picture. The frequency with which he mentioned and described thefts, robberies, brawls, fights, stabbings, murders, assassinations, and other forms of lawlessness presents evidence that such incidents were not uncommon occurrences in the Natchez of his day.

Despite the Panic of 1837, the 1830's and 1840's were mostly boom years in Natchez. Men migrated to the town from New England and the Middle Atlantic states, as well as from the country north of the Ohio River and the older South. Many were illiterate and some were well educated; most of them started at the bottom of the economic ladder, and a few entered almost immediately into the professional life of the community. The white river roustabout rubbed shoulders with foreign-born and free Negro tradesman and day laborer. Under such circumstances crime and violence were perhaps inevitable.

Excerpts from a few of Johnson's entries concerning crime both above and below the Bluff will serve as a graphic introduction:

"Flavius Fletcher Killed Iccum belonging to Mrs McCray Last night. He was shot at Mr Amatt plantation, F has got out of the way—made himself Scarce."

"A report is in the City this Morning that two of three Dutchmen and One dutch woman was taken up and it was Supposed that they had Murderd Some One Last night as there were Blood found in and about the Duchmans house."

"A Mans Hand was found wraped up in a Cloth of Some Kind to day in the old Livery Stable up at the head of Main Street. It was found in or under the Horse troft and the Stable is now Kept by Mr Chapman, the Ranger, Very Curious. The hand was taken off at the wrist; Supposed to be the Hand of a white man."

"I went under the Hill to day After Dinner To Look at the Body of a man that had been found drowned in the River   He had been Drowned Only a few hours and was a young Irishman and his name was John Whelen, Was found by Charles, a Fisherman   Was fast on a Hook—Tis Singular indeed."

As late as 1851, the *Free Trader* flayed the mayor, the city council, and the two "sleepy dunderheads who draw pay for and pretend to be City Watchmen" for not keeping order at the Natchez Landing. Throughout the first half of the nineteenth century the city officials of Natchez had been constantly harassed by demands for improvements in city lighting, public health, streets, and law enforcement. For night police work the town depended at first upon a volunteer watch which intermittently patrolled the streets. By the middle 1830's agitation for a salaried watch, in addition to the regular "Police Officer" and city constable, was reinforced by forceful statements on the editorial page of the *Free Trader:* "We have now a *volunteer watch,* numerous, active and faithful, but still not a *proper* watch . . . Can we not have a 'watch' organized in the same effective manner as in other cities, to be paid by the city?"

In 1838 the organization of a city guard, composed of a captain, a lieutenant, and seven watchmen, and erection of a "watch house" was authorized by an ordinance of the board of selectmen. Members of the guard, armed with short swords, were directed "to arrest and confine in the watch house all slaves found from home, without their masters' or mistresses' written permits, after nine o'clock." They were also expected "to apprehend and detain, for examination in the morning before a magistrate, all disturbers of the public peace, and all persons concerned in nocturnal uproar."

That the members of the guard did not always conduct themselves with proper decorum or that the city police sometimes permitted themselves to be intimidated is indicated by Johnson's diary entries. In 1842 he wrote that "Rownd tree, the Capt of the Watch, was ordered to Jail by Mr E C. Cage, the Judge—assalt and Battery was the charge VS him," and a few days later that "Rountree, the Guard, was also fined fifty Dollars—all for fighting." Seven years later he recorded an incident at the city market: "I got up Erly this morning and went to market and Found a Dr Wright cutting up and Swearing and Defying all the officers of the Place to take him to the Guard House He cursed Mr Benbrook [a city police officer] in Particular and threatnd to cow Hide Him &c. He cleared all of the officers out for none of them would tuch him."

Occasionally the situation got so out of hand that one of the city's militia units had to be called out. One March day in 1837 the diarist wrote that the Fencibles turned out to put down a crowd of Irishmen who were disturbing the peace. Later in the same year the *Free Trader* explained why it had again become necessary "for the city government to call upon the military arm to protect the civil officers in discharge of their duty." A city ordinance required every flatboat that traded at the wharf to pay an $8.00 harbor duty, the proceeds of which were used to improve the landing, and a $2.00 hospital tax, to support boatmen admitted to the city hospital. A group of flatboatmen refused to pay the charges and armed themselves with bowie knives and other concealed instruments of death; but "the cold and sullen bayonets of the Guards were too hard meat for the Arkansas tooth picks. There was no fight."

Natchez court decorum, as pointed out by several of Johnson's diary entries, also was spiced by the boisterousness of the times:

"Lawyer Tho. Armat was sentenced by Judge Cage to Jail, there to remain 48 Hours and be fined the sum of Two Hundred Dollars, for comtempt of Court &c."

"Mr McMurran told Judge Dunlap that if he was worth the notice of a Gentleman that he would cow hide Him—Judge Cage fined Mr McMurran $100 for Contempt of the Court."

"Judge Crawford Presides in Court To Day. Ju[d]ge Cage takes his in another District   Capt Cotten, not Knowing that Judge Crawford was inn, asked Mr Van Hosen How the Judge would do. He replyed that he would do very well if he would Keep sober. The Judge replied that he would try and do that—They were all of Course surprised & confused."

"To day in the Court House there was a fight between Mr McClure and Col. Sanders   It Grew Out of Some Expression that Col Sanders made, and as Soon as he went Out of the Court Room in to the Passage, Mr McClure

Knocked him Down and Jumpd on to him and was gouging Him in an instant, He was pulld off of him—Judge Cage Fined Him $200 and Sentenced Him to Jail for Four Days, Good many Persons was Surprised to find McClure So much of a Man."

The barber's diary contains numerous references to murders and assassinations. During a six-month period beginning just before Christmas, 1840, he noted several cases:

"To night at an Early Hour Mr Ruthen Isler was shot Down by a Fellow by the name of Morgan who, it is Said, stood in the street and Shot into the Buck Head Coffee House on Franklin Street. The Fellow than Ran."

"A Man belonging to the Harman Estate was murderd Last Night in the Road. The Murderers tryed to Burn up the Corpse after they Had murdered Him."

"The Little Black fellow Shedrac Murdered the Cook Ned at the Mansion House to day in a fight—it was supposed to be an old Grudge . . . There is nothing new that I Know of to day Except that the Boy Shedrack that murdered the Cook man Ned yesterday, the Fellow was tryed before Justice Robetile, Mr Vannerson in the behalf of the Prisner and no one in behalf of the State He was cleared of Course."

One of the most shocking assassinations in the Natchez area occurred in 1840, when young Colonel John T. Winn was shot while eating supper at the home of a relative. Johnson made several entries concerning the murder. For a time suspicion rested on a man named Walton; then a Negro was arrested and confessed to the crime. He was taken to the murder scene and tried but was found innocent, his confession having been the result of coercion by his jailers. Several days afterward Johnson stated that "The Investigation is still going on in that Case of Col.

Winn." The diarist became eloquent in his desire for justice to be done: "Oh that they may be able to find Out the murderer, oh the Black Hearted *wretch*." He had already paid tribute to the murdered man in strong terms, "A more Gentlemany Young man I have never seen I think, a man that the world must Love if they could but Know Him." But the murderer of Colonel Winn was never apprehended.

In late July and early August, 1843, Johnson gave details concerning the death of an old man named Tree Willow, most of which were not brought out by the Natchez newspapers:

"Poor old Tree Willow Died to day and was put in a Coffin in about 2 hours afterwards and Sent Out alone to the Grave. No one Knew that he was Even very ill— poor old man."

"Old Mr Tree Willow was dug up this Evening by a party of men to see the Condition in which he was in and other matters respecting the singularity of his death &c."

"I am told that it is the Opinion of Several persons . . . that it Looked as tho the print of Hands was on the throat and a Bruise on the Breast, tho they, to save trouble, they made a verdict to the Contrary."

Slave-stealing was a crime that greatly concerned the Southerner. In 1837 Johnson recorded that two men had left town, taking with them thirty-eight slaves belonging to the new railroad which was being constructed, but that they were apprehended. Three years later he reported that a man had run off with forty-seven slaves, also belonging to the railroad, and headed for Texas, but that a posse of citizens had gone in pursuit of them. An Irishman stole a slave belonging to Mr. Rose and a horse owned by Mr. McClure and headed for Louisiana, but the diarist related that he was caught in "the neighbourhood of Red

River." Since Southerners usually associated Negro-stealing with the rise of abolitionism, they became increasingly vigilant in protecting their slave property.

Thievery was commonplace. After stores and homes were broken into, they were ransacked or their safes were broken open. Occasionally the trunk of a traveler would be removed from a "cab" or dray between the river landing and one of the city's hotels, relieved of its contents, and tossed over the Bluff. The newspapers often complained of the "pack of thieves which now infest our city" and of the laxness of peace officers in dealing with suspected law violators.

Occasionally police officers bestirred themselves in the recovery of stolen goods. In a single day in 1840 they searched the houses of Betsy Green and grocer Sanders and found a considerable quantity of goods which had been stolen from two business firms. Two years later the diarist wrote that "The Officers was Buisy to day in search of stollen Goods They found a Considerable Quantity of Goods and Plunder in a Mrs Macens House and Celler—They have her in Custady now The Goods was in part Stollen by Moses Lee who belongs to Mrs Gemmell They have got Him and another Boy that was found also in the Same House I am told there was upwards of three Loads of a Dray found thare." But this case was an unusual one, for both the slave and the free Negro populations of Natchez were comparatively law-abiding groups.

The year 1835 was particularly rough on the gambling fraternity which frequented the Mississippi River towns. The noted Vicksburg incident came in July, when the gamblers were chased from that city after having killed Dr. Hugh S. Bodley, a member of the Committee of Vigilance. Many of them drifted down the river and continued operations. In later October Johnson recorded that handbills had been posted in Natchez ordering them to depart within twenty-four hours.

Two weeks later the Adams County "Anti-Gambling Society" met to consider the situation and to hear a report from its Committee of Vigilance. The committee reported that it had waited on a number of the professional gamblers who were established near the race track and had again ordered them to leave the city. The meeting voted to increase the number of members of the committee and selected them at once. The following day Johnson reported that "The Citizens went Out to the Race track in search of the Gamblers; the[y] Brought in Elick Piper from Mr Mardice's place—Had a meeting at the Court House for the purpose of trying him—Gridley took him from them and put him to Jail—Twas their Intention to have whipd him." The town was comparatively quiet for several years.

In 1840 professional gamblers were warned away a second time. On March 10 Johnson stated that a citizens' meeting had been held at the courthouse. The same day warning notices appeared in the city's newspapers, quoting one of the resolutions passed by the meeting, "that the pickpockets, gamblers and loafers who have no ostensible mode of making a living be allowed forty-eight hours to leave the city, and all those remaining after that time may expect to receive their just dues." This action again cleared Natchez of the undesirable element.

Though townsmen sometimes complained that the law was not well enforced, they seldom resorted to mob violence in their quest for justice. One day in 1838, however, the "Irish Turned Out prety strong . . . after a Fellow by the name of McCabe who tis believed Killed a man Last night and threw him over the Bluff so as to make it appear that he had fallen over the Bluff Himself. The Irish threw over the House that he Lived in and Let it fall Down the Bluff The Guards and Fencibles had to turn Out To Keep them from Linching him." Ten years later a "Dutchman" was accused of having "Stole $100 from George Dyer Last night under the Hill at Franks Coffee House. Dr Broom and others Hung the Dutchman for a Little while to make him tell the truth but they Could Not Come it." But such extralegal outrages were rare.

During the entire ante-bellum period Natchez was comparatively free of Negro crime, by either slaves or members of the free Negro group, and a majority of the law violations were cases of petty theft. William Johnson, who seemingly received some pleasure from recording the misdemeanors of the whites, reported Negro law violations just as faithfully. When Mr. Smith from Lake Washington was robbed of $250 at the Mansion House hotel, the diarist stated that one of the servants had committed the crime and that $150 of the money had been recovered. Occasionally Negroes were "taken up" for gambling. Cloea Pomet was "put in Jail under the Gallon Law," a statute that prohibited the selling of intoxicants to Negroes, and John Kyle was jailed on a charge of stealing horse feed from Miller's stable.

Murder was an infrequent Negro crime. While the colored members of society were generally quiet and law-abiding, some were excitable, and most of their killings were perpetrated in the height of passion. They were almost never the result of calculation, and most of them were committed against members of their own race.

One of the most important cases of Negro disturbances in Natchez occurred in 1843 when "one of Mrs Lintons Black men by the name of Rolla beat Mr Preston this afternoon up at Mrs Lintons Gate. It was Whilst he was in

Company with Some Ladies His Friend Fouler or Fuller or Some Such name was with [him] and was prevented from assisting Mr Preston by Mrs Lintons Carriage Driver, who would seize him when Ever he attempted to interfear. Considerable fuss about it to night, 8 of the Guards Ordered Out. Greate times indeed."

The next night Johnson wrote, "Nothing New but the Out Rage Committed yesterday on the Person of Mr Preston by a Black man belonging to Mrs Linton. The Boy has ran off and is not to be found at all—there has been a greate deal to say about it."

A week later the diarist recorded that the two Negroes had been brought before the justice of the peace and that carriage driver Beverly had been sentencd to thirty-nine lashes, while Rolla had been "Comited to court." He concluded his entry: "This offence was this that the black man Choked and beat Preston for striking or attempting to strike him."

In the early 1840's white slaveowners in the Mississippi River counties manifested a growing fear that free Negroes as a class constituted a grave cause of potential unrest among slaves. Demands that laws regulating the conduct of both slaves and free Negroes be rigidly enforced became more frequent. In particular, it was pointed out that a substantial segment of the free Negro population of the river towns had immigrated into the state in express violation of the law.

In 1841 the alleged abolitionist activities of free Negroes living in Natchez and Adams County brought about what Johnson termed the "Inquisition." Committees of vigilance and safety were appointed at a general meeting of the citizens to ascertain whether the free persons of color were conforming to existing laws, particularly the provisions requiring individuals to prove, before the county board of police, that they were of good character and entitled to remain in Mississippi. A typical communication to the *Free Trader* urged the people of Natchez to act promptly, "to strike a severe blow against the practices of the rogue, the incendiary, and the abolitionist," by regulating slave conduct and by "the immediate removal of every free Negro, who has intruded upon our society."

The "Horrows of the Inquisition"—to use William Johnson's phraseology—aroused his sense of justice. On August 17 he wrote: "All Sorts of Tryals going on   The different Offices has been full all day and they Continue to arrest Still—The Lord Knows how those things will terminate for I have no Conception myself." A few days later he reported that "The meetings are Still Going on in the Inquisitions Court, The Lord Only Knows the result."

While Johnson's own position in the community was secure, he nevertheless expressed his gratification when "one of Our noble, Generous and Gentlemanly young men" offered his support; and he could not but enjoy some of the humor of the situation, for he wrote one day, "Lotts of F. P. C. are running arround Town with Petitions to have the Priveledge of rama[in]ing in the State, tis laug[h]able almost."

His white friends—Bingaman, Duncan, Wilkins, Nevitt, and others—signed petitions in behalf of his free Negro apprentices, and he boasted that "those Names are Enough to make any Common man Proud—Those are Gentlemen of the 1st Order of Talents and Standing."

Johnson reported briefly on some of the individual trials:

"Yesterday Ann Perkins that was Commited to Jail some 3 days ago was tryed under Habeas Copus—She prooved that She was of Indian Decent and Came of[f] Clear—Mr. T. Armatt was her Council—Saunders & Thatcher V.S. Her—She was put in by a [two blanks left by Johnson] by the name of Sandy Parsons."

"There were a greate many Petitions hand[ed] in to day and some of them was I understand regected by the Board—Old Dr Wren adressed the Bourd at Length— Mr H Conner Got tireed of the old Fellow and Ordered him to Hush and if, seys He, you say another word I have you put in Jail—and the old Fellow stoped off I have seen a Greate many that was very Glad of the old Fellows defeat—His remarks was that old Nancy Kyle & Caroline Kept a House of ill fame, a House of asination, a whore House, &c.—but he could not Shine."

Nevertheless some of the free Negroes were deported, and the anxiety and tension of the group as a whole deeply concerned the diarist. Wrote he: "Poor Andrew Leeper was, I understand, ordered off to day, and so was Dembo and Maryan Gibson They are as far as I Know inocent and Harmless People And Have never done a Crime since they have been in the State that I have Herd of . . . Oh what a Country we Live in."

The spirit of the Inquisition persisted throughout the next two decades. After 1840 the files of the petitions and memorials to the state legislature contain comparatively few by white men for permission to manumit slaves, and very few Negroes were freed by law. Nearly a hundred emancipation papers were officially recorded in the Adams County deed records during the 1830's but fewer than ten between 1840 and 1850.

The surprisingly few cases of white injustice against colored individuals noted by Johnson suggest that the Natchez folk were in general considerate of the black population. There were, however, instances wherein slaves were treated brutally by their masters and white men committed acts of violence against both slaves and free Negroes. In 1836 the diarist recorded that Peter Lawrence had been cleared of the charge of whipping free Negro Kitty McCary—"there was no Bill found against him. Rascally. Rascally"—and two months later she died.

In 1844 Johnson described another case:

"To day there was a tryal before Esqr Potter and the Parties were a Mr Gibson VS. the Daughter of Poor Old Sam Gibson who the world Knows to be free, but during the Inquisition She and her mother went Out to Stay with this Gibson and now he puts up a Claim to her, by Saying that Sam G. her father belonged to his Father and that he had went Out of the State and was set free and returned to it again. Thus he became the Property of Said Gibson under Some old Law passed so seys Potter in 1807—Greate God, what a Country, The Suit went in favor of Gibson."

The case of "Arther" commanded considerable space in Johnson's journal; and the diarist left small doubt as to his opinions in the matter, though the Natchez press had little to say.

"Reports were in circulation this morning that Mr Simon Murcherson had beat his man Arther very Severly on Friday night with a Picket that he pulld off of the fence and that the Picket had a nail in it which Stuck in the Poor fellows head, and that the man Arther had Died Last night. There was Considerable talk about it. So much so that Several Persons had went to Esqr Woods and he sat down and wrote a note to Mr Murcheson about it. Murcheson wrote back a note Stating that he, the Esqr, could ask Dr Lyle, but in the mean time he had him *Burried* or there would have been an Inquest held on this Evening, over the Body—Reports Seys that he beat the Poor man from 9 Oclock to about 10 Oclock at night when he was herd to hallow no more. Plain case."

The following day Johnson concluded his account:

"Inquest was held on the Body of Arther belonging to Mr Murcheson   They were 14 in number. They Looked at the head, found it very much Bruised. Did cut it Open Did not strip him nor Look at his back. No One, Says One of them, is authorized to work without Pay and the Law Seys that a Dr shall have fifty Dollars for Oppening the head &c and no One would say do it So they closed the man up again and Said he Died with Congestion of the Brain, Thus it was and thus it is, &c."

But the case of Isham, a slave accused and found guilty of the murder of planter Wilford Hoggatt in the Adams County Circuit Court was barely noticed by the barber. The judgment of the lower court was reversed by the High Court of Errors and Appeals on the grounds that Isham's master had not been permitted to testify in behalf of his slave, that in "prosecutions for offences negroes are to be treated as other persons," and that Isham's confession had been obtained while he was "in great pain" from shackles and because he was in fear of the "blind fury" of an "excited company" which would have lynched him but for the intervention of a white man. The acquittal of other slaves or free Negroes also excited little comment; Johnson accepted justice to Negroes accused of serious crimes in the courts as the rule rather than the exception.

CHAPTER THIRTEEN

Pistols, Fists, and Bowie Knives

MORE than a hundred accounts of street fights between individuals, some of them related in great detail and in racy language, enlivened the barber's diary and re-emphasized the persistence of the frontier spirit even in the town that was the acknowledged social and cultural center of Mississippi. The Natchez newspapers of the period contained very few references to cutting and shooting scrapes and to duels, one editor explaining the omission by stating that it would require the services of a full-time assistant if all the "street fights" arising from "personal quarrels" were reported. It is also likely that political affiliations and friendship, as well as considerations of bodily safety, impelled some editors to omit newsworthy stories of fights. But William Johnson had no such inhibitions in his writings. He enjoyed setting down the particulars of raucous brawls and deadly affrays in a colloquial and sometimes quietly humorous style. Even more important than this factual data was his delineation of the code of physical violence regulating the conduct of the man-in-the-street as well as many of the gentility, a code that resulted in far more action than the famed dueling code.

Fights began, according to Johnson, in a wide variety of situations. Politics, legal suits, debt settlements, horse races, carousing, holiday celebrations, or family difficulties often provided the background, but quarrels might also originate over a twenty-cent bet or a refusal to take a

PISTOLS, FISTS, AND KNIVES 157

drink. Men fought "about a yellow Girl" or because a wife had been insulted. Violent affrays could originate because a person had been called a puppy, a humbug, or a liar. The record of one such contest was set down in the barber's diary entry for November 28, 1836:

"To Day we had Bloody work for a while in the streets up in Throckmortons Corner. Last night up at Mrs Rowans Bourding House several gentlemen were in conversation about a Duel that was fought in South Carolina. When Mr Charles Stewart stated that those Gentlement that fought actually fought with Bullits, Mr Dalhgreen Said that they must [have] fought with paper Bullits—Mr C. Stewart then Said if any man would say that they fought with paper Bullits that he is a Damed Lyar and a Dd Scoundrel & a Dmd Coward—this was at the Supper Table Mr Dalhgreen Jumped up and Slaped Mr C. Stewarts Cheek one very hard slapp They were then parted so young Stewart told him that they would settle it in the morning—So this morning young Stewart took a Stand up at Carpenters Drug Store for the purpose of making the attackt upon Dalhgreen as he would be going to the Bank—Dr Hubbard at the Request of his Brother went up to Carpenters with young Stewart to see him Out in the affair Elick Stewart said that he would not take any part in the affair and he took a stand over on Sorias Corner—and as Dalhgreen past the Door Stewart stepped up to him and told him that now was [the time] to Settle therr Dispute and at the Same time Struck Mr Dalhgreen with his stick, Mr D then Struck him back with an umberralla—Stewart Struck him with the Stick again—Mr D. then steped Back and Drew a Pistol and Fired at Mr S. and missed Him—Mr S. then Drew and Fired and the Ball Lodged under the arm in the Left Side of Mr Dalhgreen, Mr D. then steped in at Throckmortons Store S steped in at the Door but finding that D. had another Pistol he steped Back and stood in the caseing of the Door   D. then advanced on him, shot Him on Left Side of the face on the Temple or uper hinge of the Jaw Bone and the instant the Ball took Effect he Droped on his Knees and Fell over on the pavement as Dead, so Dead that he Barely Breathed. At the instant he fell Mr Elick Stewart ran up and struck D. with his fist   D then advanced on him with an Empty Pistol and in doing so Dr Hubbard shoved Him Back, E. S. Drew a Bouye Knife and commenced cuting at him— Mr D. had no weapon at this time and was fighting with his naked hands and Mr E. S. with the Knife—E. S cut him twice over the Head and cut his Little finger nearly off and split his hand pretty Bad   It was one of the gamest fights that we have Ever had in Our City before."

The Natchez press treated this breach of the peace with its usual reticence, although one newspaper did notice it in a paragraph headed "A Rencontre": "We shall not pretend to relate the particulars, but merely record the fact that such an affray took place, that blood was shed and probably loss of life will follow, and at the same time declare that such a disaster could never have occurred but for the abominable practice of carrying arms."

A brief flurry of agitation against blood-letting in the streets followed and was reflected in the newspapers. The *Free Trader* of December 8, in deprecating the "many sad consequences resulting from wearing weapons," stated that the practice "has become almost a passion throughout the whole south and south-west"; the same article quoted the Memphis *Enquirer:* "It is almost a strange sight in this section of the country, to see a man whose bosom heaves not under a ponderous butcher knife, brace of pistols, or glittering dirk . . . How many have fallen innocent victims to this desperate vice!" The *Free Trader* of the following day reported the proceedings of a public meeting that adopted resolutions calling for the civil authorities to put an end to such outrages, requesting business firms to refuse employment to individuals habitually carrying lethal weapons, and stating "that the practice of carrying deadly weapons, such as pistols, dirks and Bowie knives" was unnecessary "in a land of civilization and laws."

Meetings of this type were ineffectual. The pious adjurations of the editor of the *Free Trader* were not reflected in his own actions, for in 1836 and 1837 he himself was involved in several public frays. Neither of the principals in the sanguinary affair related by Johnson was prosecuted. On the contrary, one of them, Charles G. Dahlgren, achieved high community position; he soon became the master of a gracious, tall-pillared (and still famous) home by virtue of marriage to the aristocratic widow who owned it, and in the Civil War became a Confederate general. Both prominent citizens and others continued to fall to blows and to flesh their dirks and knives when heated words led to action.

The impressive list of weapons used in street and store encounters recorded by the Negro diarist included chairs, decanters, iron bars and weights, bricks, umbrellas, whips, sword canes, hatchets, dirks, bowie knives, pistols, and guns. "To day Mr James," wrote Johnson in 1837, "in a small Dispute with Mr Stanford Struck Him with his fist twice, Stanford drew a Dirk and Mr James ran into his store and got a Hatchet—Shortly after that young Rayley and Mr James Came to gether and Mr James struck him also with his fist. Rayley drew his dirk And Mr James drew a Pistol and Cocked it at him, so that put an End to the fight."

In addition to using fists, two combatants resorted to gouging and many to choking, scratching, slapping, hair-pulling, spitting, kicking, and biting. The tragedian and theatrical manager Charles Booth Parsons after quarreling with one of his actors, "takes him by the hair of his head and throws him Down and Choakes him." Two prominent doctors went at each other in one of their offices by choking and hair-pulling. Choking was common in tavern brawls, but fatalities were usually prevented by onlookers. District Attorney Will T. Martin, who later built a mansion on the outskirts of Natchez, and John Jacquemine, who was probably the most successful of the town's foreign-born businessmen, were both bitten "pretty smartley" in street fights.

"This [morning] Early," Johnson recorded in 1843, "Mr Postlethwaite and Potter has a fight Elick Postlethwaite was the first to make the attack, and I am told that if they had not been Seperated that Potter would have whipped him, and as far as the fight went Potter got the best of it for he gave P. a Black Eye and Scratched his face and neck prety smart. Postlethwaite bit Potters finger a Little—The fight was about the Settlement of Some Estate in which they acuse Each other of Swindling the Estate. They Said a good many Hard things of Each other."

The barber often set down the particulars of damage inflicted on bodies or clothing. In one pavement tussle a leading businessman pulled the stock from another's neck and tore his coat; in another Main Street bout a newspaper editor's blow drew blood from an opponent's mouth, and in return the editor "got a Blow on the forehead raising a not for a short time." In a tavern broil, "Phillips the Tavern Keeper has a fight with a Little Bar Keeper and the Little Fellow has him Down and nearly Bit a piece Out of his under Jaw or Neck and whiped him."

Another diary entry concluded with an equally graphic set of anatomical details:

"To day Old man Guinea John was Drunk . . . and an Italian by the Name of Cariscino Commenced a beating the Old man with a Stick and Continued to do so untill he was driven Clear over on the opposite Side of the Street, Here the Italian was Just in the act of throwing Him Over the wall where the perpendicular fall was I suppose about a hundred feet Just as John was about to fall, he drew a knife from his bosom and plunged it in Cariscino Just below the navle, Tis supposed that the nife has Cut a Gut—John was taken up a short time afterwards by Dillon and was committed to Jail by Rivers, the Justice of the peace."

While violence appeared sporadically in many aspects of Natchez life, the customary patterns of everyday life persisted. Blood might flow in one block while in the next a storekeeper calmly cut cloth for a customer whose mind was only upon the making of a dress. Yet in the 1830's and 1840's even a storekeeper might often be engaged in personal combat.

The group of businessmen in the immediate vicinity of William Johnson's barbershop took part in numerous altercations, many of which led to hand-to-hand clashes. Across the street Samuel T. McAlister, senior member of a commission firm, was known as a man who was ready to argue with either fists or pistols. "I saw to day a sight as follows," the barber wrote in 1843. "Mr. McAlister had taken Mr. George Powell by the Collar with his Left hand and he had a Pistol in the other and Mr. Izod was holding the hand that he had the Pistol in, Several others was holding him at the time and all this time he was holding Mr. Powell fast by the Coat Collar and he was standing Peaceably tho trembling Considerbly. He stood in that way for several minutes to the gaze of the Public tho after a while he pulled away and ran down the street fast whilst Every body was standing astonished." And two days later: "Report seys that Mr Powell made another run again today for fear of Mr McAlister." On another occasion: "I herd Mr McAlister telling Old Esqr Carson to go to the Devel—he called him a Damd Old Fool, and told him Several times more to go to the Devil." One of McAlister's neighbors, the merchant Simon Murchison, was also a redoubtable fighter, and once got an opponent "down in the mud and the mud is Just about 6 or 8 inches deep They were giving the Lye to Each other often, Neither was hurt tho M. got the better of the fight &c." But in another contest in which the weapons were chairs and knives, Murchison "got Several Sticks in the arm and side &c."

Two of the barber's immediate business neighbors were also enemies: "I herd Mr P. Gemmell walk past my Shop door Cursing N. L. Williams He was about to Flake him and did attempt to Jump the counter after him and was prevented by Mr Neibut. He cursed him for a d——d scoundrell and a greate many more things."

Several of his tenants were foreign-born tradesmen, and Johnson often watched their activities with amusement. When one of his slaves got drunk and attacked an Italian renter, the barber commented: "When he found that I was not thare he cut up Greate Shines, got in a fight with one of the men, an Italian that Lives in a part of my House, Antonio Lynch is his name, He bit the Italians hand a Little and the fellow made more talk about it than Enough—" Another Italian tenant got into a fracas with a tailor, who "Shoves Down the old Lucconio and cuts his head. Lcc. Charges him with Killing his Parrott and it was all a Mistake. L. Called him Boger, Saucey man, nasty man, poor man, Tailor, Son of a Beachee &c." A French tenant got into a "very Laughable" street fight with another Frenchman, "the one with a shovell, the other with a stick."

Other white tenants of the free Negro also fought. The "botanic" doctor tenant clashed with a painter, the bootmaker with a partner, the hatmaker with a journeyman in a sword cane–versus–brick affair. Some of them had disputes with their landlord, but not one laid rough hands on him or menaced him with dirk or pistol. From the day that he opened his shop the barber's person apparently was untouched by violence until the June day in 1851 when he was ambushed by a violent man with a shotgun.

William Johnson walked with dignity through a town where business affairs were often marked by blows and stabs. Fights over the settlement of accounts frequently occurred, but the barber's records were never questioned. His elderly but bellicose friend, Dr. Samuel Hogg, was not so fortunate:

"Roberson and Dr Hogg has a kind of a fight," the barber related. "Old Dr Hogg made him Travell prety fast. Particulars are those, Roberson Owed the Dr 12 dollars for Medical Services. The Dr gave his account to Whiting to Collect for him so he presented the Acct. to Roberson & R. said that he was not the man, so Dr suied on it, & Robs. Came to his office to abuse him about it, and the old Dr told him to Leave his office. The Dr and him came to Blowes, and the Dr struck him with a chair & R. ran in the Street and struck him in the Breast with a Brick, then ran up Street as Hard as he could split and the old Dr after him   So Roberson run throuh Thistles Stable and came out at the Back side of the Stable and went Home   The Dr & Maj Miller went around to Robs House   Dr went in & struck him with his cane and R. caught the stick and the sword came out, and the Dr would have killed him if his arm had not been caught by Mr Ross—Roberson then Broke and run as hard as he could split to the Jail, and went in for Safe Keeping—In time of the fight Robs Brother Struck Maj Miller on the head with a Brick Bat and then Run and the old Maj after him as hard as he could split   The Maj stumbled and fell and as he fell he made a cut at Robison and Cut him in the Butt."

Certain types of business houses—hotels, taverns, bars, gambling places, houses of prostitution, and coffeehouses—were most often the scenes of rows. "Big Fights" occurred at Natchez coffeehouses, now no longer exclusively lounging and reading places for gentlemen. A public house apparently provided the setting for this incident: "Last night a man by the name of Josh Smith cut Charly Brogen with a Bouie Knife Prety Severely Brogen run and Jumped Down in the Bar Room through a Hole and the other, a Mr Sterling Smith, Jerked a Door off the hinges and Sprung out of the window   I tell you they Left in Short Order." William Johnson described encounters involving the use of sticks, dirks, and pistols in the Mississippi Hotel, the Globe Hotel, the Mansion House, and the Tremont House. Even the City Hotel, which the local press boosted as possessing accommodations comparable to those of New York's Astor House, did not escape these fracases. In 1842 Johnson noted that "all sorts of fights" took place "at the City Hotell to night." A lawyer who was affronted because he had been locked out of his room for failure to pay his bill slapped the manager of the City Hotel; another customer knocked him down with a bottle and then "drew a Pistol and cut Several Shines"; and a painter gave him a black eye and forced him to run, after he had cut his assailant's head with a musket.

A surprising number of doctors, lawyers, and government officials engaged in street fights. The mayor and one of his policemen battled several times in a single day, but a lawyer "Gave Judge Rawlings a Terrible Flogging with a Large Lether Strap and the worst of it that he stood and Took it." Politicians especially tended to become unpacific at election time, as two diary entries made by Johnson in 1837 and 1844 show:

"An Election Came On to day for Major General of 2d Division of Malitia of this State, Judge [John A.] Quitman & Mr Besancon [editor of the *Free Trader*] has a fight. Mr Besancon made a thrust at him that would have killed him had not a piece of Silver in the Pocket of the Judge arrested the Progress of the sword, They were seperated by the Sherriff or some other Gentleman or two —Dr Benbrook and Mr Rivers has a fight The Dr Struck Rivers first with a stick, then Rivers struck him with a Large walking Cane with Both hands a hold of it which Knocked the Dr as flat [as] a flounder, and Struck him twice after that whilst he was down, As soon as he Came to his sinseses he hallowed Murder Like a man that was getting murderd."

"The Excitement is fast Commencing about the Election. . . . Natchez Guards at there Armory had a meeting and a marching and wound up thare meeting with a fight. In the first place Shanks and the Capt. Page has a quarrell, After a Little Capt Page and W W W. Woods has a fight Page caught him around the necke and choked Him wonderfully: untill he was Seperated. Great times, we have them."

More than any other element, the "wild Irishmen" apparently were most inclined to enjoy fighting and to give way to a blind lust to kill. They ran together in packs, and when there were no passers-by to bethwack with sticks or poke in the nose they pommeled each other. This playful trait resulted in several entries in the barber's diary, the first occurring in 1835: "Two Irishman commenced boxing in fun and then began to fight. The one kicked the other in such a seviere maner that he broke his gaul. His Head was bruised also—He Died in 8 or ten hours after the fight."

While such overseriousness in the gladiatorial art was generally deprecated, William Johnson's diary also clearly exposed the steel-fingered compulsion of the code of the Old South that brought down contempt on any show of cowardice. As usual, the barber's attitude was not far removed from the community norm, and on one occasion he even took it upon himself to assist in exposing funk. A man who had supposedly been knocked down "Lay on the Box pretending to faint—I Saw him and Said at wonce that he was using Deception for the purpose of geting off without Some more of the Same." On the other hand, he also condemned the taking of unfair advantage: "To Day [a] Fight took place over at the Barlow Conner between Hary & Mr D. Gibson—After striking several Blows the Coward Harvy Drew Out a Large Bowie Knife and Stabbed Mr Gibson." But he had no sympathy for Robert Dunbar, when it was reported that an enemy had "Cursed Him and His wife for Every thing he could think of and Mr Dunbar stood it and did not resent it."

In about twenty-five instances the Negro barber condemned men for cowardice. When a member of a militia organization allowed his opponent in a fight to chase him into "some French Ladies Room," Johnson commented, "He is a member of the Natchez Guards and to run in that maner does not become him." Often he was derisive, as in the case of the "Scuffle" between Mr. Turner and Mr. Midderhoff:

"It Commenced in this way, Turner Commenced on Miderhoff with a Cow hide, fell by accident, at that time M Jumped on him but other was too Strong for him. Miderhoff Jumped of[f] and ran away Left his hat in the fight. He fought prety well for a very Short time and at the close of the fight he made a Splendid run It was in very good time that he made the Run."

Midderhoff shortly sent a second to challenge his assailant to "cross the river" to fight a duel, but Turner declined on the grounds that "he was not a fighting man."

Midderhoff, who was a lawyer with political ambitions which would have been effectively squelched unless he had done something to counteract the story that he had turned tail and had run from a street encounter, thereupon purchased space in the newspapers to denounce his enemy as "a base poltroon and an arrant coward."

Natchez dueling challenges more often resulted in a bloodless exchange of notes whereby seconds arranged "a settlement" satisfactory to the honor of both principals. During the sixteen-year period covered by Johnson's diary, available evidence indicates that no more than twenty challenges were sent. Thirteen were settled without an exchange of shots. Fatalities resulted in three of the seven duels actually fought. One of the seven duels was between tradesmen who were settling a dispute about "a Barrell of oysters"; apparently none were fought by the authentic cotton aristocracy, the owners of several hundred slaves and of colonnaded mansions. William Johnson tried diligently to witness a duel, but never succeeded because most of them existed only in the realm of rumor.

Many Natchez homes a hundred years ago held more bottles than books and more pugnacious brawlers than dueling cavaliers.

Chapter Fourteen

Fires, Fire Fighters— and a Tornado

NUMEROUS routine entries in William Johnson's diary reveal that fire was the greatest single property destroyer in the ante-bellum Natchez community. There were periods when hardly a week passed without a blaze. As many of the smaller and less destructive fires were not mentioned by the newspapers, Johnson's entries contribute to a better understanding of pre-Civil War town life.

While the Negro diarist never belonged to one of the city's volunteer fire companies, few fires occurred without his dashing off to spend long hours with the bucket brigade or to man the hose lines or the engine pumps. He always remained until the blaze was brought under control or burned itself out.

Two factors in the contemporary situation probably accounted for his fire-fighting activities and for his consistent reporting of fires:

The barber realized, for one thing, that fire fighting was a community duty. Every good citizen responded when the bells rang not only in order to help put out his neighbor's fire but from a sense of self-preservation. Every householder and shopkeeper feared that his own buildings might be the next to burst into flame.

Probably just as important in William Johnson's case was the strong emotional outlet he found in battling fires.

He loved the excitement of the bright blaze and the clouds of smoke, of the shouts and clamor of the fighters, of the clang of the fire engines as they were wheeled down the streets, and of the streams of water—effective or more often ineffective—sprayed from the hoses by means of pressure developed by strong and anxious human backs straining over the pumps. His work was just as useful and meritorious as that of the white fire fighters; they welcomed his assistance, and they offered him, amidst the roar of the flames, a generous portion of camaraderie. Johnson never mentioned this feeling but it undoubtedly existed, for a persistent craving for companionship with respectable whites marked much of his thought and conduct.

The Natchez authorities made the first fire prevention and fire fighting regulations soon after Mississippi's admission to statehood in 1817 when they enacted city ordinances providing for certain house precautions, fire wardens, and the selection of firemen. The first volunteer fire company was soon incorporated. Additional regulations were passed from time to time, but the volunteer company remained the backbone of Natchez fire protection throughout the ante-bellum period.

The fire company was a social group as well as a fire fighting organization. It sponsored parties and balls held in the city's best hotels, participated in holiday celebrations and parades, and turned out from time to time to give exhibitions of its proficiency with hose cart or engine. Occasionally companies from other Mississippi River towns were invited to Natchez to give demonstrations or to participate in contests. Johnson once recorded in his daybook that he had paid $2.00 to help defray the expenses of a New Orleans company to come up-river to Natchez, and he was considerably piqued when the visiting firemen failed to make an appearance.

But it was the celebration of a national holiday that

gave the fire company an opportunity for a day of glory. On the occasion of Washington's Birthday in 1842 notices had appeared in the newspapers urging members of the various companies to assemble at their meeting places early in the morning, "fully equipped, for parade, in honor of the Birth-Day of the Immortal Washington." The term "fully equipped" meant, in terms of the notice of the Protection Fire Engine Company, "with heavy frock coats, belts, and fire caps." The companies were to assemble at the corner of Main and Pine streets at 8:30 A.M.

The next day the *Courier* gave its description of the holiday's festivities:

"This day was ushered in by the loud pealing thunders from our ancient cavalry, and it was truly, a lovely and beautiful morning. Not a cloud in the atmosphere, to dim the smiling rays of the rising sun, the wind as smooth and balmy as at mid-summer. Every zephyr that passed, seemed to give token of a charming parade and joyful season of hilarity. We never have observed, during the whole of our life, a more propitious time for a celebration."

The editor noticed that "every fireman's face seemed cheerful"; and he was "utterly astonished," as he "took a casual glance, at the beauty and fashion thus congregated from the various parts of our city and country." He saw the "streaming ringlets, the intent anxiety, and the noble feelings of the heart speaking through the features of each face," and noted that they "could not but animate and cheer every fireman in the patriotic duty, in which he has enlisted." And he observed "from every window and balcony," the populace "waving their snowy white handkerchiefs, in honor of the stout hearts and generous minds which composed the procession."

After expressing the thanks of the various companies to Mrs. Minor, Mrs. Linton, Mrs. Boyd, Major Chotard, Mr. Walworth, and Dr. Duncan, "for the use of their beautiful stud of horses," the newspaperman proceeded to an equally embellished description of the military companies in the parade.

And that night William Johnson wrote briefly in his diary: "Buisness has been pretty Good. Nothing new of Any Interest Only to day the Companies of this place all turned Out."

While the majority of Natchez fires were confined to small houses and outbuildings, larger buildings occasionally burned, or fires got out of control and became major disasters. Most of them were the result of carelessness—an overheated flue or an open fireplace—but a few of the conflagrations were apparently caused by incendiaries. In July, 1841, the dwelling of Samuel Woods burned, and Johnson recorded that it "was no doubt Set on Fire." In September, 1842, the diarist told of another fire which had been set: "Soon after Supper time to night we herd the alarm of Fire and we ran up the street and found that it was in the building back of the Free Trader office It was Set on fire th[e]re is not a doubt as they found a Pan that they must have fired it [with]—It was Soon put out."

The most costly case of arson, however, had occurred in January, 1836: "Just before Day this morning I herd the cry of fire I jumped up almost Naked and ran over to Mr Bells [the Mansion House hotel] with a Bucket of water The fire was then Burning in Mr Harris's ware or cotton yard, I worked at Mr Bells untill after Day Light. I then went over to the City Hotel & worked there with the water at the pump untill 12 Oclock and then the Engine quit work."

The fire gutted the square block bounded by Franklin, Wall, Main, and Canal streets, and caused a loss estimated at over $50,000. The next day Johnson noted that "A man was arrested and taken to Jail on suspicion of having set fire to the Cotten Yard of Mr Harris." He had "offered to bet $50 with a man that there would be a fire at the time the above fire took place." Johnson also heard the rumor that the man had offered to bet "that there would be a Larger fire in two weeks than the fire that tooke place yesterday night—On the strength of those Bets he was taken up and put in Jail." The Natchez press later stated definitely that the fire had been caused by an incendiary.

Within the next two weeks there were several supposed attempts to set fires. The *Free Trader* called upon the city council to "insure the organization of an energetic police or *night watch,* so that our citizens may sleep under strong assurance of safety."

A few days later "Mr Sweney was arrested and put under gard at the Gard House He was supposed to have Either set fire to Mrs Dunns House or Else he knew something about it—The fire was Discovered in the Room of Mrs Dunn." But Sweney was tried and discharged by the "Committee." That night he came to Johnson's barbershop for a shave "with his pockets full of Pistols."

A week later it was thought that a second attempt was made to fire Mrs. Dunn's boardinghouse, despite the fact that there was a "gard out side and inside of the House and yet they could not Discover how it Commenced." But Johnson did not ponder long about the identity of the arsonist. Almost immediately he wrote: "It is my Candid Opinion that Mrs Dunn must have done it Herself or had it done—public sentiment is very much against her."

The editor of the *Free Trader* estimated the total loss from the January fires, including the twenty-eight houses which burned at the Natchez Landing, as at least $165,000. Meantime the town had been constantly patrolled at night by armed men who apprehended several persons and lodged them in jail. As the editor phrased it: "Every square was guarded during the whole night, and every stranger stopped." But no arsonists were caught, just as their alleged associates, the mythical free Negroes whom the newspapers accused of abolitionist agitation, were never apprehended. Both groups probably existed only in the overheated imaginations of an outraged people who sought relief from danger and threats.

Natchez suffered several major conflagrations during the years from 1835 to 1851. Good reporter that he was, Johnson usually gave brief but graphic accounts. On the night of September 14, 1837, he wrote: "Last night about 3 Oclock I was awakened by the cry of fire & the Ringing of the Bells—I arose and Discovered the Direction of the fire, and ran Down to where it was, It was the rear work Shop at Walkers, the tinners It Burned the whole of his shop, Dicks Shop of saddlery, & Hastings upholstering Shop or store—it Burned all the Rear Buildings of all those stores—It Burned a ware house of Messrs Sprague & Howells and a two story brick of Mr Parkers in the shape [of] an L, occupied as a wash House."

On September 5, 1839, a fire destroyed a considerable amount of cotton belonging to several prominent commission merchants. "This Morning about 3 Oclock I was awakened by the Cry of Fire, Fire," Johnson reported. "I got up and ran with all possible Speed and found The Fire Burning on a stable up in Cotten Ally formily Kyles Ally —it then spread Out in Different Dirrections and both Sids of the Ally was on fire at the same time—I comme[nc]ed to work on the Cotton that was in the shed With the help of others got it all out and at Least the One half Burned up afterward. It Burned Down the following Houses—Messrs Jacob Sorias, 2 Story Ware House, Messrs. Stanton, Buckner & Com 2 Story Commission & Ware house, also their Large Cotton Shed."

But not all the embers had been extinguished, and that night a new fire started at a merchant's dwelling on Commerce Street. Johnson was much afraid that the fire would spread and that his "Little Effects would be Burned up without Doubt for the then Fearfull Element had the appearance of Breaking Out on Main St. I was for a time so bewilder that I Could not Commence to work." But the firemen rallied and performed "wonders." The diarist concluded his entry: "The People are very much Jaded from the Labour Done Last night by them at the other fire Thank God I have wonce more Escaped, wonce more from Distruction."

On September 25 Johnson recorded in his diary: "It was near 9 Oclock to night that I saw from the Country [where he was sojourning because of yellow fever] a Large fire Given Light from Natchez and I mounted my horse and in a few minutes was in town and found, I am Sorry to say, One of the Larges Kinds of Fires on the Hill in State Street." The diarist had thus briefly passed over one of the city's most destructive conflagrations, one which destroyed most of the entire block bounded by State, Canal, Washington, and Wall streets, a fire which destroyed his own home. The *Free Trader* commented that "The Demon of Destruction" was seemingly unsatisfied by previous activities and that "some incendiary, a devil in human form" was undoubtedly at work, for several smaller fires had afterward been started. But the sheet warned: "The diabolical perpetrator of these horrid enormities is informed that the vengeance of an afflicted and scourged city is not asleep or benumbed by the two fold calamities that are now entailed upon its few, but resolute and determined citizens . . . Woe to the wretch who shall be caught with the brand of destruction in his hand."

Another important Natchez fire occurred on November 4, 1840. Early in the morning over twenty buildings at Natchez-under-the-Hill were destroyed at a loss estimated by the *Courier* at "nearly $40,000." Johnson's under-the-Hill barbershop was among the buildings burned. His entry was characteristically brief. "Just before Day this morning we were all suprized to hear the alarm of Fire, and I went Down to the Bluff as soon as Possible and there I saw the Last remains of my shop. It was with the rest of the whole Block wraped in Flames and Every thing was Lost. Nothing was saved by me. There was a Large Amount of Property Lost by a greate many of the Citizens under the Hill."

The editor of the *Courier* noted that the under-the-Hill part of Natchez was "a fated spot" and that this was "the third time within the last two years that this part of our city has been burned to ashes."

Usually Johnson's descriptions were brief, giving the account succinctly and without embellishment except to add some obviously personal comment. When a competing barbershop burned he recorded that he tore his coat "all to pieces in the Back, spoiled my Boots also." When he awoke one night and "discovered a bright blaze through the window and On getting Out of bed Discoverd the property of Judge Quitman all on fire," he immediately dressed and went to work. He reported: "I never worked harder in all my Life at a fire than I did at that One." He was "Frightend by the alarm of fire and the Bells Ringing" on several occasions and after one fire began his account with the admission that he was "very much frightened" and later added that "the way I was Frightened was Curious."

When a fire broke out during an evening church service, he noted that "it produced a Considerable scatering among the people Generally." When Mrs. Lacrose's house caught fire it "Created quite a sensation." And when the loss was slight he sometimes became jocular: "We had a Smart little fire Last Night Down at the Cotten press, It was some old Buildings in the Rear of the Cotton press. The Buildings were old and worth but a trifle."

The diarist's brevity in relating his personal fire losses may have been partially caused by the fact that he kept his buildings insured. His house which had burned in 1839, for example, was insured by the Natchez Insurance Company for $2,000. His loss of about $1,000 had been more than offset by rentals, and he was able to begin construction of a new house before the end of the year. At any rate, he accepted his losses with equanimity.

Johnson had even less to say about devastating windstorms and river overflows. His descriptions of them were seldom detailed, but the few "snowstorms" received less laconic treatment. On the fifteenth of March, 1843, he wrote that the weather was cold and that toward evening an overcast sky produced sleet and then snow. "By 9 Oclock the whole face of the Country was white with Snow and was some 2 or 3 inches deep." The next morning he noted that "Several Slays" were running, that "the City Look[ed] perfectly white with Snow and Citizens was throwing Snow balls at Eeach other in Every direction about the Streets."

The most calamitous attack of nature suffered by the city on the bluffs was the tornado of May, 1840. Sweeping in from the south with intense fury, it destroyed hundreds of dwellings, business houses, warehouses, and wharves, and made the roads and streets temporarily impassable by felling trees and scattering debris in all directions. The death loss was equally high. Six months later the Natchez newspapers were still discussing the disaster.

But William Johnson's diary entry gave few details: "To Day was in the aforenoon very pleasant Day untill past One Oclock and then we had rain, with One of the Greatest Tornadoes that Ever was Seen in this place before." The next day he recorded briefly that the bodies of several persons "that was Killed under the Houses" had

FIRES—AND A TORNADO

been found, and added, "Oh what times, no One Ever seen such times."

Ten days afterward he noted the condition of the countryside: "I took my Horse together with Sterns and Jno Jackomine and went into the Swamp—We found the road in a terrible condition Indeed—trees was a Lying all over the Road in Every Direction—Maj Jno Winns Plantation Houses were all Blown over—Gin and all—and the water from the River was very high and runing over for an Hundred yards or more."

Johnson's narrations of such events—a part of the common experiences of most nineteenth-century townsmen—were brief but they had the flavor of personal participation. From his barbershop or from his home on State Street he dashed out to fight fires with his colored and white neighbors. When the tornado struck he worked with them to rescue persons and property. When the snows fell he doubtless played in the streets and threw snowballs with the rest of the "enraptured" citizens.

CHAPTER FIFTEEN

Plasters, Pills, and Purgatives

LIKE many diarists, William Johnson felt little urge to write at length about doctors, common diseases, epidemics, the practice of medicine, the most frequent causes of death, home remedies, formulas prescribed by physicians, and fatal or near-fatal accidents. The close reader of the manuscript miscellany left by the free Negro soon discovers that, with the exception of irregular notations regarding medical bills and illnesses and deaths in his immediate family, he wrote little about disease and medicine. Among matters of community health, only epidemics of yellow fever or cholera stimulated him to make regular entries that can be regarded as contributions to the medical history of Natchez.

Johnson's only connection with early Natchez medicine was that he owned a lot which at one time had belonged to Don Andres Gil, who had been a practitioner of the "Royal Hospital" during the Spanish regime. But the old Spanish hospital had already become inadequate when Major Isaac Guion arrived in 1798 and raised the American flag over the city. A few years later Charles McKiernan directed that a portion of his estate be used to support the hospital "which may at any time hereafter be built in the City of Natchez," and Stephen Minor gave five acres of land to the institution. During succeeding years the town provided hospitalization facilities through local taxation —at one time taxes for this purpose were levied on boats and billiard tables—and through some state assistance.

Meanwhile the doctors had organized the "Medical Faculty of the City of Natchez" for the purpose of establishing "rates and rules of practice." The membership of the organization included Ayres P. Merrill, David Lattimore, Samuel Gustine, John S. Cornell, Thomas Hunt, and half a dozen other physicians. They fixed charges and fees; in fact, an examination of their records suggests that few contingencies had been forgotten. A visit within Natchez during daylight hours cost $1.00 (the charge was double at night); calls "under-the-Hill," $2.00; crossing the river to the Louisiana town of Vidalia, $5.00. The examination of Negroes for purchase cost $5.00; "natural" obstetrics was $25 to $50. They agreed to cure syphilis for $25, and gonorrhea for only $15. Amputation charges ranged from $50 to $75, while those for a post-mortem examination were between $20 and $50. During a "malignant epidemic," medical charges were doubled. They also decreed that "no Physician shall in the future contract to attend any individual or family by the year."

Doctors had considerable trouble with competition from druggists, for they sometimes prescribed for the sick and sold unpatented concoctions of their own making. Johnson remarked on one occasion that "the Drs turned Out to day for the perpose of Getting The Drugests to Sign an article Promising not to prescribe for Sick Persons." And he listed half a dozen physicians who had waited upon the drugstore proprietors.

The "Thomsonians," who practiced "Botanic medicine," arrived in Natchez in the 1830's, proclaiming that their vapor baths and vegetable medicines, "simple and consistent," were in truth the "AMERICAN SYSTEM" for preserving health and life, for *"Life is Heat; every abstraction from heat is Disease; and the entire absence of heat, or cold, is—DEATH."* By 1839 they had sponsored a "Natchez Botanic Hospital."

The regular medical fraternity soon answered the challenge. Meetings of the medical society were held with increased frequency, and by 1844 its members had persuaded Adams County officials to strengthen the authority of the county board of "medical censors" by granting it the power of licensing doctors, surgeons, and those who sold medicine. The Thomsonians rose to the occasion and advertised: "If you wish *genuine* poisons, call at a *Genuine Mineral Drug Store;* but if you wish *genuine Botanic Medicine,* call at a *genuine Anti-poisoning Botanic Drug Store.*" By circuit court decision the Adams County Board of Medical Censors was declared unconstitutional, and the Thomsonians continued their work.

Physicians and dentists saw nothing unethical in advertising either their professional services or the drugs and other articles they sold. Dr. C. B. Foster, a former Philadelphian, offered to insert "complete setts of incorruptible teeth, either on springs or on the principle of atmospheric pressure. Those persons who suppose teeth cannot be inserted after the fangs have been removed, are particularly invited to give him call." Dr. P. H. McGraw, a dentist-druggist, advertised "Chlorine Tooth Wash," "Chlorine Tooth Paste," and "Chlorine Dentryfuce." Both dentists and general practitioners also sold patent medicines, white lead, paints, cold creams of various types, and even fruit trees, grapevines, and shrubbery.

Medical ethics reduced to action sometimes resulted in situations that bordered upon absurdity. Johnson recorded in 1839 that the "Steam Cars ran over an old Black woman that belongs to Mrs Horn and mashed Both of her Legs of[f]." The newspaper version gave additional details. According to the editor, the woman had apparently been "running a race with the cars" when she fell and was run over. Two doctors were summoned during the excitement. Both arrived and each took a leg and "carved to suit himself," neither assisting the other. Both legs were amputated. The story concluded with the statement that the rest of the woman's body was "now doing well."

Every regular physician was equipped to amputate, cauterize, and bleed. The records of a sale of personal effects in 1837 by Dr. John M. Hubbard, one of Johnson's friends and later city health officer, included these items:

"155 jars & vials medicines	$50.00
1 thermometer	15.00
1 pocket case of instruments	6.00
1 set amputating instruments, with case	30.00
4 sets of cupping instruments, with case	40.00
1 pump 'siringe,' with case	35.00
1 set cauterizing instruments, with case	12.00
1 set Dentists instruments, with case	12.00
1 set Midwifery instruments	50.00
1 set disecting instruments	5.00"

The doctor also listed one "Shower bathing apparatus" at $65, one tin bathing tub at $5.00, and one "thermometer for Bathing" at $10.00.

The most distressing and puzzling problem confronting the doctors of Natchez was epidemics of yellow fever and, to a lesser extent, of cholera. Yellow fever first hit Natchez in epidemic proportions in 1817 and reappeared thereafter at irregular intervals. Usually beginning in August or early September, it ran its course in from one to two months. At its first sign a number of the inhabitants left the city for the North, others went to springs or resort places in the South, while many departed for a few weeks in the country near Natchez.

No one knew what caused yellow fever but there were many theories and beliefs. In 1820 retiring Governor David Holmes, in his message to the state legislature, wrote: "Whether this destructive malady originates from local causes, or was brought from a distance, is a question concerning which there exists such opposite opinions, deduced from various facts, that in seeking for a preventative by legislative assistance, it would be unsafe to consider either position as positively correct." The governor continued that, regardless of the local or distant factors, "a peculiar state of the air is necessary to render it endemial." Just what caused this "peculiar state" of air could not be agreed upon during the entire ante-bellum period.

Many were convinced that earth had something to do with the disease. Banks of freshly dug dirt or open places left by the removal of top soil were offered as causes. On one occasion Johnson wrote that "Our Streets are remarkably Dusty, and tis [my] Humble Opinion That we will Have Sickness here in less than 10 Days."

Other causes were suggested. When several cases were reported "under-the-Hill," a meeting of physicians declared "the morbid atmosphere" of the area was at least a partial cause. The "decomposition of animal and vegetable matter" was also listed, and in 1840 many inhabitants believed that the flooding of the "vast quantities of decaying timber" left on the ground by the May tornado would lead to "an early visitation of yellow fever in Natchez." In 1837 the editor of the *Free Trader* urged "the strictest regard to cleanliness in streets and private yards" of the city and stressed that there was "at least one pool of stagnant water on Union street near Washington so greened over that a frog would not venture into it without a life insurance policy." Some believed that warm weather during the fall contributed to the disease, and Johnson once reported that, "should the wether become warm and continue so far about a week" the result would be "yellow fever in the City and quite an Epidemic."

A lower Mississippi Valley epidemic usually made its

initial appearance in New Orleans, and Natchez folk thereafter began to watch the health of their community. One September day Johnson wrote that "The accounts of the yellow fever in New Orleans by the Papers of to day seys that it is much worse—whilst this place is One of the healthiest places now that I Know of." Again he reported: "Considerable Talk about the yellow Fever in the City and the People are devided in the oppinion about the Disease. Some think that the Fever is here whilst others do not believe it and I for One is very much inclined to doubt it."

Once an epidemic became plainly evident, the city was placed under quarantine, and communication with the outside ceased, particularly with Natchez-under-the-Hill. In 1841, for example, a temporary hospital was set up just above the Natchez Landing to care for the sick aboard steamboats, who were not allowed to come up the bluff to the city, and the landing place was shifted to Bacon's Landing, about two miles below.

Johnson's recordings regarding the epidemic of 1837 were frequent and in most respects gave better coverage than the newspapers. He wrote Adelia Miller, his sister, in New Orleans: "We are all in hopes you will write shortly —for we are uneasy about yourself and family—in that Sickly place. I wish you had some healthy place to go to." He continued: "We have had a greate many casses of yellow fever in this place and we have Lost a good many persons out of town." At the time, deaths in Natchez were numbering from twenty to more than forty a week. This epidemic was unusual in that large numbers of the colored population were attacked. Negroes usually suffered proportionately less from the disease than whites.

Two years later the epidemic struck again. In late August Johnson began reporting cases of yellow fever, and by the first days of September they had reached epidemic proportions. Despite the sedulous efforts of the press to calm the people, hundreds left the city—a mass exodus unusual in Natchez history. The inland town of Washington, six miles away, prohibited the "emportation of yellow fever patients, or beds, bedding and merchandize (except food) from Natchez under penalty of $50." In early December the *Daily Courier* admitted that "the greater part of the population" had "left the city" and that as a result the total number of deaths was slightly under the record of 1837.

On September 24 Johnson moved his family to the country and the following day wrote: "I am in the Country Sound as a Dollar." During the last days of the month Charles, one of his slaves, contracted the disease and was critically ill for several days. Meanwhile Johnson read a few books and made daily hunting trips into the surrounding country. About the middle of October he wrote: "I have been too sick to Hunt or go about . . . Last night I took a Dose of Calomell—the first I have taken for years—thank be to God for it." He was indisposed for several days but took little medicine, writing that he had been on the point of taking some several times but "thank be to Heaven, I am so far able to do without it." He slowly regained his strength and gave thanks for his recovery to "the Giver of all Good." The family remained in the country a few days less than two months.

But yellow fever was not the only destroyer. Cholera broke out on several occasions during the 1830's and 1840's, and Johnson's mother died of it in 1849. Smallpox, or varioloid, as it was sometimes called, also occurred with a frequency sufficient to warrant the erection of a "pest house." And "influenza" occasionally reached epidemic proportions.

On the whole, however, Natchez was considered a

"healthy" town, and its press constantly made the most of this blessing in editorials stressing the unsurpassed advantages of the community. But the diarist got in one jab that would not have met the approval of the city's other businessmen: "Our City is Considered Healthy at Present but I think we have a Good many Billous Cases."

Although Johnson had small interest in medicine, the graveness of the cholera situation in Natchez in the late months of 1832, moved him to record a popular method of treatment:

"For Injection ½ pint of Warm Milk & Water & a Table Spoonful of the Tincture of Assofoetida—15 grams of Calomel & one of Opium every 3 hours, for 4 successive doses Should Spasams continue after the injection, take a tea spoonful of Paregorick & one of Ether—If they do not check the spasams take a tea spoonful of Paregorick and one of Tinc Assofoetida Keep the feet & Legs warm with hot water bottles."

Some years later he copied "Dr. Harper's prescription" for treating the disease: "Apply a Blister to the pit of the Stomache Give Every hour a quarter of a Grain of mophine and 2 Grains of Calomel till the vomiting Stops or till 20 Grains of Calomel have been taken Apply Large mustard Plaster to the Legs and inside of the thighs If the Purging Continues Give an Injection of ½ tea cup full of thin Gruel and 40 drops of Laudanum—to be Kept from pasing away as Long as Possible."

Like most fathers, Johnson usually prescribed for and treated the ordinary ills of his family and of the boys who were apprenticed to him. An examination of his accounts reveals purchases of such items as calomel, Godfreys Drops ("The only sure remedy for the Headache"), Dumbries Itch Ointment, Dr. Relfe's Vegetable Specific (for dyspepsia, sick headaches, nausea, and "as a preparatory to Sea Bathing"), Hygeian Pills (which cured practically every human ailment), blister plasters, castor oil, Seidlitz powders, "Liquorish Root," and "sperrits of Nitre."

He doubtless bought other patent medicines widely advertised at that time—Wright's Indian Vegetable Pills, Rowand's Improved Tonic Mixture, Doctor Cannon's Celebrated Fever and Ague Remedy, Doctor Hossack's Medicated Lozenges, Compound Syrup of Sarsaparilla, and Beal's Hair Restorative.

In 1840, druggist P. H. McGraw announced in the *Free Trader* that he had "French Leeches. Two thousand French Leeches, warranted of the best quality, imported and for sale." Druggist W. H. Fox also advertised: "Leeches. Three hundred real Hungary Leeches just received and for sale." At the end of the year Johnson's accounts recorded the purchase of four leeches for $2.00 and another group of the blood-sucking aquatic worms at $1.00. The record fails to disclose whether he administered them himself or called in a physician.

His diary noted several routine treatments. Louis, one of his apprentices, became ill in 1837. Dr. Hogg bled the boy and prescribed that he be given "in a powder 10 grs of ipacak and 12 of Calamell To take flax seed tea if it purged him, and to take warm water if it vomited Him." When Peter came home sick, Johnson gave him "Pepper & Brandy."

One of the most curious entries in the Johnson diary found the barber involved in a situation that had passed beyond the curative powers of nostrums or medical science. After Thomas G. Ellis, a prominent citizen of the community, died, Johnson went out to shave him:

"After I shaved him I assisted Mr Lee Cand & Yandel to take a Cast of his face. Mr. Bush and a Young Mr Ogdon was thare all assisting with it. The process is this. After the face was shaved and the hair all removed from the face, Eye Brows, and so forth, they then took a Brush and Oiled the face all over, puting dough in the lips and in the nose, then Bandaged up the Face in such a manner as to prevent the plaster a parris from runing down the neck They then poured in the plaster which they mixed in a pitcher with warm water untill it becomes higher than his nose. It was suffered to remain on the face about 20 minutes, it was then taken off and it presented a fine Likeness of Him."

The diarist never helped a midwife during childbirth or directly assisted a physician, but in this instance he had aided in preparing one of the most respected citizens of Natchez for burial and in preserving his facial features for posterity.

CHAPTER SIXTEEN

Thespians and Clowns

DURING ante-bellum years the majority of Natchez men were hell-bent on the accumulation of land, slaves, and other property. They worked hard and played just as strenuously. Their chief outdoor pastimes were hunting, fishing, and horse racing. As the city grew in population and wealth, both men and women became devotees of the theater, heard concerts and lectures, viewed art exhibits, and enjoyed less cultural attractions such as parties and balls, circuses, and even a few balloon ascensions and boxing exhibitions.

William Johnson enjoyed only a portion of these activities. He attended the theater and there heard both plays and vocal and instrumental music; he watched processions and parades with the rest of the black and white populace; he was present at the circus and practically any form of entertainment given in the open. But he could not participate in any of these as he did in sports such as hunting and fishing, wherein he could and did consort with white associates. Although he wrote irregularly about social and cultural gatherings, he was interested in them in a somewhat forlorn, left-out way. His diary entries, then, were usually brief and in the form of short announcements or notices, often made simply because these events were a part of the daily life of the community.

Natchez folk had never looked upon the theater with the "holy horror" which handicapped it in New England and elsewhere. A theatrical company visited the town as early as 1806. In 1809–10 a local "theatrical association" presented a season of plays; by 1814 Shakespeare's *Othello* had been performed; and regular professional actors first appeared during the season of 1817–18. In September, 1822, the "Theatre" burned, but by 1826 the erection of a new theater had been planned by a group of rich plantation owners, who had organized a subscription enterprise and had contracted with Andrew Brown, recently arrived from Scotland, to construct the building.

Beginning in the late 1820's, the town had in operation during the winter season one, and sometimes two, theaters, where such impresarios as Noah Ludlow, Sol Smith, James H. Caldwell, James M. Scott, and John S. Potter presented the standard plays with well-organized and costumed companies.

Luminaries of the stage frequently stopped for a "Natchez season" when journeying up the Mississippi toward Memphis, St. Louis, or Louisville, or down-river toward New Orleans. Tyrone Power, the noted Irish actor, visited the town and had much to say about it in his *Impressions of America*. Ellen Tree was presented in *The Lady of Lyons*. Charles Booth Parsons, who possessed a "voice like stage thunder" and "a rather successful formula for imitating Edwin Forrest," enjoyed several successful seasons. According to one commentator, James H. Hackett portrayed the character of Rip Van Winkle, "the hen-pecked Dutchman," so well that the "very respectable assemblage" was "convulsed with laughter." A. A. Adams took the leading role in *Virginius; or, The Liberator of Rome*, supported by the "celebrated" Mrs. Potter in the part of Virginia. Joshua Silsbee, as historian Allan Nevins states, "first appeared in a theater at Natchez, and . . . portrayed rural types to perfection." Others played engagements of from a few days to several weeks duration with varying degrees of box office success.

Tickets for the theater could be purchased for the season or for individual attractions. In 1836 a box cost $200, or $20 for one performance, the management urging that the "seclusion of these boxes will certainly commend itself to the elite of our city." Individual seats in the balcony were priced as low as fifty cents; William Johnson's account books indicate that from time to time his tickets cost fifty cents, seventy-five cents, and one dollar.

Most foreign travelers who visited Natchez described its theaters or theatrical performances. Tyrone Power wrote in general terms, without criticism of the planter families who sometimes came "from very considerable distances" to enjoy his characterizations. Charles Augustus Murray candidly stated his objectives in visiting the Natchez theater and was more specific in his description:

> In the course of our evening ramble we entered the theatre, not so much as faithful disciples of Thespis, as for the purpose of observing the dress, manners, and appearance of the citizens and citizenesses. The theatre is of middle size, and not remarkable for elegance of decoration; the same may be said of the stage and scenery. The orchestra was certainly very good, and the various interludes played between the acts were selected with more taste than is usually shown in such cases; for, instead of giving vulgar jigs and "dashing White Sergeants," or the opposite extreme of slow pieces of music, wanting both introduction and meaning (and generally interrupted by the bell), they played some very graceful and new German waltzes. The ladies in the boxes were neatly dressed, without any pretension or display of finery; as far as I could judge from costume, there were only three or four Frenchwomen in the whole circle. The men were in the usual stocked and cloaked attire of Americans in the evening; the pit was filled with noisy, merry fellows, and the gallery was in the undisputed possession of some dozen swarthy goddesses, wearing upon their heads and persons all the several colours which nature has denied as ingredients in their complexion.

After witnessing *The Fatal Marriage*, in which the leading lady demonstrated "considerable energy and pathos," Murray concluded that "there are few country theatres in England which would gain much by a comparison with that in this small town, which (it must be remembered) was, a few years ago, a wilderness."

Opinion as to the general deportment of the audience varied with the individual observer. Power wrote that "The demeanour of these border gallants was as orderly as could be desired; and their enjoyment, if one might judge from the heartiness of their laughter, exceeding." But a modern historian of the ante-bellum theater in the Natchez area concludes that "Theatre audiences during the 1830's were not noted for their decorous behavior. Despite the posting of notices and policemen, Natchez and Vicksburg audiences often become boisterous and ill-mannered, spitting tobacco-juice, chatting loudly, hooting and cat-calling, moving about and making themselves a nuisance generally." William Johnson, who of course sat in the gallery, sometimes became annoyed at the general conduct there and voiced his displeasure in his diary. He also noted in his cashbook: "To the Last time that I ever goes to that theatre, $.50."

During the early 1830's the Natchez barber saw many theatrical performances. Negroes, both free and slave, apparently were welcomed in the gallery if they could pay the price of admission, though at times the amateur Thespian Society advertised: "Persons of color not admitted." On one occasion, a night in 1831 when Clara Fisher was the star attraction, Johnson and his party of ladies had coffee at the theater.

The young Natchez businessman used the theater as an adjunct to courtship. His cashbooks contain such entries as "Miss B. [Ann Battles, his future wife] to the Theatre, $1.00"; "2 Tickets to see Mrs. Sharpe & Hacket, $1.00"; "To 2 Theatre Tickets Miss A, $1.00"; "took Mrs. & Miss Battles to Theatre"; and "To the Theatre with Ladies, $3.00."

Johnson's diary entries concerning the theater were

irregular and short. By no means hypercritical in judging the drama, he enjoyed the play and rarely wrote at length regarding the acting, the costumes, or the general quality of the production. The opening of a new theater usually called for a note, such as "The first Commencement of the New Theatre in Main Street." Or he mentioned the arrival of a theatrical troupe: "Parsons came with theatrical company." But often his cashbooks must be examined to determine whether he had been present at a given performance. At other times he permitted one or more of his colored apprentices to attend: "I rote a pass for John & William to the Theatre." Infrequently he gave the title of the evening's production, "The play is Hunch Back. Master Walter by Mr Parsons," or mentioned a bit of theater gossip.

After 1836 Johnson witnessed few productions. His growing business interests, his family, his hunting and fishing, and in the later 1840's his enthusiasm for farming conspired against theater attendance.

During the 1840's, when a passion for self-improvement, "to be achieved, preferably, with a minimum of self exertion," swept the nation, lecturing became a part of the general movement, the forerunner of the lyceum and Chautauqua. During those years, Natchez heard many discourses on cultural subjects.

"Mr. Tasistro," an "accomplished Tragedian and lecturer," delivered a series of lectures on Shakespeare, the drama, and "its literature at large." The "science" of mesmerism was the subject of public lectures in the courthouse given by a Dr. Benbrook, who figured in Johnson's accounts as a frequent borrower. Professor Benjamin Silliman of Yale made public appearances, his general theme being "geology in reference to the general structure of the earth." The Natchez press admitted that the subject was "too grand and important to be sufficiently collated, even by such a man." "Miss Hayden" brought her "Grand Exhibition" to Natchez, and gave "a series of splendid performances at the City Hall, in the beautiful art of polite Magic, in conjunction with the grand scriptural and moral Panorama of Jerusalem, Venice and St. Louis, on 2,000 square feet of canvas," as well as "Mechanical Automata and a variety of other performances." Other lecture subjects included "Laughing Gas," "Phonetic and Graphic System of Teaching Language," and "Electro-Biology."

By 1847 the Natchez Institute was presenting a regular course of Friday evening lectures, where local and visiting speakers interested audiences with learned as well as popular discussions. Since it was not possible for William Johnson to attend such lectures his few announcements were made without comment. "The City is Quite Lively at present and all Sort of Concerts, Lecturing and now and then a fight," he wrote in 1844.

By 1840 the Natchez City Band had become a permanent organization which gave intermittent concerts. This group, "for its size . . . 'discourses' as delightful music, as any band in the country," reported the *Courier*. The town also boasted several amateur orchestras, one or two of which considered themselves professional, for charges were made for their services. A Philharmonic Club was conducted by "Professor" Charles Gaita, who also painted and composed in his spare moments. One of its concerts included thirty complete musical numbers by the full orchestra and various soloists, and concluded with the "Marseilles Hymn" given by the "Chorus aided by the entire strength of the performers." The holder of a ticket that night undoubtedly received his money's worth.

Concert singers were often booked by Natchez theaters or hotel "saloons." Miss "E. Brienti, Prima Donna," and "Mr. Manvers, Primo Tenor," presented a "grand operatic soiree" in full costume at the City Hotel Saloon. "G.

Krollman," who was "late Solo Violinist of the French Opera, New Orleans, and formerly of Julien's Concerts, London," and his "Assistants" appeared in two concerts. "Madam Ablamowicz" (the Natchez newspapers could never agree upon the spelling of her name) gave several of "her charming Concerts." "Signora Elisa Biscaccionti, the celebrated American Prima Donna, from Astor Place Opera House, New York, from La Scala in Milano, and the principal Theatres in Italy," appeared, assisted by her husband, a cellist, and "Mr. F. Kley, Pianist, pupil of the celebrated Liszt."

During the later 1840's singing groups became fashionable. The "Philharmonic Vocalists, formerly members of the celebrated Mad. Bishop's Opera Company," gave a series of concerts featuring selections from "the most celebrated new operas." Members of the French Opera in New Orleans occasionally journeyed up-river to give programs. And a minstrel group, the "Original Ethiopian Serenaders," gave three concerts in as many nights.

In March, 1845, the *Free Trader* announced the impending visit of the renowned Ole Bull, the "Napoleon of violinists," who had inherited "the mantle of the departed Paganini." The editor concluded his lengthy article: "We are only able faintly to convey to our readers the pleasure this visit affords us, and the glorious opportunity that approaches of feasting our souls upon sweet sounds, and enjoying the matchless efforts of the acknowledged first, and foremost of living performers."

William Johnson, the diarist, was laconic in his announcement: "Ole Bull gives a Concert to night at the City Hotell. He gave One Last Saturday Night at the Same Place." If he heard the "mighty magician, whose bow, more powerful than that of the mythological Diana, subdues without wounding the heart," he made no mention of it, either in his diary or in his cashbook.

The celebrated dwarf Tom Thumb visited Natchez on at least three occasions. Hailed as "the most perfect *piece* of mankind ever exhibited," and having pleasing manners, a graceful carriage, and entertaining conversation, the twenty-five-inch-high, twenty-five-pound little man nevertheless made little impression upon the Negro diarist for, while Johnson must have seen him, he did not mention him in his town chronicle.

Natchez was overwhelmed when the newspapers announced a concert by the Swedish soprano, Jenny Lind, during her enormously successful American tour in the early 1850's. Her appearance was scheduled for March 10, 1851, but the steamer *Magnolia,* which carried her party, arrived so late that the concert was postponed until the next day. Meanwhile 790 tickets priced from $3.00 to $12.00 had sold for $6,643.

Mass hysteria took possession of the town. A great overwrought crowd awaited her arrival and escorted the "Queen of Song" to her hotel.

The Natchez press had already written many paragraphs praising her in its customary florid style. The editor of the *Courier,* however, was more critical after the concert: "Some there are, who from the extreme laudations of the press, had fancied Jenny something more than mortal. The greatest compass and highest musical skill could not satisfy such, because while they knew not what they really expected, nothing that they could have heard would have filled the measure of fancy. Others again, finding that Jenny's pieces were usually in one beaten round, thought that she could not leave it, and therefore were unwilling to accede to her the title Queen of Song . . . We only express the general voice, by saying that the concert was received with universal delight."

In another column of the same issue, a lady critic "of the highest musical taste and education" gave her impressions: the high notes were "wonderful," with "silvery liquid clearness, a delicacy and sweetness of sound"; and the low notes were full and rich, but not "remarkably beautiful." But her chief criticism was that the singer bowed too low.

Nearly a month passed before the people of Natchez returned to reality. On April 9 the editor of the *Free Trader* denied the rumor that Jenny Lind and her manager, P. T. Barnum, had given $1,000 to charity, and stated that the trustees of the Methodist church acknowledged that of the total ticket sale of $6,643 they had received only "$946.30 from the committee," after all expenses and the $5,000 guarantee had been paid. His concluding remark was one of plaintive reproach: "They did not even give or spend a cent in this city."

To the Negro barber, Jenny Lind's visit had only meant increased business, for he could not hear her sing. On the night of her concert he wrote: "Our city is full of strangers Came to see Jenny Lind. They have Came from the Country and The ajoining Counties. Buisness is very brisk. I Like to See Such very much indeed. The Shop took in to day $13.60 This is Good."

Exhibitions of paintings brought another art to the City of the Bluffs. Some were later offered for sale and purchased in Natchez, but the majority were taken to other towns for exhibition. The "truly moral and celebrated" paintings "Adam and Eve" were presented at the City Hall, where daily tickets were sold for fifty cents, or $1.00 for the season. "Christ Healing the Sick" was viewed without cost at the Methodist church. A painting of "The Last Supper" was shown at the Institute Hall. But Benjamin West's "Death on the Pale Horse" made the greatest impression upon the local critics.

By 1850 moving panoramas and dioramic paintings had become popular, and Natchez was favored with many such displays, such as those of "Mr. Brewer" which included "the Mammoth Cave of Kentucky, Niagara Falls (in summer and winter), a day's journey through the Western Prairies, Mount Vernon, and the Natural Bridge of Virginia." In 1851 Bahin's "Landscape" of Natchez-under-the-Hill was shown at Macmichael's store on Main Street "for the convenience of those who desire to see it." And from time to time portraits of noted Americans were exhibited and copies offered for sale.

William Johnson displayed no interest in these exhibitions, the one phase of Natchez life that he wholly neglected to mention in his journal. He was intensely attracted, however, by another type of spectacle then considered both diverting and educational—the circus. He attended performances regularly during his early years in Natchez and less frequently after his marriage. The records in his cashbook also indicate that he was never niggardly in furnishing money to his children and apprentices for circus or menagerie attractions.

His diary entries concerning the circus are numerous: "The Grand Carravan of Animals arrived in town, the Musicians was on the back of the Elephant as they past through the Streets"; "The Circus was in Performance and a Greate many of Our the first Familys were thare with there Children—Aristocracy with Beauty and intelegence a plenty was thare"; "the Circus fell down on the Spectators, ie the Curtain did"; "I was at the Circus to night and tis the Best Performance of the Kind that I have seen for a Long time if Ever."

More than enough circuses appeared to satisfy the diarist: Stickney's New Orleans Circus, accompanied by the New Orleans Brass Band; Rockwell and Company's Circus, which featured the "Queen City Brass Band" and a "Spanish Bull Fight"; Dan Rice's Metropolitan and Hippo Dramatic Circus; the Olympic Circus; Spalding,

Rogers and Van Orden's Circus; and numerous others. Natchez was definitely a circus town.

The diarist rarely enjoyed the relaxations and amusements of celebrations because the nineteenth-century barbershop habitually remained open on the days that they occurred.

Independence Day celebrations featured a parade of the militia units and fire-fighting organizations, speechmaking, and a city-wide picnic. In 1841, for example, the diarist wrote on July fourth, which apparently fell on a Sunday, that a "Greate many persons are Frollicing to day, tho to morrow is the set day for the Celebration, and a Large parade is expected, Good many of Our Citizens have gone over the River to take a Frollic." The next day he recorded: "To day is the day the Citizens Celebrate for the 4th The Cricket Club has a Dinner Out in the Capt Miner Pasture—Several fights so I herd, Ive not herd particulars yet." The next year he had little to say except that the music did not suit his fancy: "Oh it was dreadfull indeed, past Anything that I Ever Herd in my Life." A few years later Johnson, as was his habit, wrote briefly and without affectation: "Nothing going on very Lively to day altho tis the 4th old Roan and the Sorril mare wran off from the Commons to day Some time."

The Natchez Christmas was ordinarily tranquil and unexciting. Once the diarist wrote of "Considerable mirth" going on, but his own day was usually one of set routine, a morning's work at the shop, a savory dinner, a walk about the town or a ride to the race track, and an hour or two of fellowship with friends. During the succeeding week he recognized the holiday season by drinking a few glasses of eggnog.

Washington's Birthday also featured a parade of firemen's organizations and militia companies, which, as the press reported, generally "went off in good taste." Children observed May Day, the "Festival of the Flowers," with a procession amidst the "rush and crush of a fashionable crowd." Johnson once wrote on a May first that it had been a gay day with "hundreds of children . . . perading the streets" and "Several fairs agoing On."

Dances were popular with most classes of Natchez society, and while William Johnson never attended such functions, he often mentioned them. One entry ran: "Very much of a Dancing party at the Mansion House given by Mr Bond, There were a greate many at it indeed, full House."

Dancing instructors, such as Joseph Barbiere, gave cotillion parties for their pupils, for those feminine guests "heretofore ticketed," or for the public. Parents and guardians received formal invitations to attend the "juvenile Cotillion" parties. Sometimes the Natchez Institute, where dancing was a part of the curriculum, sponsored dances. Johnson reported one party, given in 1847: "This was to have been a Big turn out with the children at the institute. They did turn out Late and a very Large turn out it was They partook of Some Little refreshments at the City Hotell And then went to the City Hall to dance."

Public balls—sponsored or given by hotel proprietors, organizations, or individuals—were a part of holiday festivities, of the celebrations of the anniversaries of militia or firemen's units, and of the honors paid visiting dignitaries. "Mr Henry Clay is in this place at present," wrote the barber. "A Ball will be Given To Him on Thursday night at the Mansion House."

The Natchez press invariably reported these affairs in the extravagant tone of the times. The account published in the *Courier* on December 23, 1840, was typical:

THE BALL.—The Ball at the City Hotel was a delightful affair. The ladies looked well, danced well, talked well, walked well, sat down well, but did not eat anything, of course. The menfolks danced tolerably, chatted considerably, ate furiously, and drank discreetly. All was hilarity, and so influenced were we by the spirit of the scene, that we once were near unbending from the cares of state and despatching the dignity of an editor to our *sanctum,* we were actually on the point of dancing ourself . . .

Of the dancing then we speak not as one having actually participated in it.

But of the supper, we can speak, but scarcely in fitting terms.

We know not which displayed more *taste* about the supper, those who *got it up,* or those who *got it down.* There were squadrons of venison, battalions of turkeys, and whole regiments of chickens. In short there was everything from *bear meat* to *blancmange.* The onslaught was terrific and the execution tremendous —and the man of sensibility could not look upon the mangled corpses of the dead, without a tear. Unlike most conquerors, the appetite of the victors for *carnage* seemed to be appeased at the end of the attack, they sighed not for more *Turkeys* to overcome.

Johnson's notices were often terse, but occasionally he interjected a critical expressive comment: "To night is the Grand Ball at Parkers Hotel. The manergers of the Ball are all Bigist Kind of Bugs"; "This was the night in which the Bill Ball was Given at Mr Barlows City Hotell whe[re] there never has been Just Such another Mixture"; "The Ball was very well attended Last night, a good many Ladies were present and them of the big Kind"; "There are two Balls in the City to night, One at the City Hotel and the other at the Mansion House. Gerasdys at the City Hotel and Bonds at the M. H—both has a good Ball, They are Just as they Should be, Some Small Potatoes at the One and you know whats at the other"; "Several Balls about town to night, An Irish ball or two, then there were Darkey Balls."

William Johnson could attend none of these dances —not the "Grand Ball," nor the one marked by the presence of "Some Small Potatoes," nor the "Darkey Balls." He had little freedom of movement in social and entertainment circles, but there were few persons better informed about Natchez social and cultural happenings. That he was forced to satisfy this portion of his gregarious yearnings through the talk of his barbershop patrons may have become—although he never so stated—a spirit-corroding personal tragedy, for few of his contemporaries had more appetite for social intercourse. He could only listen and long as he shaved and clipped and anointed the heads of men preparing for the evening's hilarity. Later he could only scratch on a paper in the silence of his room as the pomaded ones danced.

CHAPTER SEVENTEEN

Sports of the Turf

WILLIAM JOHNSON'S avid and sustained interest in horse racing was partially an outgrowth of lifelong homage rendered to the way of life practiced by the rich planters of the Natchez area. While in his teens during the 1820's he observed their attendance at public dinners, dancing assemblies, the theater, and meetings of the Adams County Jockey Club; he noted their support of literary and library societies and their patronage of traveling artists, fencing masters, and instructors in dancing and music. He was barred from all these activities except theatrical performances and horse races, and as he grew older he became increasingly reluctant to occupy a seat in the theater gallery where slaves and free Negroes were seated together. At the track he was subjected to much less humiliating discrimination. His betting money was welcomed and freely covered by the less aristocratic white spectators, and he was a paid-up but nonvoting subscriber to the jockey club.

William Johnson and the local "sports of the turf," as contemporary newspapers referred to horse racing, grew up together. The 1820's, the decade in which the free Negro reached manhood and became proprietor of his own barbershop, was the period in which horse racing became firmly established in the Natchez community. The increasing prosperity of the plantation aristocracy, reflected in the erection of handsome country residences and the expanding estates and slaveholdings of this upper-crust minority, also stimulated the augmentation of the racing program and an interest in acquiring and producing fast thoroughbreds. In the early 1820's the Natchez Jockey Club held each year an insignificant three-day meet; by the end of the decade two vigorous organizations —the Adams County Jockey Club and the Mississippi Association for Improving the Breed of Horses—were holding meets in which substantially larger purses were offered and pedigreed horses were entered.

Natchez racing reached a period of bustling vigor in the mid-1830's. Colonel Adam L. Bingaman, who was later to become the Deep South's candidate for the newspaper title, the "Napoleon of the Turf," had begun to develop his stable at one of his plantations. In 1827 and 1828 this highly educated planter, politician, orator, and turfman and his wealthy planter kinsman, Major James Surget, had become co-owners of the Natchez race track, known first as St. Catherine's Course and later as the Pharsalia Course. In the 1820's Bingaman's stable won several races at Natchez and New Orleans, and with his own resources and the backing of the Surget fortune he began to invest in better horseflesh and to breed faster horses, and thereby he completely dominated the local races in 1831 and 1832. During the next two years his mastery was successfully challenged by young William J. Minor, another large-scale planter. But these were only skirmishes preliminary to the principal engagements between the two turfmen.

The Bingaman-Minor rivalry, which was to be a feature of lower Mississippi Valley racing for a quarter of a century, first became pronounced in 1835–36, the initial years of William Johnson's diary. Bingaman had bred Hardheart, winner under different colors of nearly a dozen races on the Natchez tracks, and had begun his longtime practice of buying promising Tennessee and Kentucky yearlings, many of them sired by Leviathan, a famous imported English stallion. William J. Minor's answer was noted in Johnson's diary late in 1835: "Mr Wm Minor returned from France, Ingland and a great many places. . . . Mr William Minor Returns home his six imported Horses also Came on the same Boat, They were Led up main street by six white men, They were imported too."

William J. Minor found time to maintain a businesslike and almost academic interest in improving race horse strains, to serve as an officer of jockey clubs in New Orleans and Natchez, and to challenge Bingaman year after year on the tracks of both places—all in addition to his many duties as absentee owner of three South Louisiana sugar plantations which eventually were valued at more than a million dollars, as owner of a famed Natchez residence, as president of a bank, and as captain of a militia company. Minor's imported racing stock included Britannia and Doncaster, both of which were later used for breeding purposes. His carefully kept account books recorded his expenses and profits in maintaining a stock farm and a "Breeding Stud & Training Stable" and in entering races; and in 1854 he published his *Short Rules for Training Two Year Olds*. But his imported horses were not often successful in actual races, and he had to wait until 1849-51 before his Voucher, Verifier, and La Vraie Reine, by winning numbers of lucrative New Orleans races, gave him a national reputation as a turfman.

Meanwhile, the free Negro barber was a careful observer of the many races which point to the latter part of 1835 and all of 1836 as a period of intense enthusiasm for racing. Another jockey club was formed. Side bets in the regularly scheduled races and the wagers in match races now sometimes mounted to $5,000, to $10,000, and even to 500 bales of cotton. Johnson noted that "sportsmen," "gamblers," and "strangers" arrived in town in large numbers during the racing season of these "flush times." Under such conditions, tempers flared, but only William Johnson described one scene completely ignored by the newspapers:

"The Race to day between Red Mariah & Cassandra was won fairly by R. Mariah But after the judges once gave it in favor of R. Mariah they afterwards turned and made it a Dead Heat—Old Dr Branch & A Stranger & Mr John P. Smith were the judges Mr Ja. Perry was perfectly wronged in the race and he told them so—abused Mr Lee Clabourn for all sorts of D— rascals & Dm thieves, rouges and Every thing else that he Could Lay his tongue to—He shoved Mr Os Clabourne Back 3 times and struck him Once—They were all armed and it was thought that they would fight but neither of the Clabournes would strike."

John G. Perry engaged in a number of boisterous controversies arising from occurrences at the race track in 1835 and 1836. After initial successes with his horse Red Maria in the summer of 1835, he became convinced that certain turf aristocrats were conspiring to defraud him of his money and to traduce his character and conduct. He claimed that they had made malicious and unfounded charges against him, had attempted to "authorise an ungenerous and unmanly course" toward him, and had subjected him "to the irresponsible machinations of wealth and personal influence." He not only quarreled with the Claibornes, but he issued a long, signed blast in a local newspaper in which he denounced the decision of the judges in awarding a $2,000 racing stake to Colonel Bingaman. In this vitriolic statement he referred to the colonel as "the Autocrat of St. Catherines," and Johnson later recorded that "Jack Perry abusees Col Bingaman for Every thing but a gentleman The[y] come very near Fighting." Perry was successful in winning a $5,000 race in rain and snow from Minor, but he was thereby stimulated to challenge publicly *"the world in general, and Mississippi in particular,"* and lost all his winnings to the same opponent in the 1836 races at St. Francisville, Louisiana, which were entered by all the chief Natchez stables.

While Perry claimed to be as gentlemanly as those among his opponents who were favored by "wealth and influence," many of the sportsmen who attended the Natchez races of the mid-1830's were unquestionably professional gamblers. In the fall of 1835 the Adams County "Anti-Gambling Society" took action to clean out a nest of professional gamblers at the race track; and at least one of the participants in leading races, Joseph Rocheleau, was later indicted for professional gambling. But this was after "Rushlow" (as Johnson spelled his name) had been relieved of his slaves and horses in racing bets with Colonel Bingaman and other aristocrats. Ante-bellum society made a distinction at once blunt and finespun between a person who made his living by professional gambling and the planter who could laugh at the loss of a $5,000 racing bet.

In common with many of his fellow citizens, Johnson took keen delight in betting on the races. He did not bet with Colonel Bingaman, but the colonel's farm manager, Samuel Gossin, would cover his money. He had a curious caution, however, for a man who was addicted to gambling, and sometimes hedged his bets or paid small sums to withdraw wagers. Besides risking money, he bet boots, bricks, cigars, or "a month of shaving," and more often lost than won. In one year he lost more than $250 in wagers on the races and won less than half that amount, and he lost $105 in four days in November, 1847. Usually he bore his losses with equanimity, as he thought a gentleman should, except when he suspected that the outcome had been framed in advance. After he recorded in his accounts that he had lost seven bets totaling $35 in one day in 1850, he stated in his diary: "I am under the impression that There is Something done in the way of Swindling out there at times."

As a willing bettor on the horse races and occasionally a paid-up subscriber to the Adams County Jockey Club, Johnson attended the races when he pleased and even enjoyed a limited use of the facilities of the track for his own horses. His horses ran there for small stakes against those of such white friends as St. Clair, a carpenter, and John Jacquemine, or less often against nags owned by other free Negroes. These contests, always for stakes of less than $50, were not a part of the official racing schedule and were not to be compared with match races on which the Adams County aristocracy wagered large sums. Johnson's horses always ran after the regularly scheduled races had been completed or on some other day. None of his horses had cost him more than $200, and they and their opponents were not pedigreed stock.

The Pharsalia Race Course in off seasons was the scene of dozens of sprint races, some hastily arranged, some scheduled informally a few days in advance. The contests were for distances of a hundred yards to a half mile, but most often for "a quarter." These quarter races provided the less affluent horseowners with a method of participating in the sport of kings, and an exceptionally fast-starting nag occasionally achieved special recognition. One was mentioned in three entries within a week in Johnson's journal in 1844: "I Saw a race to day between the Quarter horse Bull and another Horse from below, The Horse Bull gave 17½ ft to the other Horse, and beat him 21 ft." Two days later: "I Saw a race to day between Bull, the Great race Horse, a quarter, and another mans Horse from Louisiana, Bull Beat the Race 21 ft. so I herd." Six days later: "Bull ran to day and was to give the Little Horse 30 ft in a Race but was beat 7 ft Even, Causing Emerson and Farrar to Loose Every thing they had, Horses and all So I herd."

In the 1840's Pharsalia also became a community recreation center where pleasure-seekers could often find diversions other than racing. William Johnson mentioned "Shooting for Beef," pigeon shooting, "chicken fights," militia musters, a Democratic rally, mule races, and colt and cattle shows. The local newspapers were silent about most of these activities, but they did print "puffs" concerning the accommodations available on the days of the big races. In 1840 the railroad ran cars to the course each day; and the announcement appearing in the *Free Trader*, March 22, 1845, was a typical advance notice:

"To-day, the last of the season, two Races will come off, and great sport is anticipated. . . . The first race will be run between the hours of 12 and 1 o'clock. Time will then be given for the horses to recruit, sportsmen to partake of one of McNulty's best dinners, and the multitude generally to refrigerate, when the second race terminates the pleasures of the day. Those who are difficult to please, and relish neither good racing, good eating nor good drinking, may find other amusements, if they have any taste for a 'private game merely for amusement.' "

While William Johnson's diary reflected interest in all these pastimes, his attention was more acutely focused on the regularly scheduled jockey club meets, with their huge "side bets" by owners of highly regarded horses, and the special match races between "brag nags" for high stakes. The free Negro wrote accounts of dozens of these races. Here was one of the spirit-stirring spectacles of antebellum life—the long, tedious training of the thoroughbreds, the hours of conversation devoted to debating the merits of the entries, the thousands of dollars wagered by small and large bettors, all brought to concentration on a few minutes of competition between swift-pounding hoofs maneuvered by slave jockeys clad in their owner's distinctive colors. The gradually mounting delirium attending these contests was only occasionally suggested in Johnson's matter-of-fact recitals, but the space he devoted to the races was an accurate reflection of their importance to spectators and owners alike. A typical sample of his reporting occurred in an entry describing the first race of the Natchez spring meeting of March, 1836:

"A Race for the Jocky Clubb purse 2 miles Heats. Three Horses started, Hard Heart, Prince Talerand & Naked Truth Hard Heart won The First Heat. The Second Heat. Naked Truth won the Second Heat, Princ Talerand close to her heals, H. H. behind Both. Third Heat Naked Truth won beating P. Talerand a Little or about a Length H. H. was still behind. He made a Run on them Coming Down the stretch and if they had have run one Yards farther he would have won the Race very Easy It was a very unexpected Run and suprized Every person present."

Such spectator reactions furnish the racing historian with interesting supplements to the official accounts printed in the *American Turf Register and Sporting Magazine*. Johnson did not consciously write for posterity, as did the Eve of Mark Twain's imagination, when she stated that "some instinct tells me that these details are going to be important to the historian some day." In this instance the historian must turn to the *Turf Register* to discover that, in the race just described, Colonel Bingaman's jockey aboard Naked Truth wore a pink cap and harlequin jacket, while the boy riding Hard Heart wore the blue of the William J. Minor stable. Moreover, horses of different ages ran in the same race and were handicapped accordingly: the three-year-old Naked Truth carried 83 pounds; the four-year-old Prince Talleyrand, 100 pounds; and the six-year-old Hard Heart, 115 pounds. Between the three two-mile heats, which were run by the three horses and constituted the whole of the afternoon's racing, thirty-minute rest periods were allowed. If the heats had been one mile each, the rest periods would have been twenty minutes; and forty-five minutes would have been allowed between four-mile heats.

William Johnson rendered further services to racing history by relating the particulars of disagreements and fights at the track, which no sporting journal or newspaper ever mentioned. One dispute occurred on March 10, 1838:

"To day there was a Race Out at the tract and I went Out to see it. The Nags belonged to Col Bingaman, Col Smith and Mr Minor. Capt McHeath [a horse belonging to the Adam L. Bingaman stable, which was trained by J. Benjamin Pryor] won the first heat very Easy and in coming up to the stand His wrider dismounted and The Blankets was thrown on him and when Mr Minor saw that he spoke of it to Mr Prior and Mr [blank] returned him a very impertinent answer and told him that he was too Damed Smart and To mind his Own Business, &c. This made Mr Minor Mad and he Left the matter for the judges to Decide On and they Decided that Col Bingaman should not Start his Horse again, that He was Ruled off or out of the Race—The Col then stated that it was a Damed Rascally Decission and there followed a Greate deal of deal of abuse to the judges Those were the Judges, Mr Jno Steel, Mr Lief, Mr Gift. They proclaimed it Out that Col Bingaman Could not start according to Rule He swore that He would start his Horse. With that Mr. Minor sent his nag Home Mr Smith ran his mare slowly around, but the Horse ran pretty fast, Doubled Distanced her, for she did not Run—Mr Pror abused Mr Minor a good Deal—it was Laughable to see the following men Cursing the Judges—Col B., Young B, Mr Sam Gocian, Mr Prior, Mr

Joseph Smith. First One and then the other was at it. I am very sorry it Occured indeed There was no Decission on the Subject, it was Left to be Decided between parties at a meeting of the Jocky Clubb."

This was merely an episode in the usually friendly Bingaman-Minor struggle for supremacy on the track. The year 1837 marked Bingaman's rise to more than local sports prominence. His horses won not only major Natchez races against the Minor stable but also against the entries imported by the Louisiana sportsman, Thomas J. Wells. Bingaman had previously raced in Tennessee, at Louisville, Kentucky, and at Donaldsonville and St. Francisville, Louisiana, and elsewhere, but in 1837 he won every race entered at Vicksburg and New Orleans.

Colonel Bingaman's stable (including Angora, Naked Truth, and Fanny Wright) won five of eight New Orleans races held over the recently constructed Eclipse Course, at Carrollton, March 17–22, 1837. A New Orleans newspaper reported that "the lucky Col. B. . . . has been highly successful with his stable. . . . The gentleman has won, we believe, when not only his friends but he himself thought he must inevitably lose." These races, two of which were held before crowds estimated at 10,000 to 12,000 persons, are historically important because they marked the beginning of the rise of New Orleans as a racing center. Racing crowds reached Carrollton, now a part of New Orleans but then outside the city limits, by a new short-line railroad, steamboats and other water transportation, or highway. The receipts on opening day, March 17, when Angora won the principal race, were three and one-half barrels of dollars.

Colonel Bingaman's pre-eminence in lower Mississippi Valley racing was firmly established in the late 1830's and early 1840's. In 1838 six of his Leviathan-sired horses won seven lucrative races at Natchez, Port Gibson, Plaquemine, and Tuscaloosa, and six of eleven races entered at New Orleans; in 1839 his stable won four of six races in the Natchez fall meet; and in 1840 his Sarah Bladen won six races in Natchez and New Orleans. The Natchez press began to refer to him as the "Napoleon of the Southern Turf" and "king of our grounds," and in 1841 a national sporting magazine rated his Sarah Bladen among the leading "four mile horses" in the United States and dubbed her "Champion of the South West, the renowned Sarah Bladen." Although she was finally beaten in 1842 at New Orleans by a much younger horse, an issue of the *American Turf Register and Sporting Magazine* of the following year stated: "But to this day, the Turfmen of the Old Dominion and of the North will not concede that *any* performance made at New Orleans equals that of *Sarah Bladen,* who, at eight years old, *with her full weight up,* ran four mile heats in 7:37—7:40."

During the 1840's Bingaman and Minor continued their duel in spring and fall meets at Natchez and at four tracks in New Orleans, with Bingaman usually in the lead. At Pharsalia they and other horsemen contested with such prominent visiting turfmen as Duncan F. Kenner, Thomas J. Wells, and the Turnbulls of Louisiana, Col. William R. Johnson of Virginia, and Joseph G. Boswell of Kentucky, and all of them then shipped their stables to New Orleans for further competition. Both Bingaman and Minor developed other winners, and both were officials in New Orleans jockey clubs; but Bingaman attained the added distinction of giving his name to the Bingaman Race Course, across the Mississippi from New Orleans.

When Bingaman died in 1869, the New Orleans *Picayune* remembered that "Out of Mississippi Col. Bingaman was better known for his love of the turf and for his liberality and judgement in the selection of the race horse than as a politician. He was a leading authority upon all racing questions, the best judge of horses in the Southwest, and became truly the successor of Col. Johnson, of Virginia, as 'The Napoleon of the Turf.'

"Warm, hearty and emphatic in his friendships, he outlived the era in which he was born and in which he flourished and in his declining years saw the splendor of the past fade into darkness.

"He had been residing in this city some years, living a secluded and quite solitary life."

His old friend and racing competitor, William J. Minor, read another newspaper notice of Bingaman's death "in obscurity & poverty," and nine days before he himself died, wrote in his plantation diary: "For a number of years past Col. B's conduct in m^y respects has not been what his real friends could have wished   Still I am greatly affected at his death   He had a fine mind & many good traits & I had known him so long & so well, had spent so many pleasant hours with him & had so often partaken of his hospitality that I am deeply moved—"

The explanation of the cryptic remarks in these quotations about Bingaman's "conduct" and the "splendor" of his past "fading into darkness" was not a subject for open discussion in drawing-room society. The "Napoleon of the Turf" had chosen to spend his last years with his Negro mistress and their children. Portions of the story emerge in a subsequent chapter dealing with the white associates of the free Negro William Johnson.

Chapter Eighteen

Aristocrats and Lesser Men

NATCHEZ sowed the seeds of its aristocratic tendencies during the third quarter of the eighteenth century and further developed them during the years of Spanish rule when Carlos de Grand Pré, Estevan Miró, Manuel Gayoso de Lemos, and Stephen Minor (known during the Spanish regime as Estevan Minor) were representatives of the Spanish Crown. The little frontier post of Natchez could not compete with Louisiana's capital at New Orleans, but it did have a miniature court comprised chiefly of royal military and civil officials and members of the Catholic clergy.

The Natchez plantation regime began soon after Bernardo de Gálvez, Spanish governor of Louisiana, conquered the area during the middle years of the American Revolution. Spain welcomed planters to the country and was generous with land grants. Irishmen, Scotsmen, Englishmen, and Americans migrated to the rich lands of the Natchez country and soon founded estates, some of which are extant today. By the time the United States acquired the district the pattern was fixed; it did not change substantially during the entire ante-bellum era.

The Adams County tax records show that a wealthy society was rapidly maturing by 1810. The leading landowning names of that year were Minor, Bingaman, Dunbar, Barland, Surget, Hoggatt, Ellis, Wilkins, Farrar, Fitzgerald, and others. They were the first aristocrats of Natchez and—except for the heirs of Barland, Fitzgerald, and one or two others who openly left their property to mulatto children—their descendants remained among the patrician group for the next half century. Each owned one or more plantations, containing as much as and often more than 5,000 acres, manned by as many as 130 slaves. The Natchez area was nearing its mansion-building era.

During the next two decades this group increased its holdings and the number of its slaves. By 1830, however, new "cotton aristocrats" had appeared—Duncan, Green, Mercer, Purnell, Smith, and others. In 1831 Dr. William Newton Mercer owned over 5,000 acres of land, divided into five plantations, and over 200 slaves. Dr. Stephen Duncan held about the same acreage and 320 slaves. These two groups of planter-businessmen rapidly added plantations in Louisiana to their holdings—in the parishes directly across the Mississippi River, in the lower river parishes, and even in the Bayou Lafourche region far to the southward. In 1849 Adam L. Bingaman owned 230 slaves; James Metcalfe, 274; William Newton Mercer, 342; Philip Hoggatt, 389; and Francis Surget, 590. In that year the number of slaves held in Adams County totaled 13,644.

The pressure of the newly rich landed gentry upon the older strata of aristocratic society became severe, and the group rapidly advanced its position. Aided by wealth gained from recently cleared plantation land and the labor of imported slaves or by fortunate marriages into the older families, a professional class—lawyers principally, but hard-pushed by members of the medical profession and the Protestant clergy—began to gain entrance to the mansions in and near the town. And members of the middle class, composed of merchants and other groups, hoped to break into the inner circles gathered in the well-guarded halls.

The record of William Dunbar's estate, probated

during the middle 1820's, discloses that he had owned several plantations—"The Forest," "The Grange," "The Hedges," "The River Place," "Elgin," and "Bayou Pine" —as well as other tracts of farm and timber land. Three decades later the will of Francis Surget listed five Louisiana plantations and several in Mississippi, as well as some unidentified tracts and others listed simply as "wild swamp lands." The will of Philip Hoggatt, probated in 1855, admitted that "the amount of my real and personal property is considerable, my real estate is about nine thousand and forty five acres of land, some acres more or less." His "considerable" property included 450 slaves "of all descriptions, also cattle, horses, mules"; 1,860 shares in different Mississippi financial institutions; $180,000 on deposit in various Mississippi and Louisiana banks, and "also some small sums at my credit in the banks of Natchez"; and for investment purposes "in the hands of Messrs. Buckner, Stanton & Newman about one hundred and twenty thousand dollars."

As early as 1836 the Democratic press was using the phrase "aristocratic county Adams and city Natchez." Four years later, during the stirring days of the Presidential campaign of 1840, a Democratic newspaper derisively and half-contemptuously referred to "the loud talking, aristocratic, stylish leaders of the clan in Adams county." "Aristocratic county Adams and city Natchez" had come of age, for its strength was now begetting savage opposition.

By the 1840's the aristocratic group was a closely knit segment of society. Few of its members were politically ambitious but the majority were Whigs. Later, by 1860, a considerable number were Unionists who wrathfully predicted the destructive effects of the war that would inevitably follow secession. Many of them had extensive Northern and foreign investments in addition to mercantile, manufacturing, or banking interests in Natchez or elsewhere in the South.

From another viewpoint, that of the romantic plantation tradition, few Southern communities equaled the Natchez of 1860. Along with yearnings for polite society and culture had come the gradual maturing of the spirit of *noblesse oblige*. This planter-businessman-banker aristocracy founded hospitals, orphanages, and schools; aided the sick during epidemics; and in other ways expressed a paternalistic attitude toward those less economically fortunate. Several became members of the American Colonization Society. It became their almost universal practice to free favorite slaves by will, as is well illustrated by Adams County probate records. The will of Philip Hoggatt contained this small gesture of benevolence: "I will that one thousand dollars be divided between my three plantations, that is to say among the slaves of those places to be given them at Christmas, that they may be able to purchase some small articles and remember me at the same time." By these and other practices they manifested at least an attempt to maintain the standards of gentility.

William Johnson grew up on the border of this tradition. From his free Negro point of view, wealth and social position were the constant and ultimate goals of existence, and the possession of one or preferably both raised the individual to the rank of gentleman. His analysis of the white man's code caused him to believe that the ownership of property led to honor and even distinction, as well as obligations, and his conduct was therefore marked by an insatiable, restless straining to become affluent. The young Negro had fixed his eyes upon the star, and this state of mind was reflected during the early years of his diary.

Within two years after he began keeping his record he penned a revealing entry: "More Company in town than I have seen in for some Considerable time The Following are a few that I Recollect of seeing to day on the streets." Here followed a list of twenty-nine names, including such men as Governor Alexander McNutt, Colonel Adam L. Bingaman, Captain Thomas G. Ellis, Brigadier General John A. Quitman, Captain William J. Minor, Major James Surget, and Doctor Stephen Duncan. Significantly he characterized the group: "Those are the most wealthy and inteligent part of this Community." As far as the Negro was concerned, wealth and intelligence were indistinguishably fused in "aristocratic county Adams and city Natchez," the only reality worthy of esteem and emulation.

While Johnson constantly strove to elevate himself to the top of the Natchez free Negro group, he could hardly aspire to the title "gentleman." But that was exactly what he tried to be in every aspect of his daily living, and the word was ineradicably fixed in his thought patterns. Gentlemen who fell from grace in their conduct were always condemned. In one instance his remarks were particularly pointed: "Last night there were a parcell of vagabonds, I may say, for I cannot call them Gentlemen, for the[y] were hallowing and hooping through the Streets, One of the Black Gards Broke Several paines of Glass Out of the uper End of my house, ocupied by Dr Loyd, I do not Know the names of any of them Except Mr Pincterton, he was One of the partee, He I think is making rarther a poor show, for a Gentleman."

William Johnson, like other diarists, commented frequently and descriptively upon his acquaintances. And his acquaintanceship included the foremost men of the town and the surrounding countryside. In his barbershop he came to know many of their business affairs; he learned the names of members of their families; he heard their arguments; he saw them in anger; and he heard their roars of laughter over a well-told story. Association with them became a part of his daily living. If he respected them he paid tribute in brief but definite terms when they died.

"The fine and Gentlemany Dr Ker was to have been brot over To day—" he recorded in one instance. "He Died yesterday at his Plantation with 5 hours Sickness—a Disease of the Heart." And on the following day he wrote: "Dr Ker was brot over to this side of The River and Buried To day. He was a Gentleman that I Liked very much."

Again, he wrote: "Capt. Israel Barrett Died this morning near Breakfast time with Congestive fever. He is a man that is beliked by all that Knew him He was a plain, unassuming, Gentlemany man."

On another occasion, he reported an accidental death: "The Dweling House of Mr Robt McCoulough was Blown apart and He was Killed by the falling of a Brick or Bricks—Oh he was a man that Every body that Knew him had much Respect for."

Though the free Negro was personally acquainted with but few of the white women of the community, he had heard enough about them to have definitely fixed opinions. When Mrs. Woods died of apoplexy he wrote that she "was very much of a Lady"; and when "Old Madam Lear Knox" was buried he wrote: "She is Happy I have no doubt for She was a Good old woman."

Johnson occasionally was admitted to the homes of the aristocracy. His visits were usually in connection with a job of haircutting for some member of the family, and he was treated much like any other tradesman—with businesslike politeness. He wrote very little about the individuals thus met but at least once he was moved to unrestrained admiration: "I was Out to Maj Chotard to day and he had his Hair Cut and Miss Mary one of His Daughters. He then paid me the Sum of Sixty Dollars by an order on W Britton and Co. Oh the Major is a gentleman and no mistake, and Mrs Chotard is oh she is a Splendid Lady at home and abroad and Every where."

Men who treated the Negro fairly in business dealings always fared well in his diary jottings. Usually he was prepared to accept necessary risks and unless he was befooled by subterfuge had no censorious remark to make; but when white men treated him with consideration or went out of their way to accommodate him, he was grateful. Colonel William Robertson received several encomiums. In 1850 Johnson remarked that the colonel had paid him a $200 account. "We deducted The amount he had Previously Paid which was ninety Dollars. Thus he paid me in Cash to day One Hundred and Ten Dollars. This shows Conclusively That he is a Gentleman in every Respect, for I was Perfectly willing To Take $50 but he Said no The $200 was right and Thus we Settled." The next January he asked the colonel for aid in securing title to a tract of land he had bought, "which he was Kind Enough To agree to do for me, He is a Gentleman, every inch of Him." The colonel attended to the matter with dispatch, writing several letters in behalf of the free Negro. Three weeks later Johnson made his last entry concerning the incident: "Col Robertson Came up from New Orleans this morning & brought me two Deeds for the Swamp Lands that I Bot of Messrs Mott & Lee of N. Orleans. Oh he is a Gentleman, Every inch of him, I feel very Greatfull indeed to Col R. for his Kindness in this Buisness."

On the other hand, the diarist now and then added a well-chosen, mildly hostile phrase to his brief account of an incident, a phrase which marked a Johnson bar sinister on the individual concerned. He once loaned a horse but commented in his diary that night: "I think it will be his

Last wride on him—he is too Smart, too Smart." One day he met Dick Ellis and commented that "he told me that He would mak about One hundred Bales of Cotten this year. That is pretty Strong for him I think." In 1851 Johnson's small son Richard returned from a visit with his aunt in New Orleans on board the steamboat *Natchez,* and the night of his arrival the father added a line to the note concerning the son's return: "The Capt would take pay for his Passage."

Individuals who took unfair advantage of the barber or his apprentices were exposed and properly branded— not publicly, for the free Negro was always circumspect in his speech—but in the seclusion of his home and on the pages of his diary. His remarks concerning a man named Odell are illustrative: "Mr Odell was at the Shop to night and made several Bets with the Boys [Jeff and Winston, two of Johnson's apprentices] on the Reported Majority for Judge Smith and it appears that he Knew at the time what the Majority was and he Bet them $30 VS 20 that he Could guess within 30 votes of the true majority. The bets were all Closed and I am Satisfied that he Knew at the time he made the Bets."

A month later Johnson again mentioned Odell. He had made with him a "Fair Bet" on the election of the city treasurer. Odell backed out of the wager "and Mr Carpenter was present . . . & Said that if any One took him to be a Gentleman they were Damably Fooled." The barber added, "Enough Said, shure."

While Johnson sometimes was moved to denunciation when he was shaded in a business transaction, he usually considered that he had simply been outgeneraled and was solely to blame. Horse trading, however, was in a different category. His castigation of Louis the butcher is a case in point:

"I Found my fine Bay horse this morning in a Byio [bayou] with his Left hind Leg or hip knocked out of place and very much Bruised, indeed. I then on the strength of having Lost so fine a Horse Took old Pagg out & swaped him away to the meanest and most Low Life Rascally Butcher that Ever has Lived in this town, His name is Louie or Some Such Name, He is a pock marked Butcher and a most infernal Rascal, He put a young horse on me and told me that if he did not work that he would take him Back again & that he was not Blind and promised me very faithfully that if the horse did not answer my purpose that it would be no trade, Well a Day or two afterwards I tryed his horse, and I found him to be no kind of a work Horse, and blind in One Eye, and the other very near Blind—I took him back to the Rascall and he had swaped my horse away and could not he said take Back his Horse."

When men failed to pay their debts to him he sometimes noted his disparaging opinions of them in his daybook. One of these entries was about a Natchez storekeeper: "Col Throckmorton Left here on Bourd of the Steam B. Homer 11th day of June 1833 and I hope he may never Return again for he has this day Refused to pay his just account with—William T. Johnson."

But he was equally impressed with the fairness of another businessman, Andrew Brown, who ran a sawmill and lumberyard just above the Natchez Landing and from whom Johnson often purchased lumber. "I got a full Load of Plank of Mr Brown for which he charged me four Dollars Only," he wrote about one of their transactions. There is no record that Brown ever overcharged or tried to take advantage of the free Negro. William Johnson was grateful.

So ran his comments regarding the Natchez citizenry

—some laudatory, some depreciatory, some damning. A few were outbursts made during a period of anger; many were observations written during the quiet of the evening when the diarist sat at his desk and thought about the happenings of the day. They often reflected as much of the diarist as of his fellow men.

Part III

The Diarist Appraised

Wherein the Free Negro Diarist Is Appraised in Terms of His Friends, His Code, and His Community's Reaction to His Wanton Murder

CHAPTER NINETEEN

White Associates—and One Great Friend

IF William Johnson heard the Southern phrase "poor white trash," he understood and appreciated its meaning and the tone of contemptuous derision with which it was uttered. As a businessman who enjoyed material substance and community standing in a trade catering to whites, he avoided intimacy both with what he regarded as poor white trash and with poor black trash. As an individual who endeavored to pattern his conduct according to his conception of the code of white gentlemen, he avoided close association with inferior persons of any estate or complexion. Caste and class existed then, as now, among Southern Negroes, and the barber carefully maintained his position at the top of his personal social and economic heap.

Yet he succeeded in a marked degree in evading the overt antagonism which his three-story home, rental properties, and income might well have aroused among envious, less prosperous whites. Few of them openly opposed him; few aroused his enmity, and usually for a day or two only. He referred to a flatboatman who had neglected to unload wood in accordance with a promise made at the time of payment as an "infernal Rascal"; he thought a keeper of a small store who cheated him in paying a race bet must be "a Greate Rascal"; and he called a "dutchman" who had killed one of his cows and stolen the meat an "Infernal Rascal." But only one small businessman went out of his way to trouble the barber on more than one occasion. Adolphe Esdra—half owner of a low-income-producing saloon and billiard hall and considered "a mean Fellow" by the diarist—was the subject of several uncomplimentary entries in the Negro's journal. In 1836 Esdra interfered in Johnson's attempt to persuade two French tenants to move in order that a higher rent might be received from a firm of newly arrived storekeepers. Johnson received word from one of the Frenchmen that he "would stay in the store as Long as he pleased" and that he would not leave "if they were to give him $200. This Esdra put him up to say and he told him that I could not Raise the Rent more than one third." But Johnson proceeded to evict the tenants, and in this and other situations demonstrated that he was unafraid of Esdra even though the saloonkeeper was acknowledged to be a tough man in a fight.

While the barber walked and talked softly in public, he lived in no pervading tension of fear that he would make a misunderstood move or fall into gesture or intonation that would offend a white man. He had amicable if ill-defined relationships with many whites of different classes and, while there were social barriers never to be crossed, numbers of these relationships were built upon mutual respect.

Johnson's friendly association with many of the whites was admittedly of a casual nature. On hunting excursions and during his late afternoon strolls about the town and its vicinity, he frequently met and had long conversations with white men. During after-dinner rides about the countryside, he often met planters or farmers or their sons, who stopped to graze their horses along the roadside while they talked with the free Negro. On one occasion he recorded that in returning from Natchez-under-the-

Hill he "walked up the Hill and then up the Streets as far as Mr Howells Residence with Mr. R. J. Walker," who was a nationally known figure in politics.

His fraternization with other whites was less incidental. The same names were recorded again and again as his partners or competitors in shooting matches, fishing and hunting excursions, and placing bets on horse races. Occasionally some prominent white man would come forward to offer backing and assistance in a time of stress and need.

In choosing white men for more-than-incidental companionship, the free Negro was doubtless more than ordinarily limited. But the evidence is clear that he did have a range of choice, of selection or rejection.

Johnson had at least three firm sympathizers among white men who were not professional men or planter aristocrats. He was on exceedingly congenial terms with contractor George Weldon. A white carpenter named St. Clair did some work for Johnson, raced horses against him for $20 stakes, and bet on horse races with the Negro. In the summer of 1836 Johnson recorded that "To day it was that Dr Potts was whiping a Black man and St Clair walked up and took him by the Collar and Choked him and Slung him around and then Told him to get on his Horse and Clear Out, which he did do very soon." The carpenter undoubtedly would have taken similar steps if the colored barber had been mistreated in his presence.

The third white associate was John Jacquemine, proprietor of an amusement center about two miles from town, where he held shooting matches, operated a tenpin alley, and sold fruits and drinks. "John the Greek," as the barber referred to him early in their acquaintance, had been born in Greece but had married an American wife, and by 1850 was the father of eight Mississippi-born children. During Johnson's lifetime, "John the Greek" acquired few slaves but still experienced sufficient growth in status to be listed as "Capt. John Jacquemine" in the tax rolls.

The relationship between Jacquemine and Johnson was largely rooted in the eagerness with which they jointly indulged their common tastes in amusements and sports. In some weeks they were together almost constantly in after-work pastime hours. Samples of the dozens of entries in the barber's diary give his version of this association between a Greek-American and a free Negro extending over a full decade:

"Mc and Jno Jackomine and myself was Out this Evening shooting at the mark in the Minor Pasture—Mc won only 1 Bit from me and 2 from Jam and 1 Doz Segars, And I won 1.75 from Jackominee   I Beat him 2, 50 cent Matches—Oh I beat him Bad—Shure—Shore—Shuree."

"I Loaned John Jaqumine Fifty Dollars to pay for his Fruit."

"I Receved a Letter Last night from Mrs Miller [Johnson's sister, who lived in New Orleans] by the Hand of Jaqumine."

"I Started Over the River in the Afternoon with Mr Jaqumine to Hunt for Game and to Get his Saddle that has been Lost for some time on the other side of the River . . . I Got five Black Birds—did get one shot Once a[t] Ducks a Flying, never got one—Twice at Black Birds—Jakumin said He got fifteen, tho I did not see them myself."

"I went arround to Mr Jaqumine to day with him and He gave me a Puppy by his white Dog out of Flora."

"About Eleven Oclock Mr Jaqumine and myself Started down in the Swamp on a Hunt or to see if we could not get a Shot at a Deer . . . We Came home and took Egg nog, Oysters, Coffee &c."

"I made a Bet with Jaqumine to day or proposed a

Bet and we let another bet which was 1.50 that he would back Out. That taken, he did back Out and refused to pay the 1.50. He must pay it or I Shall think hard of Him, and will get Even with him when it may be Convenient &c."

"To day Mrs Miller [Johnson's sister] Bets Mr Jaqumine a ten Dollar pr of Boots Vs. a ten Dollar Bonet that Mr Polk would be Elected President of the United States."

"Mr. Jaqmine and myself wrode Out to Mr [John] Barlands to Drive in a Bull that I had Out thare, which we did with the Assistance of Mr Barland."

"I played a game of Dominos to day with Jaqumine and won his Roundabout from him."

"I bet Mr Jaqamine to day 1 pr shoes that his young heiffer from the Cow that I won of him would not have a calf in year from this date and I bet him 1 pr shoes that my Horse would out walk his &c."

Johnson also was on exceedingly good terms with several bank officials and physicians, including Colonel William Robertson, Thomas Henderson, Dr. Samuel Hogg, and Dr. John M. Hubbard. This resulted in part from the sense of financial responsibility jointly held by the barber and the white men. The Negro's two bank accounts and property-holdings made him a reliable person in the eyes of the bankers, but their treatment of the barber indicates that they also considered him an individual who merited their liking and—within limitations —their friendship. Dr. Hubbard trusted Johnson's rendering of their long, involved accounts, wherein medical services had to be balanced against barbering and loans, and later proved trustworthy himself by completely squaring the accounts on the day before his marriage. Moreover, Johnson had an unusual concept of the obligations that should exist in the informal bond between physician and patient. He wanted his doctor to respond promptly when called and to be "very Regular" in attending the seriously sick among his family and slaves, and in turn he paid bills for medical services immediately upon presentation. In the case of a doctor who had pulled one of his children through a prolonged illness in 1841, Johnson started off the succeeding New Year's Day by paying the medical man's bill covering the past year—before it had been handed to him. "I went around to Dr. Davis this morning Early and paid my Doctors bill, the amount of which was One Hundred Dollars—I paid it and then went to Breakfast."

In the late 1840's Johnson developed amicable relationships with his lawyer and his doctor. In 1843 he stated in his diary that "I herd a young man by the name of Martin speak Last Night on the Bond Question and I was much pleased with his speech, his Looks and his General appearance." Thereafter he made notes on William T. Martin's career—his public speeches, his term as district attorney, his conduct in two fights. Eventually he employed Martin as his chief attorney in the land dispute which led to his death. During the same period, the barber and Dr. Luke Pryor Blackburn, captain of the leading militia organization in Natchez, were very friendly. Johnson had a very high regard for the medical services which Blackburn gave his household and slaves, and the two men exchanged both business and personal favors.

Events subsequent to the barber's death in 1851 demonstrated that he had chosen wisely in these two well-wishers. Both Dr. Blackburn and attorney Martin were extremely helpful to Johnson's widow and fatherless children, and William T. Martin was special prosecuting attorney in the trials of the alleged murderers of both Johnson and his son Byron. Both men lived to achieve a measure of distinction, Blackburn in yellow-fever control work that was "to make him known to the entire nation" and in a controversial administration as governor of Kentucky, and Martin as the builder of a famous Natchez residence, as a Confederate major general, and as a prominent attorney.

But Johnson's stanchest friend among aristocratic whites was another individual who—at the height of his career and before it took one of the most curious turns in the annals of Southern aristocracy—was even more famous; and he, too, re-proved his friendship after the barber's death. This was Colonel A. L. Bingaman, highly educated scion of a rich Adams County planting family, leading Whig politician and orator, and nationally known turfman.

The career of Adam Lewis Bingaman prior to the 1830's, when he was frequently mentioned on the pages of the barber's account books and diary, had been one of scintillating promise. Born in 1793 near Natchez, he was regarded in the succeeding years as "brilliant" and as having "added to the graces of the body those of a most active intellect, which made him a focus of attraction," an estimate partially confirmed by his graduation from Harvard as "the First Scholar of the Class of 1812." He was connected by birth and by his marriage or the marriages of his sisters to dozens of the powerful Adams County planting aristocracy. Between 1819 and 1841 he inherited a huge estate from his father, two uncles, an aunt, a cousin, his mother-in-law (who had been a daughter of Territorial Governor Winthrop Sargent), and his mother (who had been born into one of the South's richest families, the Surgets). In the 1820's he became a planter and stock raiser, began to enter horses in races on the local tracks, and—almost alone among local inheritors of great wealth —began to dabble in state and national politics. By 1830 he had served a term in the lower house of the state legislature, had been twice defeated in races for the lower house of Congress, and had acquired the title "Colonel," partly in recognition of his aristocratic position, partly because of martial tendencies evidenced by brief services in the War of 1812 and by his organization of a mounted militia troop called the Adams' Guards.

In the 1830's and 1840's the acknowledged leaders of the Whig party in Mississippi were Colonel Bingaman and Seargent S. Prentiss, "and though the fiery eloquence of the latter gave him the greater fame, the polished periods and matchless social qualities of the former made him equally formidable to his political opponents." The colonel's difficulty in politics, as William Johnson noted, was that he belonged to the wrong party, the Whigs, that he had to wage an almost hopeless struggle against the feeling of the interior of Mississippi against the Whig-dominated Natchez community, "which is supposed to consist almost entirely of a set of *purse proud* aristocrats." Bingaman did become speaker of the lower house of the state legislature and president of the state senate, but between 1838 and 1841 he was three times an unsuccessful Whig candidate for either the upper or lower house of the United States Congress.

Meanwhile his colored admirer followed his every move in the political arena. He noted his departures on speaking tours or to meetings of the legislature, and he frequently allowed one of his barbers to accompany him as valet. Johnson was often derisive in discussing Whig speeches, but he was obviously elated when the colonel spoke "much to the delight of the audience." Johnson was a confirmed supporter of the Democratic party—he once wrote that "I have One wish and that is that the Democrats will Get a Large Majority in Every State"—but he always wished Bingaman "all the Cuccess imaginable." The colonel was playing his proper role, the barber felt, when he made a felicitously worded address of welcome to the "volunteers of Mississippi" as they returned from the Mexican War, when Colonel Jefferson Davis and Lieutenant Colonel Alexander Keith McClung of the First Mississippi veterans replied in kind, and the diary entry closed with the observation that all three speeches were "well done very indeed and much applauded too" by "The Citizens" who had "all turned Out En-masse to welcome them."

The Johnson journal adds details to Bingaman's public record in politics and in acting as a foremost community figure, in the conduct of his famous racing stable and in other sporting activities, in the operation of his Fatherland plantation and his stock-raising experiments, and in serving as administrator of a number of large estates. While many of these details are worthy of remark and occasionally amusing, they serve in the main to expand or underline a not unfamiliar picture of a Southern aristocrat whose energies were largely absorbed by sport and politics.

But Johnson also wrote diary entries which show his blue-blooded hero as a personality. "The Col.," as the barber often referred to him, intervened in a cruelty-to-child case. He accepted a challenge to fight a duel, "Came in very Early this morning and got shaved He seemed to be very wraped up in thought, he had nothing to say." But three days later, "The Difficulty that was to have taken place to Day was very Hansomely arranged," the barber wrote; "the matter was left to a Committee of Honor— I was never more glad than to hear it." A few months afterward the diarist "herd that Col Bingaman spit in Mr. Morgans face and cursed him and then threw a chew of tobacko in his face, On account of his Sueing the Col." An even less aristocratic gesture caused the Negro, who had fixed convictions concerning the way the "wealthy and inteligent part of this Community" should act in public, a measure of uneasiness: "Col Bingaman was at Kains Coffee House amoung Foureigners Speaking of the American Flag &c, playing Cards &c."

The Johnson diary and personal papers afford glimpses of another and still more unconventional Bingaman behind the public façade of the eminent figure portrayed by the newspapers. As one token of unconventionality, the association between the barber and the colonel had an atmosphere of extending beyond the sincere but guarded and circumscribed friendship which Johnson sometimes achieved with other individuals in the upper reaches of society. The colonel purchased a slave for $800, persuaded Johnson to teach him the art of shaving, and sold him within less than four months for $1,550—the only instance in which the barber performed such a service for a white man. Bingaman borrowed unusual items from the colored man—a music box, a pamphlet, a book, a seine—and accepted the barber's gift of "a pair of Large Candle sticks with a Glass vase over Each—" In reciprocation, the master of Fatherland allowed the free man of color to graze his stock on the plantation pastures and breed his nags to celebrated blooded studhorses, and he uttered not a word of recrimination when a borrowed milch cow died.

The beneficent shadow of Colonel Bingaman's friendship with the barber still lay over the Johnson family long after the free Negro was killed in 1851. Indeed the bonds between the colonel and the family were strengthened during the next two decades. In the late 1860's the elderly Bingaman wrote the family a remarkably out-of-the-ordinary series of letters from New Orleans, letters that have a tone of intimacy and were primarily intended to comfort his Natchez friends in a double affliction: the death of William Johnson's widow shortly after the confinement of her eldest son, William, Jr., in an insane asylum in New Orleans.

In May, 1866, Colonel Bingaman wrote to William Johnson's second son, Byron: "Since I wrote you William has escaped three times. Once from the Charity Hospital & twice from the Insane Asylum. . . . I went to the Principal of police & told him of it the third time. He telegraphed to the Lieutenant of this district & I believe, tho am not sure, that they have him again. . . . I shall have more & write you. I sent up a bbl of sugar to your Mother Have you received it? We are all well. Teeny sends love to all & in case Teen is so lazy that she has not written you The gowns will be up next trip of the boat with her letters. My kindest respects to all the family."

In September of the same year Bingaman wrote Byron that "Bill" had again escaped and that he was again endeavoring to trace him. "And now Byron permit me to say that I never was so thunderstruck as when I heard of the death of your dear Mother. I little thought when I was up with you and sat talking to her on the sofa that it was the last time I ever should see her. But it is a stroke of the Providence of God & you & your sisters should have a humble resignation to it. The old must die and the Lord may have done it for the best. Tell your Sisters [to] bear up . . . with humble submission & to take every care that they can of one another. I shall be up shortly & will give you a further account of Bill—My sincerest regards to Mrs Battles [Byron's grandmother] the young ladies & yourselves and Teen's & Jim's also."

In 1868 he wrote at least two letters to Byron, in which he informed him that "Teeny and your sister are both well" and ended with "My love to your sisters and accept the same for yourself." In the same year he wrote courtly letters to Byron's sister Anna, informing her of various services he had performed for her, telling her of his continued interest in the confinement and health of William, Jr., and ending one: "Your blackberry jam is excellent & I am much obliged to you & your family. The girls join me in love to you & your family. With the greatest regards, Yours as ever." In Natchez, in this year, William Johnson's daughter Anna made an entry in a notebook: "I loaned Col. A. L. Bingaman 1 volume of William Shakespere."

What was the explanation of this correspondence between the former "Napoleon of the Turf," as the New Orleans *Picayune* and other newspapers referred to him, and a bereaved Negro family? What had happened to Colonel Bingaman in the 1850's and 1860's?

The answer, which has been carefully authenticated in the course of a long search, is that he spent his last years in New Orleans with his free Negro mistress, who had formerly lived near Natchez, and their children. The irrefutable item of key evidence that emerges from behind the veil hitherto obscuring the final years of Adam Lewis Bingaman is that he made a girl with some Negro blood—the survivor among his "natural Children," "duly acknowledged" in a sworn statement—his sole heir.

The New Orleans *Times* in a highly laudatory obituary notice, which referred to him as "a distinguished Southern gentleman," ended its account of his life with this statement: "Since the war great disasters and losses had clouded his life and withdrawn him, in a great measure, from his old associations, and he died in undeserved obscurity and poverty in this city, which since the close of the war, he has regarded as his home." Several of his former friends lamented his passing but regretted the nature of his "conduct" in his final years.

Substance is added to these bare statements by the papers of the family of his friend William Johnson. The same Natchez attic in which the barber's diary was found also yielded some of the letters that Bingaman and his mistress wrote to the Johnson family before and after the

Civil War. These letters and others penned in a distinctly delicate handwriting by his "natural child," Elenora, whom he affectionately called "Teen" or "Teeny," picture the colonel in his middle seventies as still possessing a large library, as being energetic, robust, and strong-voiced—as evidenced by "his deafening halloes." The former master of 235 slaves and several plantations apparently found a certain amount of satisfaction in home life with his daughter, whom a competent witness described many years later as "of light color, small stature, long beautiful hair, and, above all, great education and refinement."

Nine months before her father died at the age of seventy-six in September, 1869, Teen wrote to William Johnson's daughter a remarkable letter which included a description of a memorable dinner which both the colonel and his daughter enjoyed in a New Orleans restaurant:

"It's Christmas you know, or rather has been Christmas & I must say I never past a pleasanter one. We went round & called on some of our acquaintences, among others Mrs Hagan, & though we intended only a visit, we ended by spending the best part of the day there, but we gave a dinner to a few friends, so I had to come home. The next night Mrs Hagan gave a hop & Oh! I tell you it was splendid. I have become so accustomed to parties that I seldom enjoy them much, but that one I did enjoy. A few days before we formed the acquaintence of Col Hancock, brother to the general [Winfield Scott Hancock, Union hero in the Civil War and candidate for President on the Democratic ticket in 1880] who commanded this department of the Gulf; he was present at the party & introduced us to a friend of his, a Mr Moore, a very pretty & a very nice gentleman . . .

"[Several days later] who should walk in but Mrs Hagan with a joint invitation from Mr Moore & Col Hancock for the family to dine with them on the 7th in celebration of Mrs Hagans & Mr Moore's birth night . . . We were to dine at John's restaurant a place I never heard of colored people being admitted to before.

"I don't wonder at nor blame those white women for clinging with such tenacity to this world, nor for wishing to exclude others from its pleasures. Certainly it is selfish but selfishness is their characteristic. The room which Mr Moore selected was very large fronting the street with a balcony & without fire it was as warm as any one could wish, it had four windows beautifully hung with rich lace curtains & scarlet velvet tapistry, the furniture was of rose wood, the floor was covered by a magnificent carpit & the room was lit by eight gilted gasburners. You can fancy how it looked. Those gentleman are the quintessence of politeness. The Col's politeness amount *almost* to officiousness. After we left the carriage (which we entered to ride three blocks), walking through that hall hanging on their arms seemed to be a strange sight for New Orleans but 'practice makes perfect' they'll get used to it   Since we have known those gentlemen we have had a delightfull time with them. The dinner was very nice but I did not know what one half of the dishes were & did not taste one third of them. The wines were very, very good.

"My father drank so much that he entered the house not exactly in a 'bee' line."

The eighteen-year-old writer of this Reconstruction letter, a lifelong friend of the Johnson family, had been born in 1851, the year that William Johnson was killed. When she died in 1937 in a New Orleans home for elderly Negroes, her life and that of her white father had almost spanned the entire history of the Republic, from the second administration of George Washington to the second of Franklin D. Roosevelt.

CHAPTER TWENTY
Colored Friends and Associates

ON the pages of William Johnson's diary, both free and slave Negroes appeared with such wide range of personalities and attitudes as to defy generalization. In the Natchez area some slaves and free Negroes were publicly humiliated and even clubbed to death by whites, just as a few whites were attacked and even killed by slaves. But slaves and free Negroes also risked their lives to save white masters and friends, and there were instances of friendship and respect between whites and blacks that must present striking exceptions to any cherished stereotypes of patronizing affection on the part of one group or abject humility on the part of the other. Among both whites and blacks, there were the sober element and the drunkards, the honest and the thievish, the thrifty and the spendthrift, the intelligent and the stupid, the proud and the meek, the strait-laced and the promiscuous.

Rewarding friendships with blacks in bondage could occasionally be achieved by warmhearted whites of unquestioned social and economic position, but the possibility of such a relationship never occurred to William Johnson. Fraternization with slaves marked by even the most admirable characteristics was out of the question— or so he thought—for this man who had escaped from slavery. Free Negroes were another matter. As the town's leading barber, William Johnson was almost forced to seek his closest friendships among comparatively well-to-do free colored persons. Even among this restricted group, however, his pride and discrimination led him to choose intimates with care.

His diary presents impressive evidence that the free Negro population in Natchez and Adams County existed in widely varying economic circumstances and maintained distinct social levels within the group. The free people of color had their own aristocracy—the Johnsons, the McCarys, the Barlands, the Fitzgeralds, and the family of George Winn. Three of these upper-class families had received legacies of land or town property from white men who openly acknowledged their parentage of the mulatto children who were their designated heirs; all were slaveowners. Usually the tax rolls and census records listed them as holding five to twenty slaves (in comparison with the one or two slaves held by the other ten or twelve free Negro slaveowners). Socially and culturally, they were several notches above other Negroes. Their marriages were officially recorded, and they would have been indignant had anyone suggested that they attend any of the numerous Natchez "darkey parties"—functions that were marked by intermingling of slave servants and lower-class free Negroes.

At a lower level were free Negroes with less prospect of advancement, such as journeymen barbers, young free mulatto apprentices, stewards and barbers on steamboats, and a hack driver or two. Still lower on the economic scale was the mass of the independent free people of color, including peddlers, hotel employees, prostitutes, draymen, day laborers, and small farmers—some hopelessly poor.

Another free Negro group consisted of those who were attached to white households. The unpublished census records for 1840, the census year in which the free Negro population in Adams County and Mississippi reached its maximum, indicate that more than one fourth of the 283 free colored persons in Adams County belonged in this dependent category. About two fifths of the white families to which free Negroes were attached owned no slaves, and in a few instances free Negroes were listed as the entire dependent connection of the unmarried white male who was named as the family head.

Under Mississippi law, the property-holding right of free Negroes was their chief advantage over slaves. Members of both groups were prohibited from voting, serving on a jury, testifying in a case in which a white person was a party, or speaking insolently to a white person. Slaves were prohibited from carrying weapons of any kind, and free Negroes were allowed to own them only if they secured licenses. These and a number of additional prohibitions and regulations were designed to circumscribe the conduct of the entire Negro population. But in actual practice, as William Johnson's diary amply demonstrated, individual slaves in Natchez were sometimes allowed a status approaching that of freedom, and some of the laws regulating free Negroes were never enforced against those with considerable property.

Among these propertied free persons of color was Johnson's mulatto friend, Robert McCary, whom he usually called "Mc" or "Old Mc." McCary, born a slave, had been freed in 1815 as the result of the will of his deceased owner, James McCary, a Natchez cabinetmaker. In 1813 the will of the cabinetmaker had commended his "Soul unto Almighty God" and expressed a desire to settle his "wordly affairs to be better prepared to leave this world, when it shall please the Authour of nature to call me hence." To achieve these pious aims, his will directed that a town lot be given a free Negro woman, that his two female slaves should be freed, and that two of the children of one of the slaves should also be emancipated. These two children were "Bob" and his sister, Kitty.

The remainder of the will contained provisions that mostly favored Bob and Kitty. Both were given town lots; both were to receive the proceeds from the work of two other minor slaves; and Bob was granted a special bequest of $1,000. The executor of the estate was admonished that Bob and his sister should be "educated and brought up in the fear of God, and in the principles and practice of true religion and morality."

Why was the white cabinetmaker so solicitous about the future of these two slave children? A document prepared in the same year by the executor of the estate, McCary's "dearly beloved friend" and a prominent businessman, provided the answer. The cabinetmaker was the father of Bob and Kitty, and he thought so highly of them that he had directed that their half brother should remain a slave for life in order that they might benefit.

The executor of the McCary estate was scrupulous in his efforts to rear Bob and Kitty as their father had directed. He contrived to have them emancipated in Ohio; he managed their property and eventually perfected their titles to it; he secured at least five white tutors for them; and he saw to it that they were clothed and lodged in various homes. Among the homes in which Bob lived were those maintained by William Johnson's mother and sister in the middle 1820's. Bob and William probably learned the barber trade in the same shop, that of William's brother-in-law, James Miller. This was the beginning of a lifelong companionship between William and Bob or "Mc."

The satisfying friendship that sprang up between the two barbers was partly a result of their complementary personalities. William was the leader of the pair. "Mc," three or four years the senior, was more relaxed and less ambitious and self-seeking; he apparently desired little beyond the reasonable income provided by his two-chair shop; by 1840 he had disposed of his slaves; and during the next twenty years he occasionally assisted his fellow man by tutoring free Negro children. Inasmuch as the two barbers were almost the only businessmen in the top bracket free Negro group, they had little choice in selecting intimates but, aside from the inevitability of the situation, genuine affection flowed between them.

William Johnson wrote into his diary dozens of entries about McCary that exhibit a similarity of tastes and interests as well as mutual trust. They not only supported each other in business deals by endorsing notes, but they were continually together—at the race track, in hunting and fishing, in card games, in Sunday walks on the Bluff, in long talks in their shops after they had been closed, and in memorable sessions at the dinner table.

"Mc got on his Horse to ride out to the tract and his Horse ran Down the Hill by his House and threw him and broke his Left Arm. . . . I went up in the Evening to see Mc and I staid up there about an hour. . . . Rode up to Mcs in the Evening Found him siting by the Bed side in a Chair We talked about a half Hour &c."

"Mc Came Down to my shop in the Evening. I Cut his hair and I Read Governer McDuffee speech to him—on Slavery and Abolition—We both got tyred of it before I had finished it."

"Mc and myself had a tolerable good Dinner—We had as follows—Mc had 2 Bottles of Medoc Clarlet, 1 Bottle of Champagne wine, Buiscuit Egg Bread, P. pork, 1 Broiled Chicken & Beef Stake, I had a pice of good bacon, wheat Bread, Oysters in Flitters, one Large Bottle of Anneset, one Dozen Orenges, 1 small Bottle of Muscat wine . . . Mc had a Bottle of Brandy & honey."

"Mcs little Bill Button is now ranaway from Mc and

he Sent Dick after him this morning and Dick ranaway himself and I caught him this night and Took him home To Mc."

"Mc, The Star Shooter, Came Out here to day and after dinner we Commenced to shoot Riffles and we Shot Eight matches and here is the way they Came off—2 best in three   they were—Mc Only win 1, Mr Purnell 3 and myself 4."

"My Little Richard very Low. . . . McCary and Mrs Gibson Sat up with him to night all night . . . My Poor Little Richard is very sick yet. . . . McCary . . . has Came to night to set up with Him."

"Mc and myself took a wride Out this Evening to the Scott old Fields and the Creek &c—There we read the Laws of Louisiana in pamphlet form &c."

"Mc was down at the House Last night and whilst He was Here to See my Little Sick Child we had some Egg nog made and Drank three glasses, Each of us—it was good."

"McCary & Brustee, Wilcox and myself were up the whole night   W. and myself Beat them ten Games, we were 30 and they were 20. Thus we Quit."

While none of William Johnson's other friendships among the small group of propertied free Negroes compared to the give-and-take trust and affection he gave McCary, he nevertheless maintained a paternal relationship with several. His association with Winslow Winn was typified in an 1837 diary entry: "Young Winn was up this morning—Took Breakfast with us—He Brought me a fine mess of fish from the swamp That he Caught in his Cein—Winn is a poor young man that [could] have been much above his present Circumstances if he had only Justice done him."

"Young Winn" or "Little Winn," as Johnson often referred to Winslow, was the mulatto son of George Winn, a free Negro who had died in 1831, leaving a home on a cotton plantation of nearly 1,200 acres (partly swampland), a tract of land in another county, and twenty-two slaves. The will of George Winn provided for the education of Winslow and his two sisters, but gave the sisters preferential treatment in the division of the property which would take place when the children became of age. Pending the division, a white businessman was named as executor of the estate.

The executor's reports constituted a striking case study of the difficulties encountered by a white man entrusted with the estate of three orphan but proud free Negroes, even when the estate produced 110 bales of cotton in a single year. The education clause of the will was especially hard to execute. He hired a white tutor, who soon quit, probably because he was reluctant to remain in a farm home with three free Negro children and a free Negro overseer. The executor succeeded in getting one sister "into a decent family in the city of Natchez with the view of improving her and continuing her education," but later she brought suit against him on the ground that she had not been properly educated. He sent another sister to a Pennsylvania boarding school—where she studied French and music among other subjects—for five years, but her complaints were numerous and vociferous. He placed Winslow in another boarding school in the same state, but the young man nursed grievances against both executor and sisters for years, even after some of the property was relinquished to him.

William Johnson liked "Young Winn." He fished and hunted with him, exchanged presents with him, entertained him at dinner, and nursed him in sickness. But his attitude toward the younger man was primarily one of commiseration. He not only thought that Winn's business sense was poor, but he had another reason for compassion: "Little Winn is at my House and has been for Several

Days," he wrote in 1848. "Poor creature I Pitty him very much indeed—I am Sorry that he drink So much."

The names of Winslow Winn's brothers-in-law appear in Johnson's diary in dozens of places, but not once did he see fit to note a curious fact about them: Here were two instances in which white farmers married women who were the daughters of a free Negro. Neither did the diarist, in discussing various members of the numerous Barland family, comment directly on the marriages of at least six of these free Negroes to white persons—marriages that were officially recorded and recognized in property transfers.

The Barland story is spread upon the ante-bellum records of several Mississippi counties and of the territorial and state legislatures. In 1814 William Barland, a rich and longtime white resident of Adams County, petitioned the territorial legislature for permission to free his slave Elizabeth and the twelve children he had "begotten on her." He had emancipated her and her first three children, he said, on the same day that he had purchased them in 1789, but the record had been destroyed in a fire. And now, in 1814 as he approached death, the present petition was "in consideration of the general good conduct of the said Elizabeth as a friend and companion during thirty years, and the love and affection your Petitioner bears for these his children." The legislature passed a law granting his request, the thirteen Negroes were soon freed, and Barland died a few months later. His will made a bequest of a minimum of $2,000 to each child and directed that his minor offspring should be "schooled and brought up in the principles of virtue and morality."

Ten years later the Barland heirs petitioned, collectively, and some of them individually, for the removal of their legal disabilities as free Negroes. The legislature failed to act on the petitions despite supporting attestations signed by more than two dozen white residents of three counties, but they nevertheless furnish convincing proof of the status to which free Negroes could rise in pre-Civil War Mississippi.

One of these petitions, signed by Andrew Barland, was an enlightening document that demonstrated that at least one free Negro in a neighboring county was accorded privileges in the 1820's exceeding those granted William Johnson in later decades. This petition was supported by the signatures of thirteen white men, including General Thomas Hinds, and by a separate document in which the county clerk and sheriff of Jefferson County stated that Barland had often served on juries and that "we view the said Andrew Barland worthy of stations in common with the free enlightened citizens of said county." Here is free Negro Andrew Barland's petition to the legislature:

"Your petitioner Humbly Sheweth That he is the offspring of a white man by a mulatto woman—that he was born in Adams County and is now about thirty nine years of age, that his father gave him a decent education and property enough to be independent, that he intermarried with a respectable white family, by which said wife he has two children, that he has resided about sixteen years in the County of Jefferson and is well known to the most respectable citizens of said County, that he has almost in every case & by every man, been treated and received as well as tho he had been [a] white man of fair character, that he has been summoned as a juror very often and served as Grand & Petit Juror and often given testimony in open Court as a Legal Witness—that his vote at elections has often been taken & for many years your petitioner has enjoyed all the privilidges of a free white Citizen—but a controversy with a bad man of the name of Joseph Hawk caused an exception to be taken to your petitioner's testimony on account of his blood, but with pride your petitioner can state, that altho his oath was refused, the Jury who tried the cause gave a verdict in favor of the word of your petitioner altho opposed by the oath of his adversary, a white man—

"Your petitioner further sheweth to your Honble bodies, that his education, his habits, his principles and his society are all identified with your views, that he holds slaves and can know no other interest than that which is common to the white population, that his sisters have all married white men of fair and respectable standing, and have always rec^d the same respect shown to white women of the same station in society.

"Your petitioner prays your Honble bodies to extend to your petitioner such privilidges as his Countrymen may think him worthy to possess . . ."

This document has a ring of authenticity and is corroborated in many details by additional contemporary evidence. In only one particular does it smack of special pleading. Johnson's single diary reference to Andrew Barland's sisters flatly contradicted the claim that they invariably received "the same respect shown to white women of the same station in society." Negro blood in an individual was generally known and then, as now, was a bar to social acceptance in the Natchez region.

William Johnson was acquainted with most of the Barland family. He once wrote that he "could not come it" to a proposal by "Mr David Barland," one of Andrew's brothers and a successful planter, that he advance a loan of $400, even though a cotton crop was offered as "Collateral Security." He did lend small sums to another brother, "Mr John Barland," who was one of the diarist's casual hunting companions. In 1841 he confidently and correctly predicted that a white jury would find John not guilty of a murder charge: "He will get clear of it as Easy as possible." But Johnson was never on terms of intimacy with the Barlands, and he remained completely aloof from the Fitzgerald clan, free Negroes who had inherited slaves and land from two Scottish brothers under much the same circumstances as the Barlands.

While the barber usually stood apart from the mass of free Negroes in Natchez, he was regarded as a business adviser and father confessor by several women. Various sums of money were deposited with him by Hester Cummings in the course of her long struggle to raise funds to purchase her sister, and he often arranged for payment of taxes on her two slaves. He solved several small business problems for a Mrs. Amie and for Mrs. Gabriel Brustie, who also sometimes "took tea with us." On one occasion he patched up a quarrel between Mrs. Brustie and her husband: "Nothing new to day," he wrote in 1843, "only I herd Brustee had been treating his wife very badly and that she was very Anxious to go home to her people." The next day "Mrs G Brustee was at my House this morning and wanted me to go get her passage on the Princess to New Orleans—I saw her afwards and told her she had better remain at my house, that I would see Mr Brustie and things would turn Out right—She thankd me and we parted."

He had a deeply felt need for friends. But his talent for enjoying himself simply, with friends, was sharply checked by the combination of the severity of his standards and of his peculiar position. He dared unbosom himself to no one except his crony, Robert McCary, his family, and his diary. William Johnson, free man of color, occupied an almost isolated position at the top of his class.

Chapter Twenty-One

Pride and Compassion

BOREDOM rarely afflicted William Johnson. Disappointment and even disillusionment came to him, as to all men, but his life was too full of profitable work and spirited play to permit even occasional attacks of ennui. Much of his time and energy was devoted to the active supervision of his barbershop and other business undertakings, but he had numerous additional outlets for his abounding enthusiasm for life. Among them were conversations with friends and acquaintances, an intellectual curiosity that led to a considerable amount of reading, and an eager absorption in all manner of sports. The continual correspondence and pleasant exchange of visits with his sister, Adelia, and her husband, James Miller of New Orleans, were part of the pattern of a multiform family life.

The observations in Johnson's diary obviously were made by a man with an alert mind who was unreservedly occupied in the daily round of activities and participated in many of them. In giving full rein to his wide range of interests, he developed a well-rounded personality, a quality which materially assisted him in becoming one of the best-liked individuals in his community.

Numerous facets of his engaging personality are unaffectedly revealed in his writings. Self-confident but not aggressive to the point of making numbers of enemies, strongly competitive but never overweeningly boastful, peace-loving but occasionally beset by "Small passions," amiable but inclined to grumble when he paid "very Tall Taxation," neighborly but not offensively ingratiating, mildly humorous but not given to cutting wit, dignified but able to unbend to play marbles, talented at "buisness" but not so ambitious to amass property that it became a monomania—this man was possessed of a balance and poise arising from the kind of self-discipline that makes a man free through mastery of himself. But among all his attributes, three emerged as dominating: a desire for self-improvement that was imperative even if it had to be largely sought in loneliness; a pride that might be publicly stifled but could not be denied; and moral convictions that were tempered with compassion.

Johnson was not only a lively, intelligent man but one who absorbed all sorts of newsworthy facts. He was a subscriber to local newspapers as well as to more distant publications such as the New Orleans *Picayune,* the *Saturday Evening Post,* the *New Yorker,* the *New York Mirror,* and the *Spirit of the Times.* He had a sizable library comprised of historical and literary works (including a volume of Shakespeare), popular fiction, dictionaries, and even French and Spanish grammars. While by no means an intellectual, he had a good command of colloquial English and could express his views in a direct and positive fashion.

After he stopped attending the theater, reading was his favorite form of cultural activity. He made numerous purchases of books at stores or auctions, and while he often neglected to list the titles of books he had bought, one lot included several volumes of Buffon's "Natural History," the *Civil Code of Louisiana,* "a Roman Catholic work," and a "Large Book on History, geography &c," for which he paid "$10 in cash." The actual extent of his reading is problematical, but on several occasions he spent an entire day in the activity. Though he took a few French lessons, it is doubtful that he became proficient in the language, for at the time he purchased the volumes of Buffon he noted that they were in "the French Language or I Should be very much pleased." In all probability he was not a critical reader, for only occasionally did he comment on the quality of a book.

Johnson's pride, it must be admitted, was justified, for his climb to the top of the Natchez free Negro ladder had been slowly accomplished by reading, observation, hard work, and careful demeanor. Once at the top, he highly prized his close and casual friendships with many of the leading citizens of the community and personal accommodations from them were warmly appreciated. His use of the word "gentleman" indicated a wholehearted respect for the term and reflected his own conduct and thinking. When he had financial difficulties with Barbiere, the "Dancing man," he wrote that he could not bring himself "to believe [that he] is a Gentleman in the full acceptation of the word." When one prominent citizen spoke abusively to another he wrote that "A gentleman would not [have] talked So seviere."

Something of an aristocrat within his own sphere, he was occasionally derisive of poor whites. When the wife of one of them struck her husband "with a Brick Bat," he observed that the action was "Just like such people." Some of his most critical observations were written in disapprobation of the actions of the small farmer group that lived in the Swamp area south of Natchez. When one Swamp group came to town to see the circus he caustically described their actions: "Jasper Winn was up to day from the Swamp, Tate, B. Winns wife and Tates wife &c. Very Green Locked arm Came up to see the Show of Animals and they were a Show themselves for Sure." He once described a fight that arose because two of the brothers-in-law of a woman who had married a "Swamper" alleged to have Negro blood had become angered, one of them having said that "any man that would take the part of a Colord Man Marying a white woman was a Damed Rascal." At other times he simply stated that a man who had cut a companion in a Natchez barroom brawl had escaped to the Swamp, or that one of its inhabitants had chained his daughter to prevent her from marrying a wood chopper. On the whole, the side glances at the Swampers in his diary present a composite picture of a group of illiterate whites—one of whom once threatened to give him "a real niger Beating"—and a few free Negroes who eked out a bare, bleak existence by raising a little corn and cotton, by fishing and hunting, and by shooting hogs and cutting timber with little regard to ownership—and this very near the famed plantation homes which were the residences of the First Families of Mississippi.

In contrast to such ill-favored characters, Johnson was justifiably proud of his high community status and did everything possible to maintain it. Despite his political and militia disqualifications, he performed many civic services and contributed to funds for the celebration of holidays and for public enterprises. These contributions were apparently expected of him by his white neighbors, and the Negro did not disappoint them. He donated more from his purse than any other free Negro in town, and on one occasion noted that he had subscribed two dollars towards "Defraying the Expences of a Delegate on to Washington City to try and get the Naval Depot and Armory Here," while his Negro friend McCary had only "put down his name for 50 cts."

The payment of credit accounts was at that time considerably less prompt than today, and Johnson, as did his friends and neighbors, sometimes let months and even years pass before settling up. But the Natchez storekeepers knew not only that he was solvent but that they could have their money at any time they asked for a settlement. That the Negro had little respect for a man who did not pay his debts is indicated by his criticism of the bankruptcy law: "To day was the greate day among the Bank Rupt Cases and oh what a Rascally Law this Bankrupt Law is." He closed his entry with a list of citizens who were taking advantage of the opportunity to clean their financial slate.

Just as he watched carefully his own code of honesty, so he watched that of his slaves. He reported one night that he had "Caught old Mary" with a basket containing "7 or 8 unbaked Buiscuit" and he had reason to believe "that she got them at the City Hotell." He continued: "And the way I cursed her was the wright way and if Ever I can hear of her doing the Like again I will whip her untill I make her faint." One of his strongest outbursts came as a result of finding Winston with a pistol in his pocket. "This Pistol I find belongs to old Mr Bryley and that his own son stoled it from him and had sold it to Winston—Oh if I could only find some honest Person that I could trust in My Kingdom for some one that is truly honest."

Uprightness in another realm of human relations also concerned the barber. In a letter to her brother, Mrs. Adelia Miller stated that there had been "a greate to do" about a New Orleans widow, presumably a free Negro, openly consorting with "a white man a merchant . . . as bold in it as if she was married to him." And she added: "I have often thought that she was a goate in sheeps clothing —now I am convinced."

In most instances William Johnson would have agreed with his sister. He condemned promiscuous crossing of the color line by whites and once bitterly castigated a Frenchman who was chasing slave wenches: "What a poor Devel this Frenchman is. To night a Black Girl of Capt Dawsons Sends him word to Come after awhile and get his hankerchiefs—the fact is he has Got a few Lace or fringed hanks and the infernal fool has given [them] to wash to Every Negro wench that he can possibly have any talk with Oh the Rascal I would give One hundred Dollars if Some Gentleman would only Cetch the Low minded Dog and Cow hyde him well Out of there yards—it would do me so much good."

But apparently the promiscuity involved in such cases was the cause of his indignation, because he wrote not one line of condemnation of certain prominent white planters, well-known to him and all Adams County, who were rearing mulatto families they had fathered. That he viewed with a disapproving eye the actions of other whites is evidenced by several diary entries. He wrote briefly but to the point after he had seen a Natchez man and woman, each of whom was married, "wriding out together": "It was Late Late this Evening—it dont Look—Enough Said."

But a capacity for moral indignation was no bar to deeply felt sympathy for those who needed it. Johnson's compassion is amply revealed in his diary, and his financial records indicate that his purse was frequently opened for unfortunates. He was not ostentatious in his charity, and it is extremely doubtful that many Natchez citizens were aware that he contributed to the welfare of those visited by catastrophe or long-running bad luck. When "Beky Fraizer" died, he recorded that "I Am told that the Poor woman has Left Six poor Helpless Children to Suffer in this wide world, Poor Children. I am Sory for the woman I hope it will be in my power to render them some assistance." Though he did not note a direct financial gift, he probably found some way to aid them in their misfortune.

His sympathy was voiced on numerous occasions. When "A Mr Hamerton Fell Dead to day up the Street," he added: "The Poor man has a Family of Some 3 children." One night he heard a shopkeeper abusing a man, and he closed his day's entry: "Poor old man I was Sorry for Him, but Such is the way of the worl." When Dinah—presumably either a slave or a free Negro—died, he noted, "God have Mercy on Her, I Pray." Charles E. Wilkins, who died in 1837, was, according to the diarist, a "poor young man . . . a Harmless young Gentleman and one that I Loved." When poor unfortunates died—either white or black—Johnson often paid his last respects by following the hearse to the graveyard.

The barbershop master occupied a peculiar position regarding the institution of slavery. Since he had once been a slave, it might be expected that he would have had deep sympathy for members of his race held in bondage. But he was also a slaveholder and from this vantage point viewed the institution in the same manner as did white owners. He wrote about the purchase or sale of slaves much as he discussed the purchase or sale of other forms of property. "I was at a Sale to day of Some of the Slaves of the Harmon Estate, 23 of them was Sold," he wrote. "They were Sold by the Sherriff Newman, A good part of them was Bot by Seth W Jones, the man for whom they were Sold, Quily Bot 2, Esdra Bot 2, Preston Bot Several, 8 or 9 I think. They were Sold at tolerable prices, I think." Nothing herein indicates that the writer was a Negro and a former slave.

He sometimes viewed the cruel punishment of slave crime just as dispassionately—a reflection of his slave-owner position and of his mental alliance with the white planter group. One diary entry, written in 1842, is significant: "Nothing new that I Know of Except that some people on the other side of the River Caught One of those Runaway Slaves that helped Kill a man by the name [of] Todd Living near Red River—They Burned Him up soon after he was taken They Caught One moore of them and they Broght him to there Concordia Jail &c. They shot the other one but did [not] Kill Him." Here again there is nothing to indicate the color or the former status of the writer.

But human compassion, deeply rooted in Johnson's character, might come to light when the diarist was personally acquainted with slaves. "To day it was," he wrote in 1847, "that Judge Dunlap told me that He had Just Sold the two Little Girls and got $650 for them, and that they were Sold to a man who lived only a very Short Distance from where they Formerly Lived. So they want now to Sell the old woman Fanny. They want $350 for Her, Poor creatures I am Sorry for them."

This thread of sympathy extended even to pet animals and birds. When "Some Outrageous Rascal" knocked out an eye of his favorite mare and left her wandering on the town commons, he wrote of her as "My Poor old Mare Kitty Fisher," and hoped for retribution. And when a pet dog died he wrote: "My Poor old Rome Died to day under [the] Table whilst we were at Dinner He Came in and Died in a minute or two after he Layd Down without a Kick or a strugle, Poor old Fellow."

Although William Johnson probably was as religious as the ordinary individual of his day, it is doubtful that he subscribed to the tenets of any single sect. He rarely attended services at white churches, probably because there was no provision for a free Negro section. He once paid a substantial sum for Masses for a deceased Negro's soul; he subscribed $5.00 to the local Catholic church in 1839; and he had his children baptized in the St. Louis Catholic Cathedral in New Orleans. But none of these actions meant that he was a church member or that he even had leanings toward any one formally organized religious group. The baptism of his children in the Catholic cathedral in New Orleans, for example, could be explained on the grounds that it furnished a means of recording the legitimacy of their birth and their free status—both matters of importance to persons of their uncertain legal position.

The free Negro also subscribed to a Methodist religious publication, and he was buried by a white Methodist minister. One of his most pointed religious comments bears the stamp of Calvinism. In commenting on an epidemic in New Orleans he wrote: "The yellow fever [is] a terable mallady: but if it is Gods will, why not? Slay Slay them." It thus appears that Johnson was a religious eclectic, perhaps an inevitable result of his anomalous situation. Certainly he would have never considered joining the Negro churches conducted in Natchez by the Baptists and Methodists; neither would he have relished occupying a seat among slaves in the black gallery of Trinity Church.

He seldom gave vent to long philosophical or religious outbursts, though while in his early twenties he once wrote that "This world is nothing but Vanity and vexation of Sperritt and that is all." One day in 1846 he recorded that he was beginning to read the Bible through again. On rare occasions he thanked "our Maker" or "Our Lord" for his family's good health and for protecting them from "any Loss or misfortune." "I feel Greatfull this Evening of Our Lord that I and all my Family are well at present," he wrote; and another time, "Thank God my Family is all well this day and all my relations in Orleans and I am very glad indeed." During the fall of 1844 when Natchez was "still Considered Healthy tho the Yellow fever is said to be in Woodville very bad yet," he wrote that "We Aught to bee very thankfull for Our good Heath to Our Blessed Redeemer." Shortly after his sister's death in 1848 his diary entries reflect his strong belief in immortality and an attitude of prayerful supplication to a "Mercifull Father."

Johnson's darkest period of melancholy came during the week in which his sister died in New Orleans. He arrived there soon after her death and in the course of his visit allowed himself to become extremely angry. But at the end of the week he wrote:

"Oh how sad, how very sad I feel to night. The future seems all dark. No ray of light illumins its dark unpenetrable gloom Truly most truly, Sin brings its own reward, that of anguish, and remorse. And I have sined most grevously, by giving vent to a passionate temper, In allowing my Lips to give utterence to angry words. O, the misery that is entailed on one by an ungovernable temper. Would that I could blot out from memory the past week, which has indeed been one of Unhappiness to me. But alas it is folly to mourn over the past, the relentless past, which all my sighs can never recall. On the future lies my only hope of happiness. In the future I may at least, in part atone for the past by a strict adhesan to duty, by endevoring to become more amiable, And by striving thus to Emulate the good I may at last enjoy at least a semillance of that Joy and contentment which they Say only the good can enjoy, But can I hope to attain that degree [of] excellence and goodness that will insure happiness I can but try, and if I fail—*try again.*"

Chapter Twenty-Two

The Last Days—and Afterward

IN the late 1840's William Johnson became involved in a prolonged quarrel with a man named Baylor Winn concerning the boundary between their lands in the Swamp, a dispute that eventually led to the barber's death. Johnson had long known Winn, who was about twelve years his senior. He had bought turkeys from him as early as 1831, and they had had other small financial transactions in later years. After Johnson purchased his farm (a transaction Winn had gone out of his way to urge), they had many casual, friendly contacts. They sometimes hunted and fished together. They discussed farm problems and mutually assisted each other in times of need. On one occasion, after Winn had helped Johnson tend a sick horse, the barber presented him with a new razor and soap.

Then in 1847 and 1848 Johnson began to hear disquieting rumors concerning his neighbor. Winn's children were in revolt against his harsh domination. His hands were sawing timber on Johnson's land and rafting it to New Orleans, or cutting cordwood for sale to steamboats. But the two men remained on moderately friendly terms. They still exchanged visits, and they met on the road and had long talks on such subjects as politics, crops, and even adultery. When Winn confided that his son Calvin had left him the night before, he added that "if he should meet him he intended to cowhide him and would do it where Ever and when Ever he Could find Him." They wagered a new hat on the Presidential election of 1848, Winn betting "that Cass would Get a Majority of 2000 over Gen Taylor in the State of Mississippi."

The open break did not come until the spring of 1849, after Winn and Benjamin Wade, a Natchez banker and businessman, had jointly purchased a large tract of swampland adjacent to Johnson's. Winn continued to cut timber with flagrant disregard of boundary lines. Johnson protested, and the two men agreed to a resurvey; but Winn changed his mind and refused to permit the survey to be made. Johnson, upon the advice of his attorneys, wrote Winn requesting him to stop timber-cutting in the disputed area until a survey could be made. Shortly afterward a friend reported that Winn had said that "if I Came in the Swamp to Survey or attempt to run the Lines On Land, that we are now in Dispute about that he wood Shoot me"; but Johnson merely thanked him for the information and recorded that he "did not think he would do it." When the surveyors appeared, Winn "Cursed and tore around at a wonderfull rate, Cursing me at times and then the Boys that was to help clear the way." Johnson did nothing but "Suffered him to go on untill he got tired or ashamed I dont Know which."

Johnson finally succeeded in securing two surveys—the last by court order—and thereupon sued Wade and Winn for trespass on his property. But in early May, 1851, before the case could come to final trial, he proposed a generous compromise, which was accepted. and the case was dropped.

Johnson now relaxed from the strain of the controversy which he believed had ended. He paid lawyers North and Martin $70 for their legal work in the suit. He made small purchases and paid some accounts, rode down to the Swamp where he talked with neighbor James Gregory "untill near Supper time." He recorded the birth of

Gabriel Clarence, his fourth living son, "born 2 minutes before 4 Oclock this morning, Mrs Bennett was in attendance." Then "Our Little Ellen," a slave child to whom he and his family were strongly attached, became ill, and on May 30 she died. The next day Johnson's diary entry was brief but intimated that he had been painfully moved: "Our Poor Little Ellen was Burried to day. She was the Daughter of Phillip & Sylvia."

June opened with "The River rising Tolerably fast," and "Buisness rarther Dull." On the tenth Johnson went to an auction and bought "½ pipe of Gin at 30 cts per Gallon." The next day he had his black mare shod all around. The day following he "wrode out" with the children and "Got a Lot of Black Berrys." But on June 14, he wrote, "I Cannot find two of my Horses to day, Jeff & Fiddler—Something wrong I think, for they were Driven out of Lanieres yesterday Evening."

On Monday, June 16, Johnson rode down to his farm to take care of several routine matters. That evening about dusk, as he was returning to Natchez accompanied by one of his sons, a slave, and a mulatto boy named Edward Hoggatt (who was one of his free Negro apprentices), he was shot from ambush and fatally wounded. He died early the next morning.

The first Natchez newspaper story of this event was headlined "DREADFULL MURDER IN NATCHEZ," and read in part:

> On Monday evening last just at dusk, Mr. William Johnson, an esteemed Citizen and long known as the proprietor of the fashionable Barbers' Shop on Main Street, when returning from his Plantation, a few miles from the City, was fired upon and killed from the road side. . . .
> About an hour after Johnson's death Mr. Baylor Winn, a planter living some seven miles below Natchez, was arrested . . . The court of examination before the Justice will commence this

morning at the Natchez Court House, and will no doubt be attended by many hundreds. Both parties being in good pecuniary circumstances, the best Lawyers of the Natchez bar have been arrayed either for the prosecution or defence.

Two days later the Natchez *Courier,* under the headline "SHOCKING MURDER," carried a more complete account of the assassination and again paid tribute to the free Negro:

Our city was very much excited on Tuesday morning, by hearing that what could only be deemed a horrible and deliberate murder had been committed upon an excellent and most inoffensive man. It was ascertained that William Johnson, a free man of color, born and raised in Natchez, and holding a respected position on account of his character, intelligence and deportment, had been shot, together with a young mulatto boy, about three miles below town, as they were returning home just before sunset on Monday evening last, in company with a son of Johnson and one of his negro slaves. From the testimony elicited before the Coroner's Jury, we learn the following facts. The party had been down the river a few miles, and in returning had stopped for Johnson to light a segar, at the house of a young man named Wynn, with whose father (Baylor Wynn) Johnson had had a legal dispute relative to the boundary of their plantations, which adjoined each other. The dispute had been decided in favor of Johnson, who for the sake of peace had dismissed the suit, settling it at less than his legal rights. While sitting upon their horses near this house, Baylor Wynn entered. Having lighted his segar, Johnson with his party rode off. About three or four miles from this place they were much astonished to see Wynn riding near them, and leaving the road to go into the bushes. Shortly after, Johnson saw him again in another direction going behind some bushes a short distance from the road. A few minutes after a gun was fired from the bushes, three buckshot therefrom striking Johnson, one entering his lungs and going through him, one passing through him along the lower part of his back and one going through his arm. His horse was also wounded. The mulatto boy with him was also badly wounded by a shot entering his back, and lodging under the skin immediately over the abdomen. Johnson fell from his horse within a few yards from where he was struck, while the mulatto boy had strength enough, wounded as he was, to ride to town after assistance. Johnson died at two o'clock, that night. His dying declarations were taken in form, charging upon Baylor Wynn the commission of the crime. The boy still lies in great danger, and it is very doubtful whether he can recover.

Wynn was arrested that same night and committed to jail. Very strong circumstantial testimony points to him as guilty of the deed. The tracks of the horse where he went behind the bushes were all measured, and identified beyond question as those of Wynn's horse. His negro slaves declare that shortly after sunset he came in riding that horse, and ordered it rubbed down and taken care of. He had previously been repeatedly heard to threaten Johnson's life, and to say that the settlement of the suit was not the end of their difficulty. The Coroner's Jury which sat on Tuesday morning returned a verdict that Johnson came to his death by a wound or wounds inflicted by Baylor Wynn. Wynn is to be brought up for examination on Saturday (tomorrow) morning, when the whole case will be thoroughly investigated. Wynn, we understand, claims to be a white man, and has voted and given testimony as such. On this point will depend the admissibility of much of the testimony against him. This murder had created a great deal of excitement, as well from its atrocity, as from the peaceable character of Johnson and his excellent standing. His funeral services were conducted by the Rev. Mr. Watkins, who paid a just tribute to his memory, holding up his example as one well worthy of imitation by all of his class. We observed very many of our most respected citizens at his funeral. Johnson left a wife, nine children, and quite a handsome property; probably twenty to thirty thousand dollars.

Johnson was buried in the cemetery of the Natchez Cemetery Association. According to the custodian his grave and those of his mother and one of his daughters who died in 1901 are the only colored graves in the white section.

The murder of William Johnson and the subsequent trials of Baylor Winn provided headline news for the Natchez press during the two years Winn was held in jail. In the preliminary examination held immediately after Johnson's death before Justice Wood, Winn offered no witnesses and was therefore committed to jail without bail on a charge of willful murder. The prosecution was careful in the preliminary charge to designate that the charge was directed against Baylor Winn, a free man of color, but Winn gave notice that, at the proper time and place, he would disprove the charge that he was a mulatto. The Natchez press, though it repeatedly stated that Winn was "supposed to be a negro," admitted that he had voted and given testimony in court. The newspapers further admitted that upon this point would depend "the admissibility of much of the evidence," as the "persons with Johnson when he was shot were negroes," and Mississippi law barred Negro witnesses in a case against a white man.

A special term of the Adams County Circuit Court was ordered and held in January, 1852. At this trial Winn was indicted as a free mulatto and to the charge he made a preliminary plea that he was not a mulatto, but was of Indian and white blood. The Natchez *Free Trader* reported that "Winn came into court with a solemn affidavit admitting an admixture of blood, but that it was Indian and not negroe, as stated in the indictment." He produced two witnesses from Virginia, where he had been born, one of whom testified that Winn was from the remnant of the Pamunkey tribe while the other named the remnant of the Mattapony tribe. Winn's attorneys moved for a change of venue but the case was sent to the jury, which remained deadlocked for thirty-six hours. A mistrial was thereupon ordered, and, upon application of the prisoner and because public opinion in Natchez and Adams County was inflamed against him. a change of venue to Jefferson County was ordered.

During the latter part of April, 1852, Baylor Winn's second trial took place at a session of the circuit court held at Fayette, in neighboring Jefferson County. It was described as "the great and exciting trial of the session."

Court sessions in Mississippi towns were always times of high excitement, not only because men's lives were often at stake, but also because contests of eloquence and legal skill between opposing counsel were always appreciated. Court Day was a recognized institution in the America of the 1850's. And in this case, a battery of four of the ablest lawyers in the state was assembled for the defense, while the district attorney was aided in the prosecution by a brilliant young lawyer, Will T. Martin, who had been one of Johnson's attorneys in his suit against Wade and Winn and later was to become a Confederate general.

The case was before the jury more than a week. Numerous witnesses were called; the defense attorneys introduced many legal technicalities; and Martin summed up the state's case in a long-remembered three-hour speech. Years later, Frank A. Montgomery, who was one of the jurymen, wrote in his *Reminiscences of a Mississippian in Peace and War:* "General Martin's speech was one of the ablest I ever heard, and though it took, as I remember, three or more hours in the delivery, the attention of the jury never wavered." But in the end the state failed to place Baylor Winn within reach of Negro testimony by proving that he had Negro blood. On April 26, the jury, after having been out three hours, brought in a verdict for the defendant, and the court ordered "that the indictment be quashed and that the said prisoner be remanded to the jail of Adams County for further proceedings."

The burden of proof in these two trials was on the state. Although a number of persons, including Johnson and other free Negroes of Natchez, thought that Winn had Negro blood, legally at least he had passed for a white man. In addition to having voted and given testimony in court, Winn showed that he had served as a road overseer, had been listed in censuses as a white man, and had married a white woman. The Johnson family sent a representative to Virginia to secure evidence concerning the Winns of King William County. He brought back documents which bore the official certification of local Virginia recording officials and even of the governor of the state, documents which traced the Winns of King William County back to 1802 and stated that all of them were free Negroes. But the defense attorneys secured a crucial victory when this written evidence, because of legal technicalities, was never admitted in evidence. This, the key decision in the whole series of cases, prevented the prosecution from putting the only eyewitnesses on the stand.

In early May of the same year the Adams County grand jury brought in a new indictment against Winn as an ordinary white citizen, for the same offense, and the next week the circuit court, on the motion of the prisoner's counsel, ordered a change of venue to Wilkinson County. The case was set for trial at the June term of court, but the state, alleging the absence of certain witnesses, succeeded in securing a continuance. In December, 1852, the case was again docketed but the state obtained a further continuance.

Baylor Winn's final trial was held in Woodville in June, 1853. The state applied for another continuance because of the absence of one witness, but when it was shown that this witness was a mulatto and if present would not be permitted to testify, the application was denied and immediate trial was ordered.

Johnson's murder and the case against Baylor Winn had attracted considerable attention throughout the state and the citizens of Woodville excitedly awaited the trial. As the Woodville *Republican* phrased it: "A formidable array of counsel and witnesses were present, and expectations were on tiptoe—that we should have an opportunity of hearing many able speeches in the course of the trial."

Nearly two days were consumed in the examination

of witnesses for the state. Then Will T. Martin, as the *Republican* reported, "who deserves all praise for his able and persevering efforts in support of the trust committed to his hands by the prosecution, stated to the court, that as the law debarred the use of the only conclusive evidence which could be brought against the prisoner, and that as consequently no positive proof could be adduced, in conjunction with the District Attorney, he would ask the Court for leave to enter a *nolle prosequi* in the case." Added the *Republican* reporter: "The anticipations of the lovers of eloquence were sadly disappointed."

Exactly two years after William Johnson died, the person whom he had designated as his murderer walked out of the Woodville courtroom a free man.

Johnson's family had watched the trials with intense interest and were bitterly disappointed at what they considered the failure to secure justice. In May, prior to the Woodville trial, Johnson's son William had written from New Orleans, where he was in school: "You wrote me word that the excitement was rising again about that trial as the time was drawing near, I hope the excitement aint died away on our side, and I trust to God he wont get clear."

Eight days after Baylor Winn had been freed by the Wilkinson County Circuit Court, one of Johnson's sons made a sworn affidavit before Justice Wood in Natchez against him for the same murder. Upon this representation Winn was again arrested, but this time he remained in jail only three days. At his preliminary examination before the magistrate, his attorneys moved to quash the affidavit, arrest the warrant, and grant the prisoner his discharge on the grounds that the affidavit had been made by an incompetent person, that the question of blood had already been adjudicated, and that the prisoner had once been in jeopardy for the same offense and was therefore not liable to be tried again. The motion was sustained, and Winn was discharged.

The last attempt to convict Baylor Winn had failed, but the memories of William Johnson's murder and of the several trials of Baylor Winn lingered in the minds of Mississippians a long time. When Johnson's son Byron was killed in 1872 by another Negro, the Natchez *Democrat* devoted two columns to recounting the tragedy and to lauding the slain man. And the article continued: "His father before him (a free man of color) had by a long life of probity and rectitude won a high place in the estimation of this community, and, about twenty years ago, died much lamented at the hands of an assassin. Byron emulated the example of his father, in whose worthy memory he ever felt a just degree of pride." Until recent years, people still lived who clearly recalled General William T. Martin discussing the Winn trials of a century ago.

Until her death in 1866, Johnson's widow was the head of the family. That she did a good job of rearing her children is obvious from their record in the Natchez community. Her sons and employees continued the barbershop through the Civil War and afterward. Byron Johnson was head of the family until his death in 1872, and afterward his sister Anna L. Johnston—the family name had been changed to Johnston—and Clarence M. Johnston, the diarist's youngest son and a blacksmith, succeeded to the family leadership.

Meanwhile, several of the Johnstons had left Mississippi. During the 1920's and 1930's the Natchez branch was led by Dr. W. R. Johnston, a grandson of the diarist. Dr. Johnston, a graduate of Wilberforce College and Howard University, was the leading colored physician in Natchez when he died in 1938. A newspaper obituary lamented the death of "one of the most highly respected colored citizens of Natchez. His going has brought sorrow to a legion of friends throughout the city. . . . He was one of the last male members of a family liked and respected by people of all races and creeds. . . . Perhaps this heritage imparted to him the quiet dignity that marked his words and actions." This obituary made him the third male of three successive generations to be praised by the Natchez press.

Mrs. Sally Johnston, the widow of Dr. Johnston, made possible the publication of the diary of the family's founder. She still occupies the home that the diarist erected, and upon her death it will descend to other members of the family. In it, there will be more repetitions of the theme of a century-old conversation: *This house was built by a man of character and high community standing, a man who was the diarist of ante-bellum Natchez, but his murder was avenged by law no more than if he had been a common slave.*

Index

Ablamowicz, Madam, 194
Adams, A. A., 189
Amer, Miss, 26
Amie, Mrs., 81, 251
Anderson (Johnson's slave), 48
Antony (apprentice of Johnson), 57
Applewhite, Dr. J. R., 41
Apprentices, 54–61, 87, 152, 192
Armatt, T., 143, 145, 152
Austin, H., 73

Barbiere, Joseph, 199, 254
Barland, Andrew, 249–50
Barland, David, 250
Barland, John, 70, 231, 250
Barland, William, 214, 248
Barnum, P. T., 196
Barrett, Capt. Israel, 219
Battles, Ann, 27–29. *See also* Johnson, Ann Battles
Battles, Harriet, 27–28, 41, 78, 191, 237
Bell, Elijah, 40, 171
Benbrook, Dr., 40, 165, 192
Bertrand, Marshall Henri, 116–17
Besancon, Lorenzo, 165
Billy (Johnson's slave), 46
Bingaman, Adam L.: career of, 233–39; daughter of, 238–40; mentioned, 85, 96, 108, 111, 116, 123, 124, 131–32, 133, 139, 140, 152, 203, 204–205, 206, 209, 210, 211–13, 215, 218
Bingaman, Charlotte C., 109, 134
Bingaman, Elnora, 239–40
Biscaccionti, Elisa, 194
Blackburn, Dr. Luke Pryor, 96, 232, 233
Bodley, Dr. Hugh S., 148
Bon, M., 98
Boswell, Joseph G., 212

Bradford, Thom, 108
Brienti, Miss E., 193
Britton, W. A., 99, 112
Brogen, Charly, 164
Broom, Dr., 94, 122, 150
Brown, Albert, 115
Brown, Andrew, 222
Brustie, Mrs. Gabriel, 81, 251
Brustie, Gabriel, 72, 82, 246, 251
Brustie, Lucy, 127
Burke, H., 47
Bruns, Ferdinand, 57
Burns, W., 59
Butler, G., 73
Button, Bill, 245

Cage, E. C., 144, 145, 146
Caldwell, James H., 189
Cand, Lee, 186
Carpenter, A. G., 109, 221
Carter, Amsted, 110
Cass, Lewis, 137
Chaplain, E. K., 114
Charivaris, 121
Charles (slave apprentice), 36, 57, 61–63, 95
Cholera, 107, 178, 181, 184, 185
Chotard, Henry, 96, 111, 117, 170, 219–20
Chotard, Mrs. Henry, 220
Claiborne, Lee, 111, 117, 205
Claiborne, Os, 205
Clark, Samuel, 47
Clay, Henry, 117, 135, 136–37, 199
Coleman, Pete, 112
Conner, H. L., 109, 153
Crime: in Natchez, 142–55; among Negroes, 150–53, 155
Cummings, Hester, 251

273

Dahlgren, Charles G., 36, 157–58, 159
"Darkey parties" and balls, 56, 57, 63, 92, 107, 200, 242
Davis, Jefferson, 235
Davis, Ruben, 133
Davis, Samuel, 112
Dembo (free Negro), 153
Democratic party, 130, 135, 234
Dick (slave), 245–46
Dunbar, Alexander, 115
Dunbar family, 120, 214
Dunbar, Mrs. Sarah, 125
Dunbar, Robert, 166
Dunbar, William, 214, 215–16
Duncan, Dr. Stephen, 19, 96, 111, 152, 170, 215, 218
Dunlap, Judge, 259
Dyer, George, 150

Elizabeth (Barland slave), 248
Ellen (Johnson's slave), 52
Ellen (slave child), 264
Elliotte, St. John, 117
Ellis family, 214
Ellis, Thomas G., 186–87, 214, 218
Esdra, Adolphe, 228, 258
Evans, Thomas, 100

Farrar family, 214
Fillmore, Millard, 137
Fisher, Clara, 191
Fisk, Alvarez, 19
Fitzgerald family, 214
Flecheux, Adolph, 44
Fletcher, Flavius, 143
Foote, Henry S., 138
Forrest, Edwin, 189
Foster, C. B., 180
Fox, George, 108
Fox, W. H., 186
Fraizer, Beky, 257
Free Negroes: "Inquisition" of, 151–54; mentioned, 11, 13, 54–57, 91, 92, 130, 142–43, 148, 150, 173, 217, 241–51, 254, 255

Gains, A. L., 125
Gaita, Charles, 193
Gálvez, Bernardo de, 214
Gambling, 148–49, 206, 230–31
Gatewood, Mary, 26–27
Gayoso de Lemos, Manuel, 214
Gemmell, P., 162
Gibson, Mary Ann, 153
Gibson, Samuel, 154
Gil, Don Andres, 178
Gilbert, Thom, 115
Gillespie, John T., 110
Gocian, Sam, 210
Gossin, Samuel, 206
Grand Pré, Carlos de, 214
Green, Betsy, 148
Gregory, James, 48, 52, 263
Guice, Jessy, 115
Guion, Isaac, 178
Guion, Walter, 112
Gustine, Lemuel, 19

Hackett, James H., 189, 191
Hancock, Winfield Scott, 239
Harris, William, 171
Harrison, William Henry, 132, 135
Hastings, Little, 125
Hawk, Joseph, 249
Hazard, Bill, 65
Henderson, Thomas, 99–100, 231
Hinds, Thomas, 99, 249
Hogg, Samuel, 85, 125–26, 163, 186, 231
Hoggatt, Edward (apprentice of Johnson), 264, 265–66
Hoggatt, Philip, 214, 215, 216, 217
Hoggatt, Wilford, 155
Holmes, David, 99, 182
Houston, Sam, 137
Howell, Garnet, 108
Hubbard, John M., 40, 157, 158, 181, 231

Isham (slave), 155
Isler, Ruthen, 146

Jackson, Andrew, 99, 116, 131, 140
Jackson, Dempsey P., 136
Jacquemine, John, 1, 71, 73, 74, 75, 88, 160, 177, 207, 229–31
Jeff (apprentice of Johnson), 57, 71, 221
Jeorgan (slave), 17

INDEX

Jim (Johnson's slave), 36, 63–64, 87
John (Johnson's slave), 72, 73, 89
John, Guinea, 160–61
Johnson, Adelia, 15, 19. *See also* Miller, Adelia Johnson
Johnson, Amy, 15, 16, 17–18, 82–84, 184
Johnson, Ann Battles, 53, 81, 82, 85, 86, 87, 89, 101–102, 191, 271. *See also* Battles, Ann
Johnson, Anna, 84–85. *See also* Johnston, Anna
Johnson Barbershop: as clearing house for news, 107; mentioned, 30–33, 36–39, 59
Johnson, Byron, 232, 237, 271
Johnson, Gabriel Clarence, 264
Johnson, John, 77
Johnson, Phillip, 86
Johnson, Richard, 84, 86, 116, 132, 141, 221, 246
Johnson, William (white), 15–18
Johnson, William: apprentices of, 54–61, 152, 192; business career of, 19, 20–22, 30–43; character of, 7–9, 13, 18, 23, 28–29, 69–70, 76, 77, 93, 94, 118, 123, 126, 165–66, 169, 218, 252–59; children of, 76, 81, 82, 84–86; as chronicler of Natchez life, 107–17; colored friends of, 241–51; courtship and marriage of, 27–29; death of, 1, 29, 46, 163, 232, 264–66; as diarist, 1–7, 9, 218–23; diary of, 12, 13; emancipation of, 15, 16, 17, 19; as farmer, 43–53, 130; firefighting of, 168, 171, 173, 175; gambling by, 206–207; as gossip reporter, 118–28; home and home life of, 78–90; and horse racing, 202, 204, 206–207, 208, 209, 210; as landlord, 40–41, 44–46, 163; life style of, 23–26; and Mary Gatewood, 26–27; as moneylender, 39–40, 118; and politics, 139–41, 234, 235; prescriptions of, 185; reading of, 253–54; recreation of, 25, 69–77, 230–31; and whites, 228–40; religion of, 259–60; slaves of, 8, 162, 256; as slaveowner, 64–68, 100, 258; social and community position of, 91–104, 193, 200–201, 202, 227, 251, 255; and Baylor Winn, 262–63; on Texas, 137–38; and the theater, 191–92; travels of, 24–26; trials of killer of, 266–70; on War with Mexico, 138
Johnson, William, Jr., 76, 84, 85, 236, 237, 270
Johnson, William R., 212, 213
Johnston, Anna L., 271. *See also* Johnson, Anna
Johnston, Clarence M., 271
Johnston, Mrs. Sally, 272
Johnston, W. R., 271–72
Jones, A. A., 41
Jones, Seth W., 258

Kenner, Duncan F., 212
Kenney, Arthur, 41, 74
Ker, John, 219
Kley, F., 194
Knox, Madam Lear, 219
Krollman, G., 193–94
Kyle, John, 150
Kyle, Nancy, 153

Lacrose, J., 73
Langford, William, 47
Lapice, Peter M., 98
Lawrence, Peter, 153
Lee, H., 57
Lee, Moses, 148
Lieper, Andrew, 153
Lind, Jenny, 195–96
Lindar, Gardner, 48
Linton, Mrs., 74, 111, 150, 151, 170
Little, Peter, 99
Livingston, A., 108
Louis (apprentice of Johnson), 186
Lucinda (slave), 67, 126
Ludlow, Noah, 189
Lynch, Antonio, 41, 162
Lynch, Charles, 139

McAlister, Samuel T., 101, 112, 161–62
McCary, James, 243
McCary, Kitty, 153-54, 243–44
McCary, Robert, 1, 26, 33, 70–71, 72, 73, 74, 75, 76–77, 86, 113, 123, 242, 243, 244–46, 251, 255

276   THE BARBER OF NATCHEZ

McCary, Robert (younger), 76
McCary, William, 76, 88
McClung, Alexander Keith, 235
McCoulough, Robert, 219
McGettereck, P., 41
McGraw, P. H., 180, 186
McKiernan, Charles, 178
McNutt, Alexander, 115, 218

Maffitt, John Newland, 94
Mandeville family, 108, 109, 133
Marshall family, 111
Martin, Gill, 134
Martin, William, 160, 232–33, 263, 268, 270
Mary (Johnson's slave), 48, 256
Mary (wife of Charles), 63
Melin, Henry, 22
Mercer, William Newton, 98–99, 112, 215
Merrill, Dr. Ayres P., 19, 99, 111
Meshio, Joseph, 41, 70, 74
Middleton (slave), 64
Miller, Anderson, 163–64
Miller, Adelia Johnson, 24, 27, 64, 83, 86, 87, 88, 183, 230, 252, 256, 261. *See also* Johnson, Adelia.
Miller, James, 19–21, 53, 83, 86, 87, 88, 244, 252
Miner family, 214
Minor, Stephen, 108, 178, 214
Minor, Mrs. Stephen, 108
Minor, William J., 110, 117, 136, 203–204, 206, 209, 210, 211, 212, 213
Miró, Estevan, 214
Mitchum, Arthur, 18, 19
Montgomery, Frank A., 268
Moore, Edith Wyatt, 12
Mosbey, William, 45
Murchison, Simon, 154, 162
Murray, Charles Augustus, 190–91

Natchez: aristocracy of, 214–18, 219; circuses in, 197–98; concerts in, 193–96; drinking in, 121–22; fires in, 168–76; horse racing in, 202–12; Johnson's news of, 118–19; Johnson records life of, 107–17; in Johnson's time, 9–12; law and order in, 142–55; lectures in, 192–93; medicine in, 178–86; money crisis in, 42, 43; recreation in, 188; sanitation in, 33–34; street fights in, 156–67; theater in, 188–92; tornado in, 176–77; mentioned, 1, 6, 7, 13
Negroes: crime of, 150–53, 155, 258–59; mentioned, 191, 241–51. *See also* Free Negroes; Slaves
Nevins, Allan, 9, 189
Nevitt, John B., 40, 152
Nichols, Thomas Low, 130, 142
Night, J. B., 62
Nix, William, 57, 60–61, 65, 73, 76, 112
North, Ralph, 140, 263

Panic of 1837, pp. 42–43, 142
Parker, William, 98, 122, 127, 139, 173
Parkman, Francis, 8
Parsons, Charles Booth, 160, 189, 192
Parsons, Sandy, 152
Patrick (slave), 100
Patterson, Henry, 112, 121
Peggy (Johnson's slave), 46, 48
Perkins, Ann, 152
Perry, John G., 205–206
Peter (apprentice of Johnson), 186
Phillip (Johnson's slave), 46, 48, 264
Piper, Elick, 149
Plantations, 11, 214, 215, 216
Planters, 11, 12, 214–18, 219
Poindexter, George, 16, 36, 40, 108, 110, 131, 139
Polk, James K., 135, 136
Pomet, Cloea, 150
Potter, John S., 154, 160, 189
Potts, Reed, 40, 229
Powell, George, 161
Power, Tyrone, 189, 190
Prentiss, Seargent S., 119–20, 133, 136, 139, 234
Prior, J. Benjamin, 210

Quitman, John A., 96–97, 140, 165, 175, 218

Rabee, Jane, 108
Rachel (slave), 58

Rawlings, Judge, 164
Railey, James, 159
Recreation. *See* Johnson, William; Sports
Rivers (Justice of the Peace), 161, 165
Robertson, William, 96, 220, 231
Rocheleau, Joseph, 206
Rolla (slave), 150–51
Rose, Thomas, 41, 97, 147, 163
Routh, John, 110

Sanders, Colonel, 145–56
Santa Anna, Antonio López de, 137, 138
Scott, James M., 189
Scott, Winfield, 138
Sessions, Colonel, 114
Silliman, Benjamin, 192
Silsbee, Joshua, 189
Slaves: brutality toward, 153–55; Johnson's, 36, 37, 46, 48, 51, 52, 54, 67–68; sale of, 115; stealing of, 147–48; mentioned, 11, 12, 13, 20, 148, 150, 151, 152, 215, 216, 236, 241, 242, 243, 244, 245, 246, 247, 259–69
Smith, Judge, 221
Smith, Calvin, 110
Smith, Robert, 101
Smith, Sol, 189
Soria, Jacob, 31, 173
Spillman, A., 40
Sports: cards, 69, 75; children's games, 76; cockfights, 74; fishing, 69, 72–73; gambling, 69, 148–49, 206, 230–31; horseback riding, 75; horse racing, 202–13; hunting, 69–72; pitching quoits and dollars, 69, 73–74; shooting, 69, 73–74; toy sailboating, 69, 76–77; walking, 69, 75
Stanwood, George, 112
Staples, J. N., 41
Steel, John, 210
Sterns, Washington, 20, 27, 60, 72, 123, 177
Steven (Johnson's slave), 64–67
Stewart, Charles, 157–58
Stewart, Elick, 157–58
Stockman, John R., 31
Stump, W. H., 46–47

Surget family, 108, 214
Surget, Frank, 111, 112, 115, 214, 215, 216
Surget, James, 53, 203, 218
Sylvia (Johnson's slave), 48, 264

Taylor, F., 40, 101
Taylor, John G., 82
Taylor, Zachary, 113, 115, 137, 140
Thomsonians, 179, 180
Throckmorton, R. L., 109, 222
Thumb, Tom, 195
Tichenor, Gabriel, 27, 28, 98
Tree, Ellen, 189
Tyler, John, 135

Van Buren, Martin, 127, 131, 132, 134, 137

Wade, Benjamin, 263
Walker (slave), 64
Walker, Benjamin, 109
Walker, Robert J., 139, 229
Waymouth, D. F., 41
Weldon, George, 32, 97, 229
Wells, Thomas J., 211, 212
West, Benjamin, 196
West, Howard, 120
West, Wellington, 57, 60
Whelen, John, 143
Whig party, 132–33, 134, 135, 136, 234
Wilkins, Charles E., 258
Wilkins family, 214
Wilkins, James, 19, 139, 152
William, French, 72, 100
Williams, Mary Jane, 120
Williams, Merrit, 112
Williams, N. L., 162
Williamson, John, 121
Willow, Tree, 147
Wilson, A. L., 63, 101–102
Wilson, Bill, 58
Winn, Baylor, 254, 262–71
Winn, Calvin, 262
Winn, George, 247–48
Winn, Jasper, 254
Winn, John T., 146–47, 177
Winn, Winslow ("Little Winn"), 45,

46, 47, 246–48
Winston, Fountain, 58
Winston, William, 57–60, 73, 92, 221, 256
Wolcott, B., 47
Wolcott, William, 49
Wood, 46, 47, 48, 49, 50, 53

Woods, Buck, 120
Woods, Samuel, 97, 171

Yellow fever, 38, 78, 107, 178, 181–84, 260
Young, Major, 61–63, 95–96

www.ingramcontent.com/pod-product-compliance
Lightning Source LLC
Chambersburg PA
CBHW052329010526
44270CB00038B/1866